The Case for Shakespeare

The Case for Shakespeare

The End of the Authorship Question

Scott McCrea

PRAEGER

Westport, Connecticut
London

Library of Congress Cataloging-in-Publication Data

McCrea, Scott.
  The case for Shakespeare : the end of the authorship question / Scott McCrea.
    p.   cm.
  Includes bibliographical references and index.
  ISBN 0-275-98527-X (alk. paper)
  1. Shakespeare, William, 1564–1616—Authorship.   2. Playwriting—
History—16th century.   3. Playwriting—History—17th century.   I. Title.
PR2937.M28   2005
822.3'3—dc22   2004017656

British Library Cataloguing in Publication Data is available.

Library of Congress Catalog Card Number: 2004017656
ISBN: 0-275-98527-X

First published in 2005

Praeger Publishers, 88 Post Road West, Westport, CT 06881
An imprint of Greenwood Publishing Group, Inc.
www.praeger.com

Printed in the United States of America

The paper used in this book complies with the
Permanent Paper Standard issued by the National
Information Standards Organization (Z39.48-1984).

10 9 8 7 6 5 4 3 2 1

Copyright Acknowledgments

The author and publisher gratefully acknowledge permission for use of the following material:

Excerpts from "The Social Background," by M. St. Clare Byrne, in *A Companion to
Shakespeare Studies*, edited by Harley Granville-Barker and G. B. Harrison (copyright 1934), are reprinted by permission of Cambridge University Press.

Excerpts from "Two Shakespeares," by Scott McCrea, which first appeared in
Skeptic (vol. 9, no. 1), are reprinted courtesy of The Skeptic Society.

GHOST. If thou didst ever thy dear father love—
HAMLET. O God!
GHOST. Revenge his foul and most unnatural murder.

—Hamlet I.v.23–25

Contents

CONTENTS

Acknowledgments

This book would not have been possible without the help, encouragement, and sometimes casual comments of the following people: my wife, Melissa; my colleagues at the State University of New York, Purchase College, especially Barbara Knowles, David Wells, Greg Seel, and Eric Nicholson; my parents, Maryann and Charles C. McCrea, Jr.; my editor at Praeger, Suzanne Staszak-Silva; my agent, Barbara Hogenson; Howard Stein; David Bevington; Albert Bermel; Michael Shermer; Carol Galligan; Jonathan Bate; Glenn Young; Steven Rattazzi; Mace Perlman; and Larry Lang.

I'm also grateful to the staffs of the British Library, Yale University Libraries, Columbia University Libraries, the Library of Congress, and the New York Public Library.

Finally, I must thank all the students who have asked me why scholars think that Shakespeare wrote his own plays and poems (especially Andrew Katz, Mike Dooly, and David Ledoux). This book is quite literally for them.

Prologue: Sleight of Hand

The voice accosted me from behind. It was a raspy voice, deep and full of confidence, a preacher's voice. It said, "I know where ya got those shoes."

I wheeled around. Slouching against a brick wall with his arms folded was a forty-year-old black man with wild hair and a professor's goatee. He must have stepped out of the shadows because I hadn't noticed him when I walked by. Dressed in new jeans and a clean white t-shirt, he didn't seem to be crazy or drunk, but it was hard to tell—anyone can be anything on a Saturday. "I know where ya got those shoes," he said again, as a challenge.

We were in Jackson Square in New Orleans. It was a beautiful day—warm, sunny, blue-skyed—and I was on vacation. Please remember that. It was a gorgeous day and I was on vacation. I pointed at my sneakers and looked him in the eye. "You know where I got these shoes?"

He nodded solemnly. He knew the answer as well as he knew his own name. "Will ya give me five dollars if I can *tell* ya where ya got those shoes?"

Now, obviously I smelled a con. Obviously he couldn't really tell me where I bought my footwear. But it was a beautiful day, and I wondered how the con played out. Maybe, like Henry Higgins, he could glean something from my accent. Maybe he was some kind of shoe mystic. In any case, I wondered what his answer would be, and if he said New York or anywhere close, I would gladly pay five dollars for the miracle—and if he got it wrong, it would cost me nothing. Right?

"I'll give you five dollars," I said.

He reached into his back pocket and pulled out a rag and a tin of clear shoe polish. And he began reciting. Almost apologetically, he began reciting something he'd said a thousand times before: "Now, I didn't say I knew where ya *purchased* those shoes. And I didn't say I knew where ya *acquired* those shoes. I said I knew where ya *got* those shoes. And ya got those shoes on the bottom of your feet, which are on the sidewalk in Jackson Square in the city of New Orleans in the state of Louisiana in the country of the United States of America. *That's* where ya got those shoes!"

I let him smear some polish on my Reeboks and paid him his five bucks. I felt like a sucker. Not because I'd been fooled, but because the con hadn't been better. The entertainment wasn't worth the price.

A few years later I had a similar experience. And I thought of the man in Jackson Square. I was reading *The Atlantic Monthly* in October of 1991, and I came across an article by Tom Bethell about the Shakespeare Authorship Question—the question of whether William Shakespeare actually wrote the plays attributed to him. I had known that since the nineteenth century there had been doubts, and I knew that, over the years, various alternative candidates had been proposed, the most famous being Sir Francis Bacon, the Elizabethan philosopher and jurist. In his essay, Bethell claims that Edward de Vere, the seventeenth Earl of Oxford, is the True Author, and I must say, reading it the first time, it seemed like a good case. De Vere, with his documented skills and experiences, appeared to have known what the man who wrote the plays knew. His attitudes and attributes matched the Author's characteristics, while what little we knew about the man from Stratford seemed to be at odds with them. I was especially taken by an incident in Oxford's life that eerily parallels a scene in the Works. In 1573 three of Oxford's retainers robbed two men who previously had been employed by the earl. The encounter took place, according to the victims' letter of complaint, "by the highway from Gravesend to Rochester." In *Henry IV Part One*, when Prince Hal's friends attempt a robbery, the prince foils it at Gadshill—which is on the highway between Gravesend and Rochester. A correspondence like that sounded too specific, too genuine, to be dismissed as happenstance.

But as I reached the last paragraph, I realized that I'd been had. Bethell very cleverly diverts the reader's attention away from the historical evidence that supports Shakespeare's authorship and toward his own conjectures about Oxford—exactly like a magician palming a card. With one parenthetical phrase, he hides the most important clues from the reader's consciousness. Here's what he says: "tremendous archival digging in the nineteenth and twentieth centuries turned up quite a bit of information about [Shakespeare's] life. But (if we exclude posthumous testimony) none of it establishes [him] as a playwright."[1] Exclude "posthumous testimony"? Ignore the remarks of people who knew Shakespeare when he was alive if they made those remarks after his death? On what grounds? Imagine a murder trial in which testimony is excluded because the victim is dead! In any case, Bethell's assertion is false. There *is* evidence from Shakespeare's life that he was a writer. (The article, I later discovered, is brimming with misinformed and misleading statements.)

Bethell's next trick is to assume there was a conspiracy in which Shakespeare acted as a front man for Oxford. The earl, Bethell suggests, wrote the plays, and the actor put his name on them. This allows Bethell to ignore all contemporary references to Shakespeare that occur in a literary context; unwittingly, according to Bethell, the litterateurs of the time were really alluding to Oxford. But not a single document or artifact supports such a conspiracy. If you're going to discover the lost city of Troy, it's not enough to argue from passages in *The Iliad*; you'd better dig up some topless towers and Trojan horses. One private letter, one diary entry that mentions a rumor that the earl was the real playwright of *Romeo and Juliet* and Shakespeare's authorship would come crashing down. Until that day comes Bethell's case is nothing but a fantasy, and the Earl of Oxford will, quite rightly, never be accepted as the True Author.

With no hard evidence, Bethell plays the game of the man in Jackson Square—he creates false expectations and then pounces. Rather than looking at the existing artifacts and fitting his theory to the evidence (as a detective or a historian or a scientist would do), he invites us to think about what we would expect to find. Wouldn't a sample of Shakespeare's handwriting have survived, Bethell asks, if Shakespeare had been a writer? Wouldn't someone have claimed to be his classmate, if he had gone to school? Wouldn't the city of London have gone into mourning when he died? We might point out that if Shakespeare couldn't write, had never gone to school, and did not seem to be the poet, he must not have been a very effective front man—but Bethell is himself confused about whether the conspiracy was an "open" or "closed" secret, whether most Elizabethans were in on it or whether the truth was known to only a select few. More persuasively, he asks us to wonder what the man who wrote the plays must have been like, what firsthand experiences we should expect to see documented in the historical record (travel to Italy? friends at the Queen's court?), and then to look into the biographical traces. Presto! All we find are business transactions and lawsuits involving money matters. The magician opens his fist and his palm is empty. Our expectations (unjustified, as we'll see) have been used to distract us from the facts and to make us look elsewhere for the Author.[2]

The year after *The Atlantic Monthly* article appeared, Charlton Ogburn's *The Mysterious William Shakespeare* was reissued in a handsome new edition. Originally published in 1984, this cinderblock-sized tome begins with the premise that Oxford wrote the plays and interprets every piece of evidence it can in that light. Piling assumption on assumption, it presupposes its conclusions instead of proving them. Columnist Joseph Sobran's *Alias Shakespeare*, which could be found on bookstore shelves in 1997, is guilty of the same thing. Much less daunting than Ogburn's book, it spreads the Oxford net even wider, capturing plenty of ordinary intelligent Americans who happened to be uninformed on this particular question. Then, in 1999, *Time* and *Harper's* featured discussions of the Authorship debate, encouraging the idea that there really was a legitimate disagreement on the issue. Today, more people than ever believe Oxford wrote the plays.

Where were the scholars? Where were the defenders of Shakespeare? They were defending all right, but they never engaged the Oxfordians in a meaningful way. They assumed the problem was misinterpretation, that the disbelievers were misreading the facts, and that all that had to be done was to present a clearer explanation of the evidence. Irvin Matus, for example, made a valiant attempt to do this in his admirable but scattershot *Shakespeare, in Fact* (1994). But the Oxfordians were already familiar with orthodox interpretations; they found them unsatisfying—that's why they were Oxfordians. The real problem was much deeper than the academics realized. What needed to be addressed were fundamental assumptions.[3]

This is why I wrote this book. I thought that if I could hold the mirror, as 'twere, up to the heretics' beliefs, I might be able to bring them to their senses, as the Knight of the Looking-Glass brings Don Quixote to his.[4] I also thought I could forearm the unwitting who may wonder if the world's greatest writer was a fraud. At the same time (and this may surprise you), I thought I could vindicate some of the Oxfordians' doubts. Some of their peripheral points are worth considering and could aid us, if we let them, in understanding the plays and poems. But most of all, I thought that by dissecting the Authorship Question I might illuminate something about Shakespeare, if only that he was indeed responsible for his own poetry. A man who has given us so much deserves, at the very least, recognition for his accomplishments—even if, to honor him, we have to drag his corpse from out of the shadows.

PART ONE

~

The Man Who
Wrote the Plays

CHAPTER 1
Two Shakespeares

The second-most important book in the history of English publishing (second only to the King James Bible) came off the presses at the end of 1623. It was about 8½ inches wide by roughly 13 inches tall, and it collected between its covers some of the most popular dramas of the age, many of which were appearing in print for the first time. Known today as the First Folio, the actual words on its title page read "Mr. William Shakespeares Comedies, Histories, & Tragedies. Published according to the True Originall Copies." People who wonder why Shakespeare is said to have written *Macbeth* or *Coriolanus* or *The Tempest*, all of which are contained in the volume, need only look at the title. (Figure 1)

It's hard to notice the title, though. Taking up most of the page is a woodcut of a balding baggy-eyed man, staring out at the viewer with an inscrutable, expressionless gaze. He's wearing a starched collar and doublet, a fashion common in the reign of James I, and he has facial hair in a style from the same era—a mustache and a patch of beard just below his lower lip. The mouth is not directly under the nose, one eye is lower and larger than the other, and the hair doesn't balance at the sides, as if he's wearing a periwig that's been jostled. But, in general, the image must have been recognizable, because the short poem on the facing leaf attests to the artist's accuracy:

To the Reader.

This Figure, that thou here seest put,
  It was for gentle Shakespeare cut,
Wherein the Graver had a strife

with Nature, to out-doo the life:
O, could he but have drawne his wit
  As well in brasse, as he hath hit
His face; the Print would then surpasse
  All, that was ever writ in brasse.
But, since he cannot, Reader, looke
  Not on his Picture, but his Booke.

                                  —B. I.[1]

"B. I." stands for Ben Jonson, the Elizabethan poet and playwright. With these ten lines, Jonson has identified the balding man and told us that "Shakespeare" was not simply a name, a pseudonym attached to anonymous plays, but an actual person. He had a "face"—a *recognizable* face—he had a "life" and, in Jonson's estimation, an extraordinary "wit." He was "gentle"—a description which today has connotations of harmlessness but in 1623 meant possessing the social graces of the gentry. Shakespeare, in other words, was a gentleman (Figure 1).

Turning the page, we find a dedicatory epistle to William, the Earl of Pembroke, who was at the time the Lord Chamberlain to King James, and his brother Philip, the Earl of Montgomery. The epistle, signed by the actors "John Heminge" and "Henrie Condell," speaks of the earls having shown favor to both the plays, "when they were acted," and to their "Author living." With clauses like "we hope . . . you will use the like indulgence toward them you have done unto their parent" and phrases like "your servant Shakespeare," it reveals that the earls, on some level, had contact with Shakespeare, or at least witnessed his corporeal existence. That existence, the epistle repeatedly laments, has come to an end. The author has died, we're told; the plays are his "remains," his "orphans"—and Heminge and Condell have taken it upon themselves to publish the works in order "to keep the memory of so worthy a Friend & Fellow alive. . . ."[2]

"Fellow" in this context means fellow player. "William Shakespeare" appears at the top of the list on the page titled "The Names of the Principall Actors in all these Playes"; "John Hemmings" and "Henry Condell" are in the same column. To celebrate the writer's dual careers, as poet and performer, the anonymous "I. M." contributes some verses, displayed on yet another leaf:

Wee wondred (Shake-speare) that thou went'st so soone
From the Worlds-Stage, to the Graves-Tyring-roome.
Wee thought thee dead, but this thy printed worth,

MR. WILLIAM

SHAKESPEARES

COMEDIES,
HISTORIES, &
TRAGEDIES.

Published according to the True Originall Copies.

Martin Droeshout sculpsit London.

LONDON
Printed by Isaac Iaggard, and Ed. Blount. 1623.

Figure 1. Title page of the First Folio (1623). General Research Division, the New York Public Library, Astor, Lenox, and Tilden Foundations.

Tels thy Spectators, that thou went'st but forth
To enter with applause. An Actors Art,
Can dye, and live, to acte a second part.
That's but an Exit of Mortalitie;
This, a Re-entrance to a Plaudite.[3]

The Folio's more famous commendatory poem is Ben Jonson's soaring panegyric, "To the memory of my beloved, The Author Mr. William Shakespeare: and what he hath left us." In addition to lauding the playwright, it avows that his personality is reflected in his works:

Looke how the fathers face
Lives in his issue, even so, the race
Of *Shakespeares* mind, and manners brightly shines
In his well torned and true-filed lines.[4]

The same poem gives Shakespeare the epithet "Sweet Swan of Avon," while other introductory verses by the writer Leonard Digges mention "his *Stratford* Moniment." These two allusions pinpoint the playwright as William Shakespeare of Stratford-upon-Avon (rather than, say, William Shakespeare of Stratford-on-Trent or William Shakespeare of Coventry).

So the Folio provides us with some basic information about its author. It gives us a name, a face, and a town of origin. It tells us he was an actor known to at least two earls, and that he was dead by 1623. Most importantly, it furnishes testimony—the testimony of Ben Jonson, John Hemmings, and Henry Condell, men who knew Shakespeare—that he wrote the plays.

But even if the First Folio never existed, we would still have enough evidence to establish Shakespeare's authorship. Other artifacts and documents corroborate what the Folio tells us. Prior to 1623, fourteen of the Folio's plays were already published in quarto editions—books smaller than folios, each containing a single play. These works were attributed to Shakespeare by sixteen publishers and printers, secondhand witnesses who must have been told Shakespeare's name. Here are excerpts from the quarto title pages[5]:

"The Tragedie of Richard the second . . . By William Shake-speare. Printed by Valentine Simmes for Andrew Wise . . . 1598."
"Loves Labors Lost . . . By W. Shakespere. Imprinted at London by W. W. [William White] for Cuthbert Burby. 1598."

"The History of Henrie the fourth . . . by W. Shake-speare . . . Printed by S. S. for Andrew Wise . . . 1599."

"The Second part of Henrie the fourth . . . Written by William Shake-speare . . . Printed by V. S. for Andrew Wise and William Aspley. 1600."

"The most excellent Historie of the Merchant of Venice . . . Written by William Shakespeare . . . Printed by I. R. [John Roberts] for Thomas Heyes . . . 1600."

"A Midsommer nights dreame . . . Written by William Shakespeare. Imprinted at London, for Thomas Fisher . . . 1600."

"Much adoe about Nothing . . . Written by William Shakespeare. Printed by V. S. for Andrew Wise and William Aspley. 1600."

"The Tragedie of King Richard the third . . . By William Shake-speare. Printed by Thomas Creede for Andrew Wise. 1602."

"The Tragicall Historie of Hamlet, Prince of Denmarke. By William Shakespeare . . . Printed by I. R. for N. L. [Nicholas Ling] 1604."

"M. William Shake-speare, His True Chronicle History of the life and death of King Lear . . . Printed for Nathaniel Butter. 1608."

"The Historie of Troylus and Cresseida . . . Written by William Shakespeare. Imprinted by G. Eld for R. Bonian and H. Walley . . . 1609."

"The Tragedy of Othello . . . Written by William Shakespeare. Printed by N. O. [Nathaniel Okes] for Thomas Walkley. 1622."

The title pages also announce the acting companies who performed the plays. The early quartos, we are told, were in the repertory of the "Lord Chamberlain's Servants," and the later ones belonged to "His Majesty's Servants" (the King's Men). These were the two troupes, as documents show, that had Shakespeare as a member. The actor, therefore, is connected to the plays, and unless there was another man with the same name, he was believed to be the Author.

At Cambridge, in about 1601, an anonymous play was produced which again points to the actor Shakespeare as the Author. In the play, which is called *The Return from Parnassus Part Two*, a character named Kempe says to another called Burbage,

Few of the university men pen plays well, they smell too much of that writer *Ovid*, and that writer *Metamorphosis*, and talk too much of *Proserpina & Jupiter*. Why here's our fellow *Shakespeare* puts them all down, [Ay] and *Ben Jonson* too. O that *Ben Jonson* is a pestilent fellow, he

brought up *Horace* giving the Poets a pill, but our fellow *Shakespeare*
hath given him a purge that made him bewray his credit.[6]
[spelling modernized]

William Kempe and Richard Burbage were two of the most popular actors of the time. They are listed in the same column with Shakespeare in
the "names of Principall Actors," and they performed with him in *Every
Man in His Humour* in 1598 (according to the cast list in Jonson's *Works*
[1616]). The Accounts of the Treasurer of the Queen's Chamber records
payment to "William Kempe William Shakespeare & Richarde Burbage
servantes to the Lord Chamberleyne" for performances at the royal
palace at Greenwich in December 1594, and the three men are named
together yet again in a lawsuit of 1619 as having been joint sharers in the
Globe Theatre. The Shakespeare who was a "fellow" of Kempe and
Burbage was the actor from Stratford. And the authors of the anonymous
play thought he was a playwright.

The hardest evidence (literally) for Shakespeare's authorship resides in
the Warwickshire town of Stratford-upon-Avon. There, ensconced in the
chancel of Holy Trinity Church, can still be seen the "Moniment," an
elaborately decorated niche containing a head-to-waist bust. Its inscription reads,

> Judicio Pylium, Genio Socratem, Arte Maronem,
> Terra tegit, Populus Maeret, Olympus habet.
>
> Stay Passenger, why goest thou by so fast?
> Read if thou canst, whom envious Death hath plast,
> With in this monument Shakspeare: with whome,
> Quick nature dide: whose name, doth deck ys Tombe
> Far more, then cost: Sieh all, yt He hath writt,
> Leaves living art, but page, to serve his witt.
>
> Obiit An˜o Do[i] 1616
Aetatis. 53 die 23 AP[r].

The Latin opening translates, "In judgment a Nestor, in inspiration a
Socrates, in art a Virgil, the earth covers him, the people mourn him,
Olympus has him." Clearly someone thought pretty highly of this man.
And the last couplet as well as the comparison to Virgil prove that that
"someone" thought the deceased was a writer. Shakespeare, however, is
not "within" the monument, nor are his manuscripts. Whoever wrote the
inscription (possibly Ben Jonson) must have believed Shakespeare would

be buried in a place where visitors would be walking by, hence the "Stay Passenger." He or she must have thought the epitaph would be engraved on a tomb, as epitaphs normally are, and had no idea the body would be buried under the floor a few feet away.

That the memorial was intended for the playwright, and not for another man named Shakespeare, can be shown from seventeenth-century documents. In 1634, the bust was identified by a lieutenant from Norwich who was making a survey of the county. He describes it as "A neat Monument of that famous English Poet, Mr. William Shakespeere; who was born here."[7] At the time, Shakespeare's two daughters and their husbands, two grandsons (who would die young), a granddaughter and her husband, a sister and two nephews, were all living in Stratford. Any doubt that the monument's subject was the man indicated by the compilers of the First Folio is removed by William Shakespeare's last will and testament. It leaves small bequests to "my fellowes John Hemynge Richard Burbage & Henry Cundell." Obviously, the Stratford Shakespeare was their associate.

After Shakespeare's death, William Basse was inspired to write an elegy that begins

> Renowned Spencer, lye a thought more nye
> To learned Chaucer, and rare Beaumont lye
> A little neerer Spencer to make roome
> For Shakespeare in your threefold fo[u]rfold Tombe.[8]

Make room, that is, in Westminster Abbey. Since Ben Jonson would refer to Basse's elegy in his own commendatory poem in the Folio,

> My *Shakespeare*, rise; I will not lodge thee by
>   *Chaucer*, or *Spenser*, or bid *Beaumont* lye
> A little further, to make thee a roome:
>   Thou art a Moniment, without a tombe

we know that Basse's poem must predate 1623; it was not composed many years after Shakespeare's demise, when a myth of authorship might have taken hold. When it was published, Basse or his editor supplied the title "On Mr. William Shakespeare, he dyed in Aprill 1616." Note the date. It matches the month and year on the monument. Basse was certainly of the opinion that the Stratford man was the Author.

When the plays of Francis Beaumont and John Fletcher were collected into a folio of their own in 1647, a dedication to the Earl of Pembroke and Montgomery (Philip had survived his brother and assumed his title) reminds the earl of his former patronage of "the flowing compositions of the Sweet Swan of Avon, Shakespeare." The dedication was signed by the ten surviving members of the King's Men, including John Lowin, who had acted with Shakespeare in Jonson's *Sejanus* (1603). Lowin associated the Bard with the Avon.

That the playwright was born in Stratford was remarked in 1630 by an anonymous writer who calls the town "most remarkable for the birth of famous William Shakespeare,"[9] and thirty years later by Thomas Fuller in his *Worthies of England* (1662).[10] Also in 1662, Stratford's new vicar, John Ward, noted in his diary, "Mr. Shakespeare . . . frequented the plays all his younger time, but in his elder days lived at Stratford: and supplied the stage with two plays every year."[11] Ward was acquainted with Shakespeare's daughter Judith, who was still living in the town.[12]

With all of the historical evidence pointing in one direction (and I've produced only a fraction of it so far), it's hard to believe anyone ever doubted who wrote the plays and poems. Indeed, although many legends cropped up about Shakespeare in the seventeenth and eighteenth centuries—that he was godfather to one of Ben Jonson's children, that he was prosecuted for deer stealing, that the playwright Sir William Davenant was his illegitimate son—not one apocryphal story claims the plays were mistakenly ascribed to Shakespeare or ghostwritten by someone else. All of the myths presume his authorship, even those that create an image of the poet as an ignorant country bumpkin. Yet, ironically, those same myths would become the seeds of the Authorship Debate.

What happened was simple. In the Folio, Jonson wrote,

> And though thou hadst small *Latine* and lesse *Greeke*,
>   From thence to honour thee, I would not seeke
> For names; but call forth thund'ring *Aeschilus*,
>   *Euripides*, and *Sophocles* to us . . .

He isn't sure how much Latin and Greek the Author knew—"And though thou hadst" means "And even if you had"—but he's willing to make an educated guess based, probably, on his reading of the plays. Unlike other contemporary writers who stuffed their works with classical quotations, the Author makes only a limited number of references to

Roman texts and even fewer to Greek: so "small Latin and less Greek" is a natural inference. On the other hand, it's possible that Shakespeare knew those languages well but revealed only a fraction of that knowledge overtly in his plays. Thus Jonson prudently uses the subjunctive form of the verb, which conveys uncertainty: *hadst* instead of *had*. Nonetheless, some would read "And though thou hadst" as implying Shakespeare did not have *even* small Latin or less Greek. It was only a small step for Jonson's observation to be interpreted as *no* Latin and *no* Greek.

In 1640, for the book *Poems: Written by Wil. Shake-speare, Gent.*, Leonard Digges was asked to compose commendatory verses, as he had done for the First Folio. These begin,

> Poets are borne not made, when I would prove
> This truth, the glad remembrance I must love
> Of never dying *Shakespeare*.[13]

His remembrance may be literal. Digges was the stepson of Thomas Russell, Esq., one of the overseers of Shakespeare's will, and he may have known Shakespeare personally. Of the poet's art, he writes,

> Nature onely helpt him, for looke thorow
> This whole Booke, thou shalt find he doth not borrow,
> One phrase from Greekes, nor Latines imitate,
> Nor once from vulgar Languages Translate,
> Nor Plagiari-like from others gleane,
> Nor begges he from each witty friend a Scene
> To peece his Acts with, all that he doth write,
> Is pure his owne, plot, language, exquisite.[14]

In fact, Digges is wrong on every point. Scholars have determined that the Works are chock-full of borrowed classical phrases, imitated Latin lines, translations from French, scenes by other hands, and plots and text stolen from others. But the average seventeenth-century reader would have taken Digges at his word, especially his insistence that "Nature onely helpt him." The university men who wrote *The Return from Parnassus Part Two* knew Shakespeare wasn't one of them, but Digges implies Shake-

speare had no learning whatsoever—and his proof, notice, is the plays and poems themselves.

Digges's assertion became common lore in the seventeenth century. In *Worthies of England*, Fuller grants the poet "very little learning."[15] Vicar John Ward notes that he has heard that "Mr. Shakespeare was a natural wit, without any art at all."[16] By 1709, Nicholas Rowe takes it on faith that the poet's Latin was "small" and relates a whimsical anecdote that explains why: "[His father] had bred him, 'tis true, for some time at a Free-School, where 'tis probable he acquir'd that little Latin he was Master of: But the narrowness of his Circumstances, and the want of his assistance at Home, forc'd his Father to withdraw him from thence, and unhappily prevented his further Proficiency in that Language."[17] About twenty years later, an early encyclopedia called the *Magna Britannica* begins its entry on the playwright with "William Shakespeare was an eminent poet but no scholar."[18] Meanwhile, an anonymous *Essay against too much reading* asserts that when it came to history, Shakespeare "could scarce speak a Word on the subject." The essay imagines he kept a historian as an assistant whom he would consult frequently. "Instead of Reading," argues the pamphlet, "he stuck close to Writing and Study without Book. How do you think reading could have assisted him in such great Thoughts? It would only have lost time."[19]

As the 1700s progressed, Shakespeare ascended to his present place, atop the promontory of English letters. Accompanying him was his popular image as an uneducated, spontaneous genius. But for the first time, scholars began to question how much learning Shakespeare really had. They examined the plays, as Leonard Digges had challenged them to do, and they found everything Digges had denied—Latin translations, French translations, the works. Now, suddenly, there were two Shakespeares: One was the ignorant deer poacher and the other was the Author of the Plays, a man literate in several languages who gathered a great deal of his knowledge from books. Even as biographers dis-spelled the first of these Shakespeares as a myth, the notion that he was unlearned refused to die. For a hundred and fifty years, it had been an article of faith that he was "born not made," and investigators could find no record of his education. Never mind that the Stratford grammar school rolls had been lost in one of the many fires that plagued the town; to the credulous, that didn't matter. For the Bardolators of the eighteenth century and the Romantics of the nineteenth, it was important that Shakespeare be a "child of nature," unsullied by other men's

ideas, a poet whose every scribble flowed purely from the Dionysian spring. The greater his ignorance, the more his imagination could be revered.

So the false Shakespeare was not supplanted by the true, and it was only a matter of time before the inevitable syllogism would be formulated. Ergo: If Shakespeare was unlearned, but the man who wrote the plays had learning, then Shakespeare was not the man who wrote the plays. And so, the Authorship Question was born.

I suspect that by 1800 there were hundreds of people who had fallen prey to the above logic. But it was not until 1848 that the Authorship Question emerged from the obscurity of private murmurs into the daylight of public debate. That year, Joseph C. Hart, a New York lawyer and the United States consul at Santa Cruz, published *The Romance of Yachting*, a book ostensibly about seafaring but which meanders its way from digression to digression, pausing for an extended shore leave on Shakespeare. The latter was a vulgarian, Hart believed; he "grew up in ignorance and viciousness"[20] and purchased or stole the plays from others. His sole contribution was to add obscenities and "impurities," while the best in the Works, the profound philosophy in *Hamlet* for example, was probably swiped from Jonson.

Though Hart's book sold poorly, it was certainly in touch with the zeitgeist of its time. Four years later, an unsigned article in *Chambers's Edinburgh Journal* expressed skepticism that Shakespeare, who bought and sold land and wrote a prosaic will, could have been the National Poet. *Putnam's Monthly*, a New York magazine, followed with a feature in its January 1856 issue titled "William Shakespeare and His Plays; an Inquiry Concerning Them." Its thesis was the same: The "stupid, ignorant, third rate play-actor" could not have written the plays. Only someone with "learning broad enough, and deep enough, and subtle enough, and comprehensive enough, one with nobility of aim and philosophic and poetic genius enough" could claim as his own the "immortal progeny."[21] The article's author does not name whom she has in mind, but here's a hint: Her own name was Delia Bacon. She would elaborate on her idea the next year in *The Philosophy of the Plays of Shakspere Unfolded*. The True Author was not a man, according to Delia, but a group, a secret cabal of aristocratic poets, headed by Sir Walter Ralegh, whose principal writer was Francis Bacon.

At the same time, an Englishman named William Henry Smith circulated a pamphlet that asked the provocative question *Was Lord Bacon the Author of Shakespeare's Plays?* In 1857, he expanded his tract to book length and gave it the title *Bacon and Shakespeare: An Inquiry Touching Players, Playhouses, and Play-Writers in the Days of Elizabeth*. This slim volume, just over a hundred pages, would be the real dam buster of the Authorship Question. It was widely read and its case was simple. Shakespeare was a mere itinerant player, whereas the Author of the Works, who writes with the well-bred tone of a courtier, must have been a nobleman and a scholar—like Bacon.

A deluge of books and articles followed, thousands by century's end. Some advocated Sir Francis's cause, others more cautiously preferred to simply denounce Shakespeare's. Still others, with more imagination than scholarship, proposed new candidates. It wasn't long before Bacon was joined in the circle of claimants by every major figure of the Elizabethan age—every poet, every playwright (Christopher Marlowe, among the latter, attracting the most partisans), the Earl of Derby (popular in France), the earls of Rutland, Salisbury, Southampton, Devon, Stirling, and Essex, groups like the one suggested by Delia Bacon, and even Queen Elizabeth and King James, to name just a few. Each of these candidates managed to snare a handful of converts, but none besides Bacon generated worldwide enthusiasm. Then, in 1920, a significant contender was put forward by J. Thomas Looney (pronounced LOE-ny) in *"Shakespeare" Identified in Edward De Vere the Seventeenth Earl of Oxford*, a book that might have come out a year earlier but its author had to find a new publisher when his first one insisted he use a pen name. Looney would have the last laugh, though. By the year 2000, thousands would regard his surname as that of a prophet and his candidate would be the anti-Stratfordian idol with the most devotees.

The sheer number of alternative Bards—fifty-six, by some counts—has caused many people to dismiss the Authorship Question outright. But we should remember that all visions of the True Author are spawned from the same germinal belief—a belief in the inadequacy of Shakespeare. His meager education, middle class upbringing, and insufficient experience render him, in the eyes of the heretics, incapable of being the Poet. The question is, Was his education really so meager and his experience really insufficient? Or, to put it another way, Is there evidence in the Works that their Author was someone else—a university graduate, for example, or a courtier? Were there two Shakespeares or only one?

We can investigate these questions. But before we do, we need to remember the artifacts that point to the man from Stratford. To deny that Shakespeare wrote the plays is to deny the evidence that says he did. Can that material, which features testimonials from people who knew him, be easily dismissed? For the would-be anti-Stratfordian this is the initial hurdle. "Ben Jonson must be answered first,"[22] the great essayist Ralph Waldo Emerson told Delia Bacon, and his warning is still best heeded today.

CHAPTER 2
The Third Man

Delia Bacon was unfazed by historical witnesses. She imagined, as Hart had done before her, that Ben Jonson was lying, perhaps under duress, as part of a conspiratorial effort to hide the truth. Instead of suspecting there might be something wrong with her vision of the Author, or her conception of Shakespeare, or both, she had faith it was the evidence that was amiss. The Stratford monument, naturally, was a sham, the epistles in the First Folio a hoax, and Shakespeare (whom she calls "Will the Jester") a conniving pretender, hellbent on gain. Not surprisingly, though very sadly, Delia spent her last days in a madhouse, shrieking her unorthodox notions like a Victorian Cassandra.

But that doesn't mean she was wrong.

Maybe there *was* a conspiracy. Maybe her accusations were more than just the by-products of a disintegrating mind. One has to admit, there's something fishy about Jonson's connection to the crucial pieces of the puzzle. It's Jonson's word that the Folio engraving resembles Shakespeare, and it's Jonson who seems to have composed the epitaph on the monument. Even the dedication and preface signed by Heminges and Condell are believed by some to have been ghostwritten by Jonson. What's most germane, though, is that it's Jonson who tells us "the father's face lives in his issue." Is he being dishonest? Is he slyly fabricating a likeness between the actor and the Author to make their identity more convincing? Or, perhaps, he's misremembering his "beloved"—re-inventing the dead man and then projecting him into his supposed handiwork. Only one thing is certain: For there to be an Authorship Question at all, Jonson must be wrong. Either he was a dupe, taken in by a persuasive front man (an actor, after all) or, as most heretics assert, he was a central figure in a conspiracy.

To give an air of credence to this latter idea, anti-Stratfordians observe how Jonson's esteem for his older colleague fluctuates over the years. The author of *Volpone* is downright caustic when he speaks of Shakespeare, in 1619, to William Drummond of Hawthornden. Jonson, then at the pinnacle of his career, having become King James's principal poet and a great favorite at court, had embarked on a walking tour of England and Scotland. Visiting Edinburgh, he stayed for two or three weeks with Drummond, a poet in his own right and a laird of the Scottish gentry. As the two men shared meals and liquor, Jonson regaled his host with anecdotes from his life and with bilious criticisms of his fellow writers, all of which Drummond jotted down as soon as his guest departed. The most notorious comment in the notes, and the one seized upon by unbelievers, is "Shaksperr wanted arte."[1] This is a far cry from the "Soul of the Age!" of the commendatory verses. In fact, it's a direct contradiction of the lines,

> Yet must I not give Nature all: Thy Art,
>   My gentle *Shakespeare*, must enjoy a part.
> For though the Poets matter, Nature be,
>   His Art doth give the fashion. And, that he,
> Who casts to write a living line, must sweat,
>   (such as thine are) and strike the second heat
> Upon the Muses anvile: turne the same,
>   (And himselfe with it) that he thinkes to frame.[2]

What's going on here? Jonson praises Shakespeare in the Folio for the very thing he reproves him for, just four years earlier, to Drummond. This reversal seems mysterious, and one can understand the doubters' doubts. But it's typical of Jonson.

He treats Edmund Spenser, whose *Faerie Queene* may be the greatest epic poem in English, in exactly the same way. To Drummond, he complains that "Spencers stanzaes pleased him not, nor his matter,"[3] yet in his *Discoveries*, a book published posthumously in 1641, Jonson says of Spenser, "I would have him read for his matter."[4] Sir Philip Sidney fares no better. Jonson told Drummond that Sidney "did not keep a Decorum in making every one speak as well as himself,"[5] but in the intended-for-publication *Discoveries*, Sidney is described as a master of "wit and language, and in whom all vigor of Invention, and strength of judgement met."[6] In Jonson's epigrams (1616), John Donne is the "delight of Phoebus and each Muse"[7] and to Drummond he's called "the first poet in the world in some things" but "for not keeping accent deserved hanging" and had written "all his best pieces ere he was 25 years old."[8] As for Michael Drayton, Jonson wrote a long poem in 1627 lauding him as a modern Ovid ("who can/With us be called the *Naso* but this man?"); however he privately sniffed to Drummond that Drayton's "long verses pleased him not" and "he esteemed not of him."[9]

When it comes to Shakespeare, though, it's possible Jonson is not as inconsistent as he appears. The artistry he praises in "To the memory of my beloved . . ." is the craftsmanship of the Author's poetry, whereas the "arte" he believed Shakespeare lacked may have been a different art altogether—the skills of play construction. In his Prologue to *Every Man in His Humour* (1616), Jonson obviously had the Author in mind when he glances at *The Winter's Tale* (in lines 1 and 2), *Henry VI* (in lines 4 and 5), and *Henry V* (in line 9):

> To make a child, now swaddled to proceed
> Man, and then shoot up, in one beard, and weed,
> Past threescore years: or, with three rusty swords,
> And help of some few foot-and-half-foot words,
> Fight over *York*, and *Lancasters* long jars:
> And in the tiring-house bring wounds, to scars.
> He rather prays, you will be pleas'd to see
> One such, to day, as other plays should be.
> Where neither Chorus wafts you o'er the seas;
> Nor creaking throne come down, the boys to please.[10]

[spelling modernized]

The neoclassical principles, such as unity of time, unity of place, and unity of action, were Jonson's credos; they were his rules for writing plays. Anyone who violated them, as Shakespeare willfully did, was playing tennis without a net, even if he was an accomplished poet.

The word *art* also meant "learning" in Renaissance England. It could be that Ben was unimpressed with his friend's scholarship. He can't resist mentioning Shakespeare's "small Latin and less Greek" even when eulogizing him. Jonson himself was the most erudite of Elizabethan playwrights and recommended a long list of Latin writers to Drummond. Yet he confessed to his host that his degrees from Oxford and Cambridge were honorary and that he received them late in life. The stepson of a bricklayer, he may have attended the Westminster School as a boy, but there's no record of it—only his casual remark to Drummond that he owed all his education to "his Master Camden," who taught the younger pupils at Westminster when Ben was of grammar school age.[11] His condescension toward Shakespeare's learning—if he felt any—was not that of a socially superior university graduate but that of a self-made scholar, looking down on a less studious colleague.

Needless to say, the anti-Stratfordians have a different view. They see "Shaksperr wanted arte" as referring to the ignorant actor who did not write the plays. The True Author obviously possessed artistry and learning, so Jonson must be talking about someone else, namely the phony front man. A few years later, Jonson's praise for Shakespeare in the Folio must actually be addressed to the True Author—except, perhaps, for the "small Latin and less Greek" comment, which some read as an ironic aside, a knowing wink at the untutored impostor.

This may sound plausible, but there's a problem. Drummond precedes Jonson's remark with the heading "His Censure of the English Poets was this." Clearly, he thought his guest was reproaching the Author. Jonson went on to tell Drummond that "Sheakspear in a play brought in a number of men saying they had suffered shipwrack in Bohemia, wher ther is no sea neer by some 100 miles."[12] Since in this comment, Jonson is certainly mocking the Poet, are we to believe he would refer to the actor in one instance and the Author in another without distinguishing them to his listener? Unbelievers point to the different spellings of the name ("Shaksperr" and "Sheakspear"), but remember: it's Drummond's spelling, not Jonson's. And how does Jonson know *The Winter's Tale* was by Shakespeare? It had not yet been ascribed to him by anyone or published with his byline. Jonson must have had inside information.

The heretics have an even bigger challenge when it comes to the *Discoveries*. Jonson's collection of critical essays includes a passage that's a cornerstone of the orthodox, Stratfordian case. It specifically identifies Shakespeare the man with Shakespeare the dramatist:

I remember, the players have often mentioned it as an honour to *Shakespeare*, that in his writing, (whatsoever he penn'd) he never blotted out line. My answer hath been, would he had blotted a thousand. Which they thought a malevolent speech. I had not told posterity this, but for their ignorance, who choose that circumstance to commend their friend by, wherein he most faulted. And to justify mine own candor, (for I lov'd the man, and do honour his memory (on this side Idolatry) as much as any.) He was (indeed) honest, and of an open, and free nature:

had an excellent *Phantsie*; brave notions, and gentle expressions: wherein hee flow'd with that facility, that sometime it was necessary he should be stop'd: *Sufflaminandus erat* ["He needed a chariot brake"]; as *Augustus* said of *Haterius*. His wit was in his own power; would the rule of it had been so too. Many times he fell into those things, could not escape laughter: As when he said in the person of *Caesar*, one speaking to him; *Caesar thou dost me wrong*. He replied: *Caesar did never wrong, but with just cause:* and such like, which were ridiculous. But he redeemed his vices, with his virtues. There was ever more in him to be praised then to be pardoned.[13]

[spelling modernized]

The first sentence harkens back to Heminge's and Condell's preface, "To the Great Variety of Readers," in which the actors marvel, "His mind and hand went together: And what he thought, he uttered with that easiness, that we scarce received from him a blot in his papers."[14] If, as some scholars contend, Jonson ghostwrote those words, the thoughts must have been the actors' because here, in the *Discoveries*, he takes issue with their opinion. His response to the players, his "malevolent speech," shows that the man he "lov'd," and whose personality he could describe, was the same one that Heminges and Condell were talking about in the Folio.

That man was their "friend," the actor. It would be ludicrous for Jonson to say of a nobleman—and most alternative candidates are noblemen—"He was (indeed) honest" or "Many times he fell into those things could not escape laughter." In the England of the time, the whole passage would be seen as gravely impudent. Anti-Stratfordians, therefore, are left with no recourse except to cry "Conspiracy!" Jonson must be perpetuating the fraud. As he did in the Folio, he must be intentionally linking the Author and the front man. Maybe he's fabricating his conversation with the players, too. Who knows? There may be no end to his deceptions.

A more boring theory would be that Ben Jonson was telling the truth, that he honestly believed Shakespeare wrote the Plays. Perhaps he was fooled by the clever impostor, but that seems unlikely since he tells us the "race of Shakespeare's mind, and manners brightly shines" in his poetry. The man he knew was visible in the plays. Perhaps he was a key participant in a conspiracy, the main accomplice to the True Author and the false one, but that's unlikely too. How could he hope to get away with such a thing when other people, who were still alive, had known Shakespeare and could see for themselves whether "the father's face lived in his issue"? Although his involvement with the Folio and the monument puts

Jonson in a prime position to orchestrate a cover-up, a more plausible scenario is that he was Shakespeare's closest literary friend, and thus he was asked to write the epitaph, epistles, and verses.

As for Jonson's fluctuating opinion, it's true he is more negative in his critical essay than in his effervescent commendatory poem, but that's not exactly surprising. Since the eulogistic "To the memory of my beloved . . ." was hardly the place to quibble about the Author's shortcomings, his balanced, honest assessment would rightly wait for the appropriate milieu in the *Discoveries*. But in neither text does he separate the man from the Author. He doesn't denigrate the player while he effuses over the Poet. There's no indication, anywhere, that he believed in more than one Shakespeare.

Nonetheless, some anti-Stratfordians allege that Jonson's epigram "On Poet-Ape," written some time before its publication in 1616, reveals Jonson knew an actor was being used as a front man. This is the poem:

> Poor Poet-Ape that would be thought our chief,
>   Whose works are e'en the frippery of wit,
> From brokage[15] is become so bold a thief,
>   As we, the robb'd, leave rage and pity it.
> At first he made low shifts, would pick and glean,
>   Buy the reversion of old plays; now grown
> To a little wealth, and credit in the *scene*
>   He takes up all, makes each man's wit his own.
> And, told of this, he slights it. Tut, such crimes
>   The sluggish, gaping auditor devours;
> He marks not whose 'twas first; and aftertimes
>   May judge it to be his as well as ours.
> Fool! as if half eyes will not know a fleece
> From locks of wool, or shreds from the whole piece.[16]

[spelling modernized]

"Poet-Ape" was the current derogatory term for actor-dramatists, coined by Sir Philip Sidney.[17] This mocking sonnet's subject is being accused of plagiarizing from Jonson and from other writers, not of concealing someone else. Many scholars think that Jonson's "Poet-Ape" is Shakespeare, who indeed stole lines and ideas from Marlowe and from old plays like *The Famous Victories of Henry V*, but other scholars prefer the player-playwright Thomas Heywood. Whomever Jonson had in mind, the epigram shows he was a stickler for who wrote what.

What about the Stratford memorial? Is there a whiff of conspiracy hanging around the famous effigy?

Some say yes. They assert the statue did not originally depict a poet. Even though, today, the bust shows a man holding a sheet of paper under his left hand and a quill in his right (the fingers have been sculpted to grip one), they assert it wasn't always that way. Their proof: The earliest known drawing of the monument omits the pen and paper. When William Dugdale sketched the effigy for his *Antiquities of Warwickshire* (1656), he neglected the writing accoutrements, and his drawing, and the engraving made from it, contain other anomalies. The subject's mustaches droop rather than curl upward; leopards' heads sit atop the Corinthian columns; and the small nude figures representing Labor and Rest dangle their legs off the cornice, the latter having traded his downturned torch and skull for an hourglass. Similar discrepancies can be found between other illustrations in the book and the monuments they're supposed to represent, so, apparently, Dugdale liked to improve the funerary he sketched according to his own taste. Most of his inaccurate renderings were replaced, by more meticulous hands, in the 1730 edition of his book. Unfortunately, the engraving of Shakespeare's monument was not among them (Figure 2).

The anti-Stratfordian alternative interpretation is that Dugdale had it right, that he drew what he saw and at some point the sculpture was recast. But the bust has been examined and those kinds of serious changes were never made to it. The earliest record of repair is from 1749 when the sculpture was "beautified," but drawings by George Vertue from 1725 and 1737 show the monument in its present state—with the Poet and his quill (Figure 3).

In any event, it's not the effigy but the inscription that tells us the Stratford man was a writer. Dugdale notes the first words of the Latin opening and uses ellipses for the rest so there can be no doubt that, from the beginning, the inscription was present and an author was being honored. And a pretty good author at that—"In art, a Virgil."

Still unsatisfied, some people believe the memorial is part of the conspiracy, that its installation was intended to further the lie that William Shakespeare wrote the plays. If that's true, then the conspirators weren't very smart. Monuments like Shakespeare's cost £60 (roughly $60,000 [US] in today's money), and this one is tucked away in the chancel of a church, in a small town, among people who never went to the theatre, many of whom were illiterate. Whom were the hoaxers trying to convince? The vicar? We should also keep in mind that the early seventeenth century was a deeply religious time. To commit a fraud in the chancel of a church, a few feet from the altar of Christ, was surely to risk eternal damnation. Really, there is only one explanation for the monument. Those who paid for this marble and limestone tribute (whoever they were) thought its subject was the Author.

In the floor, a few yards away, lies the slab that covers Shakespeare's grave. This is what appears on its face:

> Good frend for Jesus sake forbeare,
>   to digg the dust enclosed heare:
> Bleste be ye man yt spares thes stones,
>   and curst be he yt moves my bones.

Nothing else is engraved—no name, no dates. With the monument on the way, perhaps a second "in memoriam" seemed redundant. But whatever the reason, the anonymity of the great man's burial plot is odd and disconcerting. In addition, the poor quality of the doggerel has fed the suspicion that this is a true writing sample of the man, while the plays and poems are not. But there's no guarantee that Shakespeare wrote it, except the word "my." And even if he did, he may have felt a simple jingle would be the most effective way to protect his remains. As early as 1694, a student named William Hall suggested the verses were aimed at the clerks and sextons. "There is in this church," he wrote to a friend, "a place which they call the bone house, a repository for all the bones they dig up; which are so many that they would load a great number of wagons. The Poet being willing to preserve his bones unmoved lays a curse upon him who moves them."[18] A believer in the Second Coming might fear a mix-up in the charnel room, so that on Resurrection Day he would find himself with a neighbor's arm, the apothecary's leg, and his wife's pelvis! The remains haven't been touched since their burial, so the curse, whosoever it is, has worked extremely well.

Another lightning rod for heretics is Francis Meres, a divinity student and enthusiast for English literature who assigned plays to Shakespeare before anyone else did and who seemed to be one of his private friends. In his book *Palladis Tamia: Wits Treasury* (1598), Meres wrote:

> As Plautus and Seneca are accounted the best for comedy and tragedy among the Latins, so *Shakespeare* among the English is the most excellent in both kinds for the stage. For comedy, witness his *Gentlemen of Verona*, his *Errors*, his *Love's Labor's Lost*, his *Love's Labor's Won*, his

Figure 2. Shakespeare's monument in Holy
Trinity Church, Stratford-upon-Avon. General
Research Division, the New York Public Library,
Astor, Lenox, and Tilden Foundations.

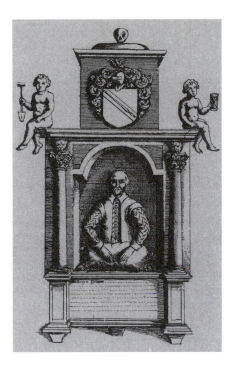

Figure 3. Engraving of Shakespeare's monument from *Antiquities of Warwickshire* by William Dugdale (1656). General Research Division, the New York Public Library, Astor, Lenox, and Tilden Foundations.

Midsummer's Night Dream, his *Merchant of Venice*; for tragedy, his *Richard the 2., Richard the 3., Henry the 4., King John, Titus Andronicus,* and his *Romeo and Juliet.*[19]
[spelling modernized]

A quarter of a century later, all but one of these titles would be included in the First Folio. The exception, *Love's Labor's Won*, may be an alternative name for another play—such as *Taming of the Shrew* or *Much Ado About Nothing*—or it may have been left out of the collection. One paragraph earlier, Meres praises Shakespeare's "sugared Sonnets among his private friends." Since none of the Poet's sonnets had been printed yet, Meres must have been one of the "private friends" or was acquainted with one; otherwise, he couldn't have read the poems he calls "sugared."

Theorists, however, claim he was deceived, a victim of the guardians of the secret, who let him peek at a few sonnets and gave him a list of plays, knowing full well he would broadcast the Shakespeare myth in his *Palladis Tamia*. More cynical heretics think he was in on the secret all along, that he carried it throughout his life (most of which was spent as the rector of a parish in Rutlandshire) and never told a soul before his death in 1647. For unbelievers, either version will do—and will have to, since there's evidence of neither. The only unacceptable interpretation is the simplest: that Meres knew Shakespeare and knew he wrote the Plays. Besides the Author, Meres praises twenty-eight poets of comedy and tragedy, yet he names plays by only two other writers: Thomas Nashe, whose notorious *Isle of Dogs* had caused the Privy Council to close all London theatres in 1597, and Dr. Leg of Cambridge, "who hath penned two famous tragedies, one of Richard the Third and the other of the destruction of Jerusalem."[20] His special knowledge of Dr. Leg and Shakespeare suggests personal acquaintance.[21] If he was not in Shakespeare's circle, how else could he learn so much about the Author's unpublished canon and yet demonstrate so little familiarity with anyone else's? Unquestionably, he knew the poet Michael Drayton, who, like Shakespeare, hailed from Warwickshire and had no university degree. Meres can report that Drayton "is now ... penning in English verse a poem called Poly-olbion," and he commends the poet for a long list of virtues, including his "honest conversation."[22] Maybe the divinity student was misled about Drayton's authorship too.

Deceived or in on the lie—the same explanations are used to dismiss the quarto publishers and the Cambridge authors of the *Parnassus* plays as well as the many contemporaries who refer to Shakespeare. No document is above question, and therefore none can be permitted into evidence. Such is the power of an assumed conspiracy. It effectively silences all external materials. The voices of history are deemed untrustworthy. Only Shakespeare's inadequacy, the guiding premise of anti-Stratfordians, is indisputable. It is the one unshakeable fact to any Authorship theorist. If it's true, if the actor could not have written the Plays and Poems, then paranoia would be justified. Scholars would have to hypothesize an intrigue to explain why Jonson and friends were misleading posterity. But if Shakespeare is not inadequate, if the Stratford man *could* have been the Author, then reason dictates that the evidence might be what it seems, and the deceived, for all their clamor, are the doubters themselves.

CHAPTER 3
The Vacuum

In the imaginations of his detractors, William Shakespeare is at best a semiliterate actor and theatre manager who, because of judicious investments, rose in worldly status to become a respected provincial burgher; at worst he is a criminal, a venal Elizabethan ruffian, tax cheat, and grain hoarder. But whatever man an anti-Stratfordian envisions, the image is based on incomplete information. The heretics construct their wicker Shakespeares out of a few business records, which have been removed from historical context. Rigidly confining themselves to documents bearing Shakespeare's name, they ignore circumstantial evidence and logical inferences which investigators always use in sculpting a biography. Like Baconian Mark Twain, they believe Shakespeare is a "brontosaur: nine bones and six hundred barrels of plaster of Paris."[1] And in a way, they're right. Historians' pictures, like paleontologists' models, are not derived from wishful fantasy but from outside sources of evidence that reveal what the nine bones imply. Willfully or ignorantly, anti-Stratfordians disregard contextual evidence so their brontosaurs are misshapen, unfinished, and inaccurate.

The fact is, we have a lot more information than the heretics think we do. We may not have the curriculum of the Stratford grammar school, but we do know what books were taught at similar schools. If no single record declares Shakespeare acted in plays at the royal palaces, several tell us his theatre company performed before the reigning monarchs. By making a few legitimate assumptions, researchers have been able to discover a great deal about the life of William Shakespeare.

This is what we know:

He was baptized, according to the Stratford Parish Register, on 26 April 1564. His birth must have been at least three days before, because the inscription on his monument states he died in his 53rd year ("aetatis 53") on 23 April 1616, which means he had to have been born on April 23rd or earlier. It wouldn't have been too much earlier because his parents had watched their first two children die in infancy, and we can assume they would have been quick to baptize William in case he died early too.

His father, John Shakespeare, was a glover—a maker and seller of gloves, belts, aprons, purses, and other soft leather goods—as well as a whittawer, one who cured and prepared "white-leather," which was made from the skins of deer, horses, goats, sheep, and dogs. This may sound like a humble trade, but Tudor master craftsmen represented the bourgeoisie of their time. In addition to practicing their principal metier, they often owned farmland and had diverse financial interests. John, for example, dealt in barley, timber, investment real estate, and, most famously, in wool. He was a prosperous man. Tourists tramping through the double-house on Henley Street, which is today known as Shakespeare's Birthplace, are usually unaware that at the time the famous man was born, his father also owned a house on Greenhill Street, held a cottage and nearly sixty acres of farmland and meadow at the freehold estate of Asbies, and was about to inherit a ninth share in two houses and one hundred acres at Snitterfield. By the time William was twelve, John had bought two more houses with gardens and orchards in Stratford and held the lease to fourteen more acres at Ingon Meadow in Hampton Lucy.

The family was among the wealthiest in town. In all likelihood, they employed servants who helped with the household chores and who may or may not have lived under the same roof. We don't normally think of Shakespeare as growing up with servants, but if his family was similar to other families of comparable income and status, then that would have been the case. His mother, Mary, the daughter of the yeoman Robert Arden, had grown up with domestics, and it's doubtful she would have married John Shakespeare if he could not have promised her a continuation of her lifestyle. Observing Mary as she commanded the help or hearing his father give orders to the stitchers in his shop, the apprentices hanging sheepskins in his drying shed, and the laborers tilling his fields, young Will could not have failed to absorb that his social place was a privileged one, that in a class-conscious society most people were beneath him.

The lesson would have been reinforced by his father's high position in the municipal government. John had been chosen as one of the town's fourteen burgesses in 1557. Four years later, he was responsible for the Corporation of Stratford's property and finances as one of the two chamberlains who prepared the borough accounts, and he continued to keep the books for two years after his term expired. But his real elevation came in 1565, when he was selected to become one of the thirteen aldermen. Aldermen had the honorific "Master" prefixed to their names and were entitled to wear black cloth gowns trimmed with fur, to distinguish them from ordinary mortal workaday non-aldermen. The Author refers to aldermen's rings (in *Romeo and Juliet* and *Henry IV Part One*) which Shakespeare would have noticed on his father's fingers. In 1568, the council elected John to their highest civic office, High Bailiff, the equivalent of mayor. During his one-year term, he presided at the Court of Record, which was a court of the Crown, as a judge and justice of the peace. He issued warrants, negotiated with Stratford's lord of the manor, and decreed the weekly price of grain. Uniformed sergeants-at-arms, bearing maces, escorted him from his house to council meetings, to court sessions at the Gild Hall, and to the market on Thursdays (market day); they were by his side at the fair on fair days and paraded his family to church on Sundays.[2] The pomp and ceremony showered on his father would have been among Shakespeare's earliest memories. If he was too young to attend the Stratford court and see his father pronounce judgments from the bench, he had another opportunity in 1571 and 1572, when John was elected deputy bailiff and his duties included serving as the town's other justice of the peace. But even if he never witnessed his father acting in official capacities, Will would have been surrounded with reminders that he was the eldest son and heir of one of Stratford's most prominent citizens. The daily courtesies shown to John, who remained an alderman throughout Shakespeare's childhood, the family's wealth, even the fact that both of his parents had seals to press in wax (John's was a ring-seal and bore his initials while Mary's pictured a running horse) would have instilled in Shakespeare a sense of superiority. When anti-Stratfordians observe that the Author does not enter the souls of characters from the lowest castes with as much sympathy as he reserves for those from the highest, they believe their perception amounts to evidence that the Poet was a nobleman. But a lordly attitude is not inconsistent with Shakespeare; quite the opposite.

Though William was the eldest, he was not an only child. His mother raised six children beyond infancy: four boys and two girls. Gilbert

(1566–1612) never married, and like his brother had business interests in both London and Stratford; he was a haberdasher in St. Bride's. Joan (1569–1646) married a hatter and had five children. Her bloodline continues to the present day. The next sister, Anne, died at the age of eight in 1579. Nothing is known about her, and not much more is known about Richard (1574–1613). The youngest, Edmund, became a player in London like his eldest brother and died there in 1607 at the age of twenty-seven.

As the sons of Alderman Shakespeare, the boys were entitled to a free education at the Stratford grammar school—called the King's New School. The student rolls, as I've said, have been lost (there is no record of anyone attending before 1800), but we can be certain William and his brothers learned to read and write at the attached petty school. Gilbert witnessed a Stratford lease in 1610, signing his name "Gilbart Shakesper" in a fine Italian script. William and Edmund became actors, and actors—unless they're mimes or improvisers—have to be able to read. Their sisters, surprisingly, were eligible for the petty school too. A court case from 1603 reveals that a woman and her female friend had gone "to school together at Stratford upon Avon."[3]

The children might have had help mastering reading from their father. Though John may not have been formally educated, he does seem to have been literate. A lawsuit of 1595 demands the return of a "book" from "Mr. Shaxpere," when John was the only man in town who would be identified as such. Presumably, he wouldn't borrow a book if he couldn't read it.[4] The number of books he owned himself is unknown, but it need not have been many to produce a writer son—Christopher Marlowe's father died in 1605 possessing only one volume, a Bible.[5] The lawsuit, by the way, was brought by the widow Margaret Young against Joan Perrott to recover "deceitfully" obtained goods, including three prayer books. Margaret and Joan could read too. Because John signed his name with a mark, usually an indication of illiteracy, some commentators continue to insist on his ignorance. But Adrian Quiney, who served as a town alderman with John, also signed with a mark, and yet we have a letter from Quiney to his son Richard. Often men such as John could read but not write. Writing was not a necessary skill in Tudor times, and most people had few opportunities to practice it. Reading, on the other hand, was something they had occasion to do on a regular basis. When John served as chamberlain, for example, he would have needed to read the items in his accounts. But whichever the case, literate or illiterate, as a man involved in public affairs, he was entitled to a free education for his offspring, an entitlement no alderman would have turned down.

If Shakespeare did attend the petty school and then the grammar school, what would he have learned? The curriculum hasn't survived. But we do know that the man who became the vicar of Stratford in 1561, and who stood at the font when the infant William was baptized, was John Bretchgirdle. Bretchgirdle had been a schoolmaster and curate at Witton in Cheshire, where he had set down the following curriculum for the grammar school scholar:

> I will the children learn the Catechism and then the *Accidence and Grammar* set out by Henry VIII, or some other, if any can be better, to induce children more speedily to Latin speech; and then *Institutum Christiani Hominis*, that learned Erasmus made; and then *Copia* of the same Erasmus, Colloquia Erasmi, *Ovidius Metamorphoses*, Terence, Mantuan, Tully, Horace, Sallust, Virgil, and such other as shall be thought convenient.[6]

This syllabus is typical of Elizabethan grammar schools, and something like it must have been used at Stratford. If it seems strange to us that pre-pubescent boys, from age seven to age fifteen, would study Roman classics and memorize Latin passages daily, the Elizabethans would be amazed by the science and math that children learn today. The education wasn't better in those days; it just prepared them for a different world. At a time when legal documents were often in Latin, it would behoove a man to know the language, if he could, in order to protect his interests.

In 1571, the year Shakespeare would have matriculated, the council of bishops asked every British schoolmaster to teach books "whereby the fullness and fineness of the Latin and Greek tongue[s] may be learned,"[7] and there's no evidence their pronouncement was ignored in Warwickshire. When eleven-year-old Richard Quiney Jr. of Stratford writes a letter to his father, he writes in Latin and even quotes Cicero.[8] From Shakespeare's generation, Abraham Sturley, in another letter to Richard Sr., switches to Latin in the midst of instructing him how to deal with Shakespeare in a matter of some tithes.[9] Unless the Quineys and the Sturleys had an unusual affinity for Latin, I think we can conclude that the leading citizens of Stratford were generally bilingual and that the town's burgesses were more cultured than they're often given credit for.

The masters they hired to teach grammar, rhetoric, and logic were Oxford graduates. Shakespeare was probably too young to benefit from Walter Roche, a fellow of Corpus Christi College whose tenure ended in 1571, but over the next three years, when Oxford man Simon Hunt wore the flat cap and stood before the class, Will was in the same room, being drilled in vocabulary by an usher, while Hunt taught the older boys on the other side of a partition. Shakespeare's principal teacher would have been Thomas Jenkins, a fellow of St. John's, Oxford (M.A. 1570), who was Stratford's schoolmaster from 1574 to 1579. Like Sir Hugh Evans, the parson-schoolmaster in *The Merry Wives of Windsor*, Jenkins was a Welshman. He was succeeded by John Cottom, whom Shakespeare may have had a year under, and who was also an Oxford graduate. Six days a week, then, throughout his boyhood, young Will was exposed to university-trained minds. On Sundays he listened to sermons given by Henry Heicroft, the parish rector from 1569 to 1584, who was a fellow of St. John's, Cambridge.

As far as we know, Shakespeare himself never studied at Oxford or Cambridge, or if he did, there's no record of it. Like Ben Jonson, Michael Drayton, Thomas Kyd, Thomas Dekker, George Chapman, Cyril Tourneur, and other dramatists, he seems to lack university education. The Cambridge men who created *The Return from Parnassus Part Two* did not believe Shakespeare was an alumnus when they had their character Kempe sneer,

> Few of the university men pen plays well, they smell too much of that writer *Ovid*, and that writer *Metamorphosis*, and talk too much of *Proserpina & Jupiter*. Why here's our fellow *Shakespeare* puts them all down, [Ay] and *Ben Jonson* too.[10]

Kempe is made to seem ignorant here, like his stage characters, which is why he thinks "Metamorphosis" is a poet instead of a poem. Since the Author's plays and poems are also redolent of Ovid and speak of Jupiter and Proserpina, the joke may be that Kempe doesn't realize his "fellow" writes like the scholarly graduates. But Shakespeare and Jonson are clearly contrasted with the university men.

Some people doubt Shakespeare even finished grammar school. Persuaded by Nicholas Rowe's dubious report that "the want of his assistance at home" interrupted his studies, anti-Stratfordians insist on his early withdrawal from Master Jenkins's class. Hard times did befall the Shakespeares in the late 1570s, but the evidence indicates their straits were never so desperate that William was forced to give up his education.

What we know is this: As late as 1576, his father John was applying to the College of Heralds for a coat of arms and official admittance into the gentry. But he didn't follow up on his petition. After December of that year, John stopped attending borough council meetings, a sure sign that something was wrong. In January 1578, when a levy was passed for equipping local soldiers, John was assigned to pay half the assessment for aldermen—the amount asked of burgesses. His fellow townsmen, at that point, must have seen his circumstances as reduced, but hardly poverty stricken. In November, they excused him from a poor tax of four pence per week. Was his situation worse? Probably, in the sense that he was deeper in debt. Four pence was not a large sum, but over time, week after week, it would further burden a man who already owed money to members of the council. How his fortune was lost in the first place is a mystery. One possibility is that John had come to rely on illegal wool dealing as his main source of income, and when a 1576 crackdown by the Privy Council forced him to abandon it, he found himself short of cash to pay his outstanding debts.[11] Moneylending at high interest was another revenue source for him (in 1570 he was twice accused at the Royal Exchequer of usury for charging £20 interest on loans of £100 and £80), and perhaps, carrying a strongbox of coins to a lendee, he was robbed on the highway. (There would be no court record of the theft unless the culprit were apprehended.)

Whatever the reason for his troubles, John Shakespeare reacted as any businessman would. First, he borrowed money, hoping his prospects would improve. When they didn't, he conveyed real estate and sold off his satellite investments. In November 1578, he mortgaged part of his wife's inheritance to his brother-in-law Edmund Lambert and leased eighty-six acres in Wilmcote to another relative. The £40 he owed Lambert was due in two years, which shows his confidence that he would soon be able to reclaim this property. A year later, however, that confidence was gone and he sold his ninth share in the Snitterfield estate. Still, things must have gotten a little better after that; in 1580 he was able to come up with £10 to bail the Stratford tinker Michael Price out of jail. By then, William would have finished grammar school and might have been earning money. The slight improvement in the family's economic position after 1579 suggests as much.

No one knows what the sixteen-year-old William's occupation was. In the 1680s, the son of Christopher Beeston, a Lord Chamberlain's player who had performed with Shakespeare, said that Will had been "in his younger years a schoolmaster in the country." Perhaps the future Bard became the usher at the Stratford school or a tutor at a manor house. It's also possible the player's son was wrong, and Shakespeare plied a different trade entirely. We just don't know. And until we find some hard evidence to confirm it, we can't rely on an old man's hand-me-down memory.

At the age of eighteen and still legally a minor, Will married Anne Hathaway, twenty-six, of Shottery. Their marriage licence was recorded in the Bishop's Register at Worcester on 27 November 1582. Or rather, it was misrecorded. The clerk, who was sloppy with names, in one instance writing "Darby" instead of "Bradeley," entered the bride as "Anna Whateley." But the next day, the marriage licence bond was more accurate (as we would expect when money is involved); it was issued to "Willm Shagspere" and "Anne Hathwey."[12] Nonetheless, Anne Whateley had been "born." Conjured up by a clerk's mistake, centuries later she would be the wraith-like cynosure of countless fantasies. For some romantic souls, like the novelist Anthony Burgess, she was the angelic woman Shakespeare truly loved, while for others, even more romantic, she was a great literary artist and (I'm not making this up) the secret Author of the Plays! Whateley may be the only Authorship candidate who never actually existed.

The other Anne, the woman Shakespeare married, came from a background similar to his. She was not, as some would have it, a proletarian country wench. Her father, Richard Hathaway, was a substantial farmer who owned a large house and outlying buildings. He held between fifty and ninety acres of fields, pasture, and orchards and employed servants, shepherds, and farmhands. When he died in 1581, he left her ten marks (about six and half pounds) to be paid upon her marrying. Ten marks could buy the equivalent of $6,500 worth of today's goods, but at a time when there were less goods available, the sum actually represented much more. If, at twenty-six, Anne was older than the teenage brides of the upper class, her age was not a sign of poverty. She was not an old maid, lamentably unwed because she was poor, shrewish, or homely. In the Stratford environs, twenty-six was the average age for first-time brides. Anne was a good catch, and she came with a dowry.

She was also pregnant. There are signs of haste in the circumstances of the nuptials—the banns were published for only one week instead of the customary three—and less than six months after the wedding, their daughter Susanna was christened on 26 May 1583. Two more children,

the twins Hamnet and Judith, were born twenty months later and baptized on 2 February 1585. They were named after Hamnet Sadler (called
"Hamlett" in Shakespeare's will) and his wife, a Catholic couple whose
consciences were troubled, as they told an ecclesiastical court, about attending the required Protestant services. Shakespeare's parents were
Catholics too, evidence reveals, though they outwardly conformed to the
Church of England. It should not surprise us, then, that the Author's plays
show familiarity with Catholic practices and sympathy for Catholic characters, even if the Poet's personal beliefs are impossible to discern.

Throughout the 1580s, problems continued for Shakespeare's father.
After attending one meeting in nine years, he was replaced on the borough council in 1586. He may have been having financial difficulties as
late as 1591 when his name appears on a list of nine who "it is said come
not to church for fear of process for debt." (Sunday was allegedly the day
regional sheriffs would seek debtors at the churches, but they could have
found him at his shop or at the Court of Record juries on which he sat.
More likely his debt was to the church itself, and it was his creditors in
the pulpit John was trying to avoid.) Among the nine absentees, by the
way, are "Bardolphe" and "Fluellen"—two names used by the Author in
Henry V. In 1589, John brought a lawsuit against Edmund Lambert's son
(Lambert had died two years earlier), in a futile attempt to reclaim his
lost property. Shakespeare's name is joined to his parents' in the court papers filed at Westminster, probably because the land in question was to
have been his inheritance. But there's no evidence William was in the
courtroom when the case was heard. In fact, there's no evidence he was
anywhere.

The years between the births of his children and his emergence in
London are often called the "lost years." Researchers have been unable
to discover what he was doing during that period, nor have they found
enough circumstantial hints to make an educated guess. No one knows
when he left Stratford or when he became an actor.

The trail doesn't pick up again until September 1592 with the publication of *Greenes Groats-worth of witte, bought with a million of Repentance*.
A thirty-nine-page pamphlet, ostensibly by the playwright Robert
Greene, its title page claimed it was "Written before his death and published at his dying request." Near the end of the book, Greene addresses
"those Gentlemen his quondam aquaintance, that spend their wits in
making plays." First he upbraids a "famous gracer of tragedians" who
"hath said . . . there is no God" and for the next thirty lines Greene tries
to dissuade his friend from atheism. "Why should thy excellent wit,

[God's] gift be so blinded, that thou shouldst give no glory to the giver? Is it pestilent Machivilian [sic] policy that thou hast studied? O peevish folly!" Because of the reference to Machiavelli (who appears as the chorus character in *The Jew of Malta*) and because the addressee is a writer of tragedies and an atheist, scholars conclude this first playmaker is Christopher Marlowe. But Greene never names him. It was a commonplace of Elizabethan invective to attack one's targets obliquely, giving the reader clues but never directly identifying the censured person. Next Greene turns to "young Juvenal," probably Thomas Nashe, "that biting satirist, that [lately] with me together writ a Comedy" whom he "advises," in eight lines, to "inveigh against vain men" but "name none" and "blame not scholars . . . if they reprove thy too much liberty of reproof." The third, "no less deserving than the other two, in some things rarer, in nothing inferior; driven (as my self) to extreme shifts, a little have I to say to thee: and were it not an idolatrous oath, I would swear by sweet St. George, thou art unworthy better hap, sith thou dependeth on so mean a stay." In other words, number three deserves the same fate as the dying Greene since he depends on the same means for his livelihood. The diatribe goes on:

> Base minded men all three of you, if by my miserie you be not warnd: for unto none of you (like mee) sought those burres to cleave: those Puppets (I meane) that spake from our mouths, those Anticks garnisht in our colours. Is it not strange, that I, to whom they all have beene beholding: is it not like that you, to whom they all have beene beholding, shall (were yee in that case as I am now) bee both at once of them forsaken?: Yes trust them not: for there is an upstart Crow, beautified with our feathers, that with his *Tigers heart wrapped in a players hyde*, supposes he is as well able to bombast out a blanke verse as the best of you: and beeing an absolute *Johannes fac totum*, is in his owne conceit the onely Shake-scene in a countrey. O that I might intreat your rare wits to be imploied in more profitable courses: & let those Apes imitate your past excellence, and never more acquaint them with your admired inventions. I know the best husband of you all will never prove an Usurer, and the kindest of them all will never prove a kind nurse: yet whilest you may, seeke you better Maisters; for it is pittie men of such rare wits, should be subject to the pleasure of such rude groomes.[13]

The line "O tiger's heart wrapped in a woman's hide!"[14] is from *Henry VI Part Three* (I.iv.137), which thirty-one years later, in the First Folio, was attributed to the actor William Shakespeare of Stratford-upon-Avon. By parodying Shakespeare's name as "Shake-scene," Greene provides a second, unmistakable indicator as to whom he has in mind. The actor had performed in a play of Greene's ("beautified with our feathers"), and now he's taken up playwriting: he thinks he can fill out ("bombast out") a line of blank verse as well as the three base-minded wits. Being a *Johannes fac totum*, "John do-all," a Jack-of-all-trades, he fancies himself ("is in his owne conceit") the only playwright ("Shake-scene") in the country; he doesn't need Greene in other words because he can do the writing himself. The actors, who in the past had been "beholding" to Greene for scripts, are buying plays only from Shakespeare, rejecting Greene's latest works and thus "forsaking" him in his hour of need.

Though this is the most plausible interpretation of the passage, it's not the only one. Marlowe biographer A. D. Wraight, for example, argues the "upstart Crow" is not Shakespeare at all, but the actor Edward Alleyn.[15] Apparently it is only an amazing coincidence that Greene would satirize a line later attributed to Shakespeare and then call the object of his scorn a "Shake-scene." Others allow that the passage refers to Shakespeare but only as an actor who ad-libs lines and makes too much noise moving scenery.[16] How these things could be the cause of Greene's present "miserie" and make actors tantamount to "usurers" is a mystery, but the fact that the parodied line is a written one, not an ad-lib, undermines this argument. Blindly grasping at straws, the heretics resist doing what any historian would do: use one document—in this case, the Folio—to understand another. They refuse to put two and two together because they don't like four.

Unquestionably, Greene believes the actor has turned to writing. Such a career move, despite Greene's complaints, was not unusual; Anthony Munday, Samuel Rowley, Thomas Heywood, Ben Jonson, Samuel Daniel, William Barksted, and others were players as well as playwrights.[17] Taking up the pen would have been natural for an actor with Shakespeare's middle-class upbringing since, as the son of a glover, he had a background similar to that of the other dramatists of the time: Greene's father was a saddler, Marlowe's a shoemaker, Chapman's a farmer; Jonson was stepson to a bricklayer, Thomas Kyd was the son of a scrivener, and Middleton and Webster were the children of a bricklayer and a tailor, respectively.

Groats-worth was edited, and possibly ghostwritten, by Henry Chettle. Three months after it was published, Chettle wrote an apology, saying that the letter to "diverse play-makers is offensively by one or two of them taken." He explains,

With neither of them that take offence was I acquainted, and with one of them I care not if I never be: The other, whom at that time I did not so much spare, as since I wish I had, for that as I have moderated the heat of living writers, and might have used my own discretion (especially in such a case) the author [Greene] being dead, that I did not, I am as sorry, as if the original fault had been my fault, because my self have seen his demeanor no less civil than he excellent in the quality he professes: Besides, diverse of worship have reported his uprightness of dealing, which argues his honesty, and his facetious [i.e., elegant] grace in writing, which approves his art.[18]

[spelling modernized]

The two playwrights likely to take offense would have been Marlowe and Shakespeare since they were the most easily recognizable and the most viciously attacked: Marlowe for atheism, which was a crime, and Shakespeare for not being as good a writer as the others. Chettle hasn't met one of the affronted poets and doesn't care if he ever does. But he has recently had a courteous conversation with the second, a man who has been vouched for by members of the gentry—"diverse of worship" refers to gentlemen, not noblemen of high rank who would be "diverse of honour." The phrase "quality he professes," which was often attached to actors, identifies the polite second writer as Shakespeare. The playwright must have felt his integrity and talent had been criticized or else Chettle wouldn't make a point of defending them. Perhaps Shakespeare was nettled by the charge of usury, which is why Chettle certifies his "uprightness of dealing" and his "honesty."[19]

Whatever his complaint was, in the ensuing year Shakespeare would have had graver concerns than his reputation. At the end of January 1593, the playhouses in London were closed because of plague and didn't reopen until December. Then, two months later, they were ordered to shut their doors again, which they did throughout February and March 1594, until the plague finally lifted. It is surely not coincidence that this period saw the publication of the narrative poems *Venus and Adonis* (1593) and *The Rape of Lucrece* (1594), both dedicated to the nineteen-year-old Earl of Southampton, a known patron of the arts. Unable to make a living from the theatre, Shakespeare tried, as most Elizabethan poets tried, to secure a benefactor.

The poems were printed by Richard Field, a man who had grown up with Shakespeare in Stratford. Three years the actor's senior, he would have known young Will at school as well as through their parents. Shakespeare's father had helped appraise Field's father's estate when the latter died in 1592. Less than a year later, Field was publishing *Venus and Adonis*, the first literary work to bear (in this case, on its dedication) the name "William Shakespeare."

"Shakespeare," let me pause to say, was the most common variant spelling of the Stratford man's surname. It's how the name appears on cast lists, tax records, purchase and mortgage documents, the license for the King's Men, legal depositions, and his wife's gravestone. To argue, as some do, that the Author was a different person because his name was spelled differently is to be ignorant of the evidence. At this time, everyone's name was rendered in multiple ways. Marlowe, for example, appears as Marlow, Marloe, Marlyn, Marlin, Marlen, Marly, Marlye, Morley, and in his sole surviving signature as "Christopher Marley."[20] John Shakespeare's surname was construed in seventeen different permutations in Stratford documents. When the civil servant Richard Stonley bought a copy of *Venus and Adonis* in 1593, he ignored the dedication's authority and cast the poet's name as "Shakspere" in his diary. Fifteen years later, the actor Edward Alleyn did the same thing, recording his purchase of *Shake-speares Sonnets* in 1609 as "Shaksper sonnetts." That the name was sometimes hyphenated (Shake-speare) doesn't prove anything either. Irvin Matus has shown that other writers' surnames, like "Charles Fitz-Geffrie," were commonly bisected at the whims of printers, as was the name of the then mayor of London "Sir Thomas Camp-bell"; "Sir John Old-castle"; and even "Saint Dun-stan." And some printers, like Robert Walde-grave, used hyphens in their own names.[21]

The name is spelled "Shakespeare" in the very next chronological record, the 1595 payment to "Willm Kempe, Willm Shakespeare & Richarde Burbage servantes to the Lord Chamberleyne" for performances before the Queen. As a player in one of Elizabeth's favorite companies, Shakespeare would have been at court several times a year, and he would have had many opportunities to observe the behavior of courtiers and to remark the opulence of palace furnishings. Floors "inlaid with patens of bright gold," "Tyrian tapestries," and "cushions bossed with pearl"[22] would have met his eye and, not surprisingly, they found their way into his poetry. The Lord Chamberlain's Men presented plays at many of England's great houses, as we know from records, and an actor in their company was in a good position to study the lifestyles, attitudes, and manners of the nobility.

On 11 August 1596, Shakespeare's son Hamnet was buried. Did the actor ride home to Stratford on hearing the news? We don't know.

Later that year, on 29 November, William Wayte "craved sureties of the peace" against Shakespeare and three others for "fear of death and so forth." Does this mean the player was a belligerent thug, intimidating his enemies with death threats? Anti-Stratfordians think so. But they neglect the context of Wayte's petition. A few weeks previously, Francis Langley, who is named with Shakespeare in Wayte's appeal, had himself sought sureties against Wayte for the same cause: "fear of death and so forth." Langley held the minor civic office of inspector of woolen cloth in London, and he was wealthy enough to buy the Southwark manor of Paris Garden in 1589.[23] He was also the owner of the Swan Theatre, located on his Paris Garden estate. Since Wayte worked for Southwark's local judge, William Gardiner, who was his stepfather, possibly he was trying to enforce a theater closure and was meeting with resistance. We know that Gardiner tried to suppress Bankside playhouses in 1597; he was ordered to do so by the Privy Council, Elizabeth's cabinet. Regardless of the issues involved, though, whether their suits and countersuits claiming "fear of death" should be taken at face value or were only legal devices, the disputants were not low-life gangsters. If Shakespeare indeed threatened Wayte, he did so in the company of Langley, a theatre owner and civic official. Again we find the Stratford man associating with citizens of substance.

Meanwhile, fittingly, he became a gentleman. Twenty years after his father first applied to the College of Heralds, a coat of arms and admission to the gentry was awarded to the family because, according to the grant of arms (dated 20 October 1596), the old glover had served as a justice of the peace and a Bailiff, possessed lands and tenements worth £500, and married a daughter and heir of Arden, a gentleman "of worship."[24] His successful son was probably responsible for re-submitting the application. For a lowly actor to join the gentry was bizarre at this time— Shakespeare may have been the first, though the comedian Richard Tarlton had been a Groom of Queen Elizabeth's Chamber in the 1580s—but the social status of the profession was changing. In the next few years, Edward Alleyn, Richard Burbage, Richard Cowley, John Heminges, Augustine Phillips, and Thomas Pope all acquired coats of arms and became gentlemen. Others followed. This social evolution did not go unnoticed at Cambridge, where the authors of *The Return from Parnassus Part Two* mock "those glorious vagabonds" with their

> Coursers to ride on through the gazing streets,
> Sooping it [swaggering?] in their glaring satin suits,
> And pages to attend their masterships:

> With mounting words that better wits have framed,
> They purchase lands and now Esquires are named.[25]

To secure his new title, Shakespeare must have amassed a chestful of coins. In 1597, he purchased New Place, the second-largest house in Stratford, for a downpayment of £60 and, probably, another sixty to follow. Wages for servants, without whom daily life at New Place would have been nearly impossible, demanded more coins. And yet, a year later in London, he still had a purse large enough to lend Richard Quiney £30—though he may have merely interceded for Quiney with a moneylender.

Around the same time, Shakespeare defaulted on his taxes. From 1597 to 1598, the "petty collectors" of St. Helen's parish, Bishopgate ward, were unable to collect 13 shillings and 4 pence from him. A note on the Exchequer's list of 1599, however, refers the matter to the Bishop of Winchester, implying he had moved to Southwark. After 1600, he disappears from the rolls of people owing money, so presumably he was found. Although this episode is the only instance in his life when he failed to pay tax, it looms large for those who wish to make Shakespeare into a scoundrel.

A much more ignoble incident came in 1598 when he stockpiled "corn," what today we call grain, in a time of famine. A Midlands grain shortage had created poverty, discontent, and high prices, which speculators drove even higher by hoarding. One of these speculators, "wicked people" the Privy Council called them, may have been Shakespeare. Though almost every house in Stratford had corn holdings, his 10 quarters (80 bushels) of malt was an amount suspiciously above the average. Still, the schoolmaster had more, and compared to Sir Thomas Lucy who had $28\frac{1}{2}$ quarters or Richard Quiney who had 47 quarters of barley and 32 of malt just a year or so earlier, Shakespeare could not be called a hoarder. The reason there was so much corn in Stratford was that brewing was the town's "especial" trade, as a petition for relief from taxes describes, "our houses fitted to no other uses, many servants among us hired only to that purpose."[26] To cease brewing so that the wheat and barley could be used for food was to risk becoming one of the hungry oneself. The moral choice facing Shakespeare was more complicated than one of greed versus generosity. In any case, as he was spending most of his time in London at this point, he may not even have known about the grain storage in his name. Whoever was looking after his household in Stratford was the real malt speculator.

Shakespeare was busy acting. In Ben Jonson's *Works* (1616), he heads the list of "principal Comedians" who performed *Every Man in His Humour* in 1598, and he's among the cast of Jonson's *Sejanus* in 1603.

Also in 1603 the Lord Chamberlain's players became the King's Men. In March, Queen Elizabeth died, and the King of Scotland, James VI, was named as her successor. Two months later, the new King—now James I of Great Britain—showed special favor to Shakespeare's troupe by placing them under his personal patronage and protection. The formal royal patent licenses and authorizes

> these our servants Lawrence Fletcher, William Shakespeare, Richard Burbage, Augustyne Phillippes, John Heninges, Henrie Condell, William Sly, Robert Armyn, Richard Cowly, and the rest of their associates freely to use and exercise the art and faculty of playing comedies, tragedies, histories, interludes, morals, pastorals, stage plays and such others . . . for the recreation of our loving subjects as for our solace and pleasure.[27]

[spelling modernized except for names]

These same nine men are designated "Players" in a 1604 list of Grooms of the Royal Chamber who are to be issued scarlet cloth for the King's official ceremonial entry into London. Shakespeare was now, theoretically, a member of the King's household as he had been a member of the Lord Chamberlain's. He was at court much more often than in the previous reign; he and his fellows played the palaces about thirteen times a year.[28]

Compensation from the royal coffers was not generous enough to make a man rich (King James's grooms made £60 a year), but as a sharer in his acting company, and in the Globe Theatre after it was erected in 1599, Shakespeare was earning an enviable amount of money. This he invested. In 1602, he bought 107 acres near Stratford (with his brother Gilbert making the purchase for him) and a cottage near New Place. From Ralph Huband, a former Sheriff of Warwickshire, he obtained a lease of tithes in 1605 for £440. Tithes were payments of a tenth of produce paid to whoever held the lease. For the next thirty-one years, Shakespeare and his heirs received half the tithes (since he bought only a moiety interest) of corn and hay from three Stratford hamlets. Still, his investments were few. For a man with a reputation as an entrepreneur he seems to have spent little time or energy pursuing wealth.

Was he litigious? In an age when the local court of law was used to settle almost every minor dispute, he sued exactly two people for debt. Through an attorney named William Tetherton, an action was brought against Philip Rogers, a Stratford apothecary, who owed Shakespeare for some malt in 1604. Because of the use of the attorney, it's impossible to say whether Shakespeare brought the suit or someone else of his household did. The other case, in 1608, involved a debt of £6 and damages of 24 shillings. While the litigation dragged on for more than a year, the defendant, John Addenbrooke, skipped town, and the court ordered his surety, the local blacksmith, to pay Shakespeare.

In another lawsuit, Shakespeare served as a witness. This was in 1612. Eight years earlier, he had been lodging in London with the family of Christopher Mountjoy, a Protestant émigré from France who supplied ladies' wigs and hair ornaments to the royal court. At the urging of his landlady, Mountjoy's wife, the actor had served as a go-between in the marriage arrangements of her daughter Mary and Mountjoy's apprentice, Stephen Belott. Now, Belott was suing Mountjoy for not living up to what had been agreed upon in the way of a dowry, and Shakespeare was called to testify. Under oath on the witness stand, he could not remember the exact amount that had been promised. After eight years, who would? Yet some anti-Stratfordians insist that a man with such a bad memory couldn't have been the Author.[29]

Also giving evidence in the 1612 suit was the playwright George Wilkins, with whom Stephen and Mary lived when they left her father's house. Wilkins wrote a novella based on the Author's *Pericles* and many scholars believe he penned the first two acts of the play as well.[30] Though the court papers don't specifically link Shakespeare with Wilkins, they do connect the actor to a person of quality in Daniel Nicholas, the son of the former Lord Mayor of London Sir Ambrose Nicholas, who testified about his conversations with Shakespeare.

At the time of his Belott-Mountjoy deposition, William no longer seems to have had a London address: He's described in the transcript of his testimony as "of Stratford upon Avon in the County of Warwick gentleman." Had he retired? And if so, when? We know it must have been after 1608, because Cuthbert Burbage (Richard's brother) remarks to the Lord Chamberlain in a 1635 letter that "Shakspeare" had been a "player" at the Blackfriars playhouse, the indoor theatre which the King's Men occupied in 1608.[31] That same year, Shakespeare's mother died, and his sister Joan and her husband, William Hart, were summoned by the vicar's clerk to administer the estate; Joan's eldest brother, we can assume, was still in London.

One reasonable guess for when he hung up his socks and buskins is 1611, the year *The Tempest* received its earliest-recorded production. The imminent retirement of its author would account for that play's undeniable valedictory quality as well as its unique epilogue, in which the magician Prospero solicits applause not for the play (as in the post-show appeals of *A Midsummer Night's Dream*, *As You Like It*, *Henry IV Part Two*, *All's Well That Ends Well*, and *Henry VIII*), but for himself:

> Now my charms are all o'erthrown,
> And what strength I have's mine own,
> Which is most faint. Now 'tis true,
> I must be here confin'd by you,
> Or sent to Naples. Let me not,
> Since I have my dukedom got,
> And pardon'd the deceiver, dwell
> In this bare island by your spell,
> But release me from my bands
> With the help of your good hands,
> Gentle breath of yours my sails
> Must fill, or else my project fails,
> Which was to please. Now I want
> Spirits to enforce, art to enchant,
> And my ending is despair,
> Unless I be reliev'd by prayer,
> Which pierces so that it assaults
> Mercy itself, and frees all faults.
>   As you from crimes would pardon'd be,
>   Let your indulgence set me free.

The Author has written an unprecedented solo curtain call for the actor playing Prospero. Did Shakespeare take the bow? If he did, his farewell was only to his acting career. Like his friend John Heminges, who retired from the stage at around this same time but continued as the troupe's business manager until his death in 1630, Shakespeare didn't sever his ties to the King's Men. He wrote three more plays over the next two years, all in collaboration with John Fletcher[32] and, in March 1613, he purchased the Blackfriars gatehouse, a dwelling next door to one playhouse and a water-taxi ride directly across the Thames from the Globe. It would seem he was looking forward to many more years of spending at least part of his time in London. But even when he was home in the country, he continued to write. Seventeenth-century vicar John Ward implies as much when he recalls hearing that "in his elder days

[Shakespeare] lived at Stratford: and supplied the stage with two plays a year."[33]

For the gatehouse purchase, three men served as trustees: his colleague Heminges; John Jackson, who may have been a shipping magnate but whose identity is in doubt; and William Johnson. Johnson was the proprietor of the Mermaid Tavern, a famous meeting place of the literati, remembered fondly to Ben Jonson by the playwright Francis Beaumont:

> What things have we seen
> Done at the Mermaid? heard words that have been
> So nimble, and so full of subtle flame,
> As if that everyone from whom they came
> Had meant to put his whole wit in a jest
> And had resolved to live a fool the rest
> Of his dull life . . . [34]

[spelling modernized]

That Shakespeare engaged in wit combats at the Mermaid may be a fictitious tradition, but as a friend of the owner, he was almost certainly a patron.

At the end of the same month (31 March), the account book of Francis Manners, sixth Earl of Rutland, records a payment of 44 shillings in gold to "Mr Shakspeare . . . about my Lord['s] impreso" and another 44 shillings in gold to "Ryc Burbadge for painting and making it."[35] An impresa was a heraldic design, displayed on banners and paper shields. Claims have been made that the "Mr Shakspeare" in this entry refers to the King's "bit-maker," John Shakespeare, to whom payments for bits and spurs are found in royal and private accounts after 1617. But the fact that the man in question is linked to Richard Burbage, receiving the same fee—probably two 22-shilling gold coins which were minted that year[36]—makes it hard to believe that the entry refers to anyone but the actor William Shakespeare. Rutland paid Burbage alone for another impresa in March of 1616, when the Stratford man lay dying in his bed. It should not surprise us that two actors would be familiar enough with the symbols of heraldry to design an impresa. Coats of arms and heraldic insignia were everywhere—painted on banners, carved into pub shingles, sewn into doublets and jerkins. Badges on the coats of liveries indicated which nobleman a servant worked for. The symbolic meanings of colors and im-

agery were common knowledge and were the equivalent, in a largely illiterate society, of a pictorial language.

If Shakespeare did retire, he may have done so when he was prompted
by a catastrophe. On 29 June 1613, the Globe Theatre burned to the
ground. Unwilling to part with the sixty pounds demanded of each
sharer for rebuilding, the theory goes, he sold or surrendered his interest to Heminges and Condell (whose families did indeed hold Shakespeare's shares years later) and trundled home to Stratford for a life of
gardening and the gossipy conversation of friends, never more to put
quill to paper. It's an appealing idea, appealing in its simplicity, and it
would explain why he may not have worked on any plays after the dis-
astrous fire. But the truth is probably more complicated. A 1619 law case
implies that Shakespeare was a sharer in the Globe even after the fire,
meaning he paid the assessment and remained with his theatre company.[37]

After 1613, Shakespeare still spent weeks at a time in London, according to the memoranda of Stratford's town clerk, Thomas Greene. He
was there in November 1614 and still there a month later, presumably
residing at his gatehouse.[38] As a royal groom, he likely attended on the
King during these stays when his troupe played at court. And it's not in-
conceivable that he continued to doctor other men's scripts. During the
Christmas holidays of 1614, while he was away in the capital, an incident
occurred in Stratford that heretics sometimes cite to paint Shakespeare
as miserly. A visiting preacher stayed at New Place and consumed one
quart of sack and one quart of claret, which the borough corporation paid
for. Unaware that the town burgesses often supplied wine and sugar to
visiting clergy and justices, anti-Stratfordians alight on the 20-pence re-
imbursement, believing it demonstrates that their nemesis was ungener-
ous. He may have been so, but this ledger item doesn't prove it:
Shakespeare was out of town. On what date he returned home is unknown, but he joined a Chancery bill of complaint (relating to his Blackfriars gatehouse) in April 1615, which suggests he was in London then,
and there are no traces of his presence in Stratford until September.[39] For
a man allegedly retired, he wasn't tightly tethered to his hometown. It's
probable, though, that he was spending most of his time there, and it was
there he died.

In January 1616, Shakespeare dictated his will. As per the custom of
the age, the testator enumerated his bequests to his lawyer—in this instance, Francis Collins of Warwick—who translated them into legalese
as he jotted them down. Normally, Collins would have had his clerk make

a clean copy of the three-page draft, but for this will he didn't. Changes were expected. And two months later, on 25 March, they came. A new first page was substituted, which was written in a smaller script to accommodate the many new provisions. On the remaining sheets, interpolations were added (unless they were made in January), including bequests to "Hamlett Sadler" (the recusant Catholic), "William Raynoldes gent" (another recusant Catholic), and "my fellowes John Hemynges, Richard Burbage and Henry Cundell" of 26 shillings 8 pence each "to buy them Ringes." The most famous addition, squeezed between two lines on the last page, is the only acknowledgment of his marriage: "unto my wief the second-best bed" with its furnishings.

It was all he left her. A four-post bed with its linens, valences, and hangings. Possibly it was the one they shared, and it had some sentimental value (the best bed in a household like Shakespeare's was usually reserved for guests). Michael Wood, in his *In Search of Shakespeare* television series and its companion book, speculates the bed was a Hathaway family heirloom,[40] but it's still a paltry legacy. Early biographers assumed she received one third of the estate as her dower right, but dower rights don't seem to have been recognized in Stratford; other wills, including that of Francis Collins, expressed the widow's entitlement.[41] Consciously and deliberately, Shakespeare left her unprovided for. Even in his purchase of the Blackfriars gatehouse he had taken special legal steps to ensure she would never inherit it. Why would he cut her off like that? Out of spite? As revenge for infidelity? Because she was senile? The simplest explanation is that he wanted to keep his estate intact and in his bloodline, and he feared that anything left to her would end up in the hands of her relatives or, if she remarried, her future husband. He had observed such a situation when his fellow actor Augustine Phillips died and his widow's new spouse gained control of his theatre shares. So Anne's unusual inheritance really tells us nothing about their relationship, though biographers often regard her supposed snubbing as evidence of friction. As for Anne's well-being, Shakespeare would have had every confidence she would be cared for by his daughter, Susanna, and her husband, John Hall. Hall was a celebrated physician who declined a knighthood in 1626 and counted the poet Michael Drayton among his patients; Susanna was equally respectable—she entertained the Queen of England, Henrietta Maria (Charles I's wife), for two nights in 1643 (the Queen no doubt sleeping in the best bed.) It was to them that Shakespeare bequeathed the bulk of his estate.

What's surprising, at least at first, is the absence of books or manuscripts in the will. It may seem odd that a writer would leave no books, but he's in good company. Manuscripts and books are missing from the wills of playwrights Samuel Daniel, John Marston, and James Shirley, and there are no books mentioned in the testaments of writers Thomas Campion, Reginald Scot, and even Sir Francis Bacon. The same goes for Thomas Russell, Esq., one of the overseers of Shakespeare's will. Unless books were bequeathed separately from other goods, they were not separately itemized; this was the case with his son-in-law, John Hall, who left his books to one person and his goods to another. Books would have been listed in the inventory post-mortem, which the endorsement of the will (located under Shakespeare's signature) tells us once existed. "Inventorium exhibitum," it reads—inventory attached. Unfortunately this inventory has been lost. As for manuscripts, the King's Men would have them. Heywood and Middleton both complain about actors retaining their manuscripts and preventing them from coming into print.[42] Playwrights, it seems did not normally keep copies.[43]

A more debateable question is whether the will is holographic—in Shakespeare's own hand. The words "By me" preceding the signature and the fact that the document was signed and witnessed without being copied over has led some to believe it's self-penned, but the spelling of his name in the body of the will—"Shackspeare"—is different from any of the six known signatures, and it's not likely he would refer to himself as "the saied William Shackspere."

Like the other wills executed by Collins, Shakespeare's is a document without personal feeling or poetic phrases. Its lack of emotion, which kindles the doubts of anti-Stratfordians, might be significant if such a lack were unusual, but a quick glance at other Collins-prepared wills shows us that it's not. For example, the last testament of Stratford's wealthiest citizen, Shakespeare's friend John Combe (who left the actor £5 when he died in 1614), is equally devoid of tenderness. Like his modern counterparts, Collins must have discouraged (or simply ignored) any of his testators' sentimental adjectives or clauses; these, he knew, could lead to lawsuits and wrangling among beneficiaries. Then, as now, verbal artistry was hazardous in legal documents (though it was often permitted by less cautious solicitors).

Earls like Pembroke or Southampton and writers like Drayton or Jonson or Fletcher, who tradition has it were Shakespeare's friends, go unmentioned in the will, and anti-Stratfordians, like Joseph Sobran, find the omission significant. That he might not have been as close to these men as tradition assumes never occurs to them. As usual, they find Shakespeare wanting when he doesn't meet their personal expectations of him. Rather than making sense of the evidence we have, they prefer to imagine what *should* exist and then howl "Fraud!" when it doesn't.

Now we come to the only real curiosity in the life of Shakespeare—the six signatures (Figure 4). On the 1612 Belott-Mountjoy deposition, the Stratford man signs himself "Willm Shakp": an abbreviation, as the lines over the first *l* and under the *p* signify, the equivalent of modern initialing. Similarly, on the gatehouse deeds, he writes "Shakspe" with a swirl above the *e* that denotes he's using an abbreviated form. (The final *r* was added later, possibly by someone else.) The second of the gatehouse signatures looks different from the others because it's written in an Italian, or "Latin," script. Elizabethan schoolchildren learned two scripts: an English, or "secretary," hand and an Italian, or "Latin," one. None of this is mysterious. The shakiness of the will signatures is also understandable, given that he was dying. (Even though the will's second sentence states he's in "perfect health and memorie," this is doubtful given that he's making a will at all and then died a few months later.) So what's the problem? Well, first of all, on the will he seems to spell his name in two different ways: "Shakspeare" on the last page and "Shakspere" on the first two. What could account for this? The first two signatures could be forgeries, but I think there's a better solution: He signed the document at two different times. The last page he signed first, presumably in January when his health was only beginning to deteriorate, and the other two pages in March, when he was dying and likely to choose the briefest spelling possible. It may seem strange to us to have multiple renderings of our name at our disposal, but that was the case in Elizabethan times. Sir Walter Ralegh spelled his name four different ways, and the theatre impresario Philip Henslowe signed himself Hensley and Henslow in letters to his son-in-law.[44]

Another mystery is Shakespeare's letter formation. In a space of four years, he uses two distinct *W*'s, two capital *S*'s, three *a*'s, two *k*'s, two small *s*'s, and two *p*'s. And yet the signatures are similar enough that they're all almost certainly written by the same person. Either he didn't sign his name very often and thus his autograph never developed a consistent pattern, or he was a man so creative he never let it become static, or both.

The autographs are curious, and it's easy to see how one might question them. But they don't prove that the man who signed them wasn't a writer. Their oddness might just as easily reveal their maker's teeming imagination.

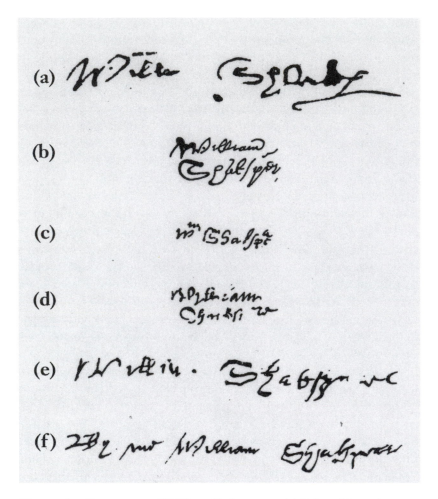

Figure 4. Signatures of William Shakespeare: (a) Belott-Mountjoy deposition (the National Archives, London); (b) Purchase deed for the Blackfriars gatehouse (Guildhall Library, Corporation of London); (c) Mortgage deed for the Blackfriars gatehouse (by permission of the British Library); (d), (e), (f) First, second, and third pages of Shakespeare's will (the National Archives, London).

∽

Not much more can be said with confidence about the life of William Shakespeare. Some of what we know is based on logical inferences, but inferences are not the same as idle conjecture. Literary historians, though they differ on a few minor points, have not dishonestly made the man seem like a poet: the evidence has done that for them. While it's true that none of the contemporary references to Shakespeare identify him as hailing from Stratford-upon-Avon, why would they? Is Drayton, who also came from Warwickshire, identified like that? Their literary lives were in London. It may not have been commonly known where they were from.

The problem, if there is one, is not what we know about Shakespeare, but what we don't. Little is certain about the great man's life, and it's easy to sympathize with anti-Stratfordian frustration that this is so. If he were the only writer of the time with few biographical traces, then we would have cause to be suspicious; but we have a lot of information about Shakespeare compared to his playwriting contemporaries. We know less about Marlowe, Kyd, Dekker, Heywood, Fletcher, or Webster—to name just a few. No one knows how many children Ben Jonson had. In some cases, though, what we know about a writer's beliefs—Marlowe's alleged atheism, for example—is perceptible in his plays. Jonson and Heywood left prose works, written in the first person, which reveal their personalities and which can be compared to their fiction. But for Shakespeare, we have no personal letters or books of criticism. This is unfortunate, but not suggestive. Because he's not alone. Other playwrights, like Fletcher, have large missing periods in their biographies, no manuscripts of their plays, and even fewer signatures—in Fletcher's case, only one.

Why is there such a paucity of information? There are several reasons. First of all, when the Globe Theatre burned down, some of Shakespeare's correspondence or manuscripts may have been lost in the blaze. Second, during the English Civil War (1642–1660) Puritans seized power, closed the theatres, and burned impious books. War being a time of deprivation, one can imagine all sorts of uses paper might have been put to. Then, in 1666, the Great Fire of London destroyed a third of the city and undoubtedly documents. There was also a different attitude toward manuscripts from what exists today. No one saved writers' letters; they were not considered valuable. Only in later centuries was a fetish made of every scratch of a poet's pen. The Elizabethans had a cavalier indifference when it came to preserving personal papers. And as for plays, no handwritten draft that went through a print shop prior to 1700 survives.[45] No manuscript by Molière, France's greatest playwright, survives either.

But did Shakespeare write the Plays and Poems in the first place? Certainly it was believed he did (more on that later), though the bare facts of his life remain silent on the question. To see if what little we know conflicts with the experience revealed in the Works, we have to compare the scraps of Shakespeare's biography to the Plays and Poems themselves.

CHAPTER 4
Reasonable Doubts

In 1919 the father of Oxfordianism, J. Thomas Looney, created a kind of police profile of what the man who wrote the plays must have been like. Based on his reading of the Works, Looney made a list of what he took to be the Author's personal qualities:[1]

1. A mature man of recognized genius

2. Apparently eccentric and mysterious

3. Of intense sensibility—a man apart

4. Unconventional

5. Not adequately appreciated

6. Of pronounced and known literary tastes

7. An enthusiast in the world of drama

8. A lyric poet of recognized talent

9. Of superior education—classical—the habitual associate of educated people

10. A man with feudal connections

11. A member of the higher aristocracy

12. Connected with Lancastrian supporters

13. An enthusiast for Italy

14. A follower of sport (including falconry)

15. A lover of music

16. Loose and improvident in money matters

17. Doubtful and somewhat conflicting in his attitude to woman [*sic*]
18. Of probable Catholic leanings, but touched with skepticism

Needless to say, William Shakespeare did not fit the description. He was not a man "of superior education" nor "a member of the higher aristocracy" nor "loose and improvident in money matters," so Looney concluded that the Author was someone else. But there's an obvious flaw in Looney's reasoning: His portrait of the Artist is entirely subjective. Others read the plays and poems and envision a very different Author: young, middle class, conventional, self-educated, involved in his world. Critics C. L. Barber and Richard Wheeler, for example, believe the "particular constellation of the burgher family [Shakespeare] grew up in is consistent with the thematic preoccupations visible in his works."[2]

The fact is, it's impossible to glean much about a writer by extrapolating from his fiction. If we knew nothing about Chekhov but had only his plays and stories, would we guess he was a middle-class doctor? His doctor characters are usually insensitive or incompetent; it's the cultured landowners who have his sympathy. Or take Dickens and Dostoyevsky. They depict the psyches of criminals with an accuracy that has been verified by psychological research; if we only had their novels, would we think they had committed murder? Would we guess Georg Büchner, the author of the world-weary *Danton's Death*, died at twenty-three? Or that Marlowe lived only to twenty-nine? Or that Keats was dead at twenty-five? Would we think Tennessee Williams was a man? His female characters are often more fully developed and lifelike than his men. Noel Coward was the son of a piano salesman and left school at the age of nine, yet his plays are about upper-class sophisticates. Joseph Conrad, the great stylist, was born in Poland and didn't begin teaching himself English until the age of twenty; he never knew how to pronounce many of the words he used in his novels. The erudite Tom Stoppard, who often populates his plays with academics, never himself attended a university, nor did George Bernard Shaw; the creator of Professor Henry Higgins had no formal schooling after age fourteen. And with "Shakespeare," the problem is even worse. As the director Peter Brook observes, "it's not for nothing that scholars who have tried so hard to find autobiographical traces in Shakespeare have had so little success. . . . The fact is that there is singularly little of the author's point of view—and his personality seems to be very hard to seize—throughout thirty-seven or thirty-eight plays."[3] To those who would try, T. S. Eliot wrote: "I am used . . . to having my personal biography reconstructed from passages which I got out of books, or which I invented out of nothing because they sounded well; and to having my biography invariably ignored in what I did write from personal experience; so that in consequence I am inclined to believe that people are mistaken about Shakespeare just in proportion to the relative superiority of Shakespeare to myself."[4]

Of course, since we don't know what William Shakespeare was like, it's impossible to say his personality doesn't match the Author's. But we can make some reasonable deductions about Shakespeare's life. Most likely he never went to a university, never was a soldier, and never traveled in Italy—we can't be certain; he may have done all three—but there are no records or historical clues that hint otherwise. Reading the Works, though, one might see the hand of a scholar in the classical allusions, the hard experience of a soldier in the military metaphors, and the eye of a tourist in the Italian settings and atmospheres. This is why people who question the authorship are not cranks or fools. But their doubts are based on impressions, and impressions can be misleading. As John Rigby Hale, author of *The Art of War and Renaissance England*, reminds us, "On the basis of Tasso's epic poem *Gerusalemme Liberata* with its range of military information, metaphor, and character, it could be argued that Shakespeare's Italian contemporary had been a soldier. But, with no missing year in his biography, we know that Tasso had not been."[5]

We have to ask if the knowledge the heretics attribute to experience was not obtainable from other sources, like newspamphlets and Elizabethan literature, and if the Author really knows more about university life, a soldier's lot, or foreign lands, than his untraveled, unscholarly, nonmilitary contemporaries.

SOLDIER'S HEART

In the 1930s, Caroline Spurgeon wrote her landmark study *Shakespeare's Imagery*, in which she isolated and analyzed the Author's metaphors, similes, and analogies in order to discover his personality and experiences. Since metaphors are by definition comparisons of the unfamiliar to the familiar, it's logical to look at them in order to discover what's familiar to a writer. Spurgeon, however, read a great deal into her findings and many of her conclusions, such as that the Author was "Christ-like," are subjective and questionable. Even so, her methodology has become widely influential in understanding the Works and their author. Looking at the Poet's military imagery, Spurgeon declares, "I find nothing which indicates any direct knowledge of war or of fighting. They mostly belong to the usual common stock of Elizabethan war images, the explosion of powder and fire, the shot of cannon, the recoil of a gun, the cut of a sword or a dagger, the action of 'bruising irons', stabs and darts, a siege, an encampment, a barricade, a flag."[6] The dramatists George Chapman and Thomas Dekker, in contrast, create detailed depictions of battle. Chapman's

> (like a murdering piece, making lanes in armies,
> The first man of a rank, the whole rank falling)

in *Bussy D'Ambois* (III.ii.469–70) and Dekker's reference to the "desperate" fighting of Dunkirk pirates (*The Honest Whore Part Two*, I.i.51–3) seem to suggest firsthand observation. Yet it's not known for certain whether either served in the military.[7] As for the Author, even what Spurgeon calls his "most vivid and individual" martial image, the "powder in a skilless soldier's flask" which is set afire by the soldier's own ignorance so that he is dismembered with his own defense (*Romeo and Juliet*, III.iii.132–34), does not prove the Poet's presence on a battlefield. Hobbling through London streets were legless veterans who had suffered such an accident, and they easily could have inspired the simile.

In the Author's mind, Spurgeon perceives, the action of war is chiefly associated with noise, "whether he wants to convey dislike of it or delight in it on the part of his characters."[8] To see the truth of this statement, one need only recall Petruchio's comment in *The Taming of the Shrew*,

> Have I not heard great ordnance in the field,
> And heaven's artillery thunder in the skies?
> Have I not in a pitched battle heard
> Loud 'larums, neighing steeds, and trumpets' clang?
>
> (I.ii.202–5)

or Othello's lament,

> Farewell the plumed troops and the big wars
> That makes ambition virtue! O, farewell!
> Farewell the neighing steed and the shrill trump,
> The spirit-stirring drum, th' ear-piercing fife,

The royal banner, and all quality,
Pride, pomp, and circumstance of glorious war!

(III.iii.349–54)

Similar passages can be found in *Richard III*, *Troilus and Cressida*, *King John*, *Richard II*, and *Julius Caesar*. But as the scholar Paul A. Jorgensen points out, the Author was not alone in describing battles in terms of sound.[9] The Author, in his imagery, is merely following George Peele, Thomas Kyd, Christopher Marlowe, and other dramatists who routinely invoke clamoring trumpets, drums and fife, cannon thunder, human screams, and horses neighing when they allude to warfare.[10] Rather than showing familiarity with armies in the field, these writers know only the noises and props used to simulate combat in the Elizabethan playhouses or, at best, in a military parade.

What knowledge they do have is often discoverable in published sources. For example, consider the Author's couplet

Like soldiers when their captain once doth yield,
They basely fly, and dare not stay the field.

(*Venus and Adonis*, 893–94)

The image seems to be an eyewitness observation, but it was more likely inspired by passages like the following one from Raphael Holinshed's *Chronicles*, a book that supplied the Author with several of his plots:

[The Englishmen] never fled back one foot till their captain the Lord Talbot was sore wounded at the back and so taken. Then their hearts began to faint and they fled, in which flight were slain above twelve hundred.[11]

[spelling modernized]

Likewise, the chorus's vivid evocation of a night before a battle in *Henry V* has convinced some that it must have been based on actual experience:

Now entertain conjecture of a time
When creeping murmur and the poring dark
Fills the wide vessel of the universe.
From camp to camp, through the foul womb of night,
The hum of either army stilly sounds,
That the fixed sentinels almost receive

The secret whispers of each other's watch.
Fire answers fire, and through their paly flames
Each battle sees the other's umber'd face.
Steed threatens steed, in high and boastful neighs
Piercing the night's dull ear, and from the tents
The armorers, accomplishing the knights,
With busy hammers closing rivets up,
Give dreadful note of preparation.
The country cocks do crow, the clocks do toll,
And the third hour of drowsy morning name.
Proud of their numbers and secure in soul,
The confident and overlusty French
Do the low-rated English play at dice;
And chide the cripple tardy-gaited night,
Who like a foul and ugly witch doth limp
So tediously away. The poor condemned English,
Like sacrifices, by their watchful fires
Sit patiently and inly ruminate
The morning's danger; and their gesture sad,
Investing lank-lean cheeks and war-worn coats,
Presented them unto the gazing moon
So many horrid ghosts. O now, who will behold
The royal captain of this ruin'd band
Walking from watch to watch, from tent to tent,
Let him cry, "Praise and glory on his head!"
For forth he goes, and visits all his host,
Bids them good morrow with a modest smile,
And calls them brothers, friends, and countrymen.

(IV.chorus.1–34)

Though crackling with vibrant realistic images, the speech's phrases and details have been culled from the depiction of Agamemnon's nighttime visit to outpost encampments in Chapman's famous translation of Homer's *Iliad* (1598).[12] More general insights into soldiers' psychology, such as their contempt for civilians (particularly courtiers), their self-perception as men who "speak plainly," and their self-conscious awkwardness when it came to wooing women were provided, in tracts and fiction, by Barnabe Rich, whose stories were the basis of *Twelfth Night* and *The Merry Wives of Windsor*, and other less well-known writers. That common soldiers were generally considered cowardly and piratical is clear from non-Shakespearean texts, such as Thomas Heywood's *Edward IV Part One*, in which the character Falconbridge castigates his fleeing men as,

> these base rogues
> This dirty scum of rascal peasantry,
> This heartless rout of base rascality.
> A plague upon you all, you cowardly rogues,
> You craven curs, you slimy muddy clowns,
> Whose courage but consists in multitude,
> Like sheep and meat that follow one another,
> Which if one run away all follow after.[13]

Marlowe makes the same observation in *Tamburlaine Part One*, when a Persian lord assesses the conqueror's invading troops as,

> being void of martial discipline,
> All running headlong after greedy spoils,
> And more regarding gain than victory.
> (II.ii.44–46)[14]

The stereotype of the greedy, fearful soldier was born from the reality of Elizabethan inductees. They were recruited by notoriously corrupt captains from the lowest ranks of the peasantry, lured by promises of steady pay and intermittent pillage but nonetheless terrified of never returning home. One did not have to leave England to pity conscripted recruits,

> Pale cowards, marching on with trembling paces
> (*Rape of Lucrece*, line 1391)

or sympathize with jittery sentinels, whom one could meet on any frosty *Hamlet*-inspiring night at their stations in London. Nor did one have to go abroad to see soldiers carrying out military exercises. Twice in the plays, in *Henry IV Part Two* and in *All's Well That Ends Well*, the Author refers to the practice ground at Mile End Green; observing this famously noisy parade field might account for much of his knowledge. Perhaps it was there he overheard shouts of

> Advance your standards, and upon them, lords;
> Pell-mell, down with them! but be first advis'd,

In conflict that you get the sun of them.

(*Love's Labor's Lost*, IV.iii.364–66)

These are the words, as the writer Duff Cooper notes in his book *Sergeant Shakespeare*, of a musketry instructor.[15] Familiarity with Mile End Green may also have prompted the Poet's recurring picture of men attacking in formations of squares and rectangles. Though training manuals dating from as early as 1562 emphasize drawing up and drilling soldiers in such patterns, no memoir or chronicle reports this sort of drill as being carried out by English troops in the course of a campaign or refers to "squares" of men.[16] Yet, in *Henry V* (IV.ii.28), *Antony and Cleopatra* (III.xi.39–40), and *Coriolanus* (II.i.23), *file* and *square* are used by the Author in the context of campaign soldiering.[17]

An even greater curiosity is the Poet's apparent ignorance of field-grade (upper-eschelon) officer ranks. In the early history plays, there is little acknowledgment of any rank other than general. It's an omission he inherits from Holinshed, who never chronicled the exploits of lower-grade commanders. Though he's familiar with captains (who led men into battle and were responsible for their pay) and knows well lieutenants, ancients (or, ensigns), sergeants, corporals, and pioners, he never mentions sergeant-majors (the second in command to a general) or colonels (the chiefs of regiments). Even when a character enumerates a general's subordinates, the Author avoids naming the ranks:

> The general's disdain'd
> By him one step below, he by the next,
> That next by him beneath; so every step,
> Exampled by the first pace that is sick
> Of his superior, grows to an envious fever
> Of pale and bloodless emulation.

(*Troilus and Cressida*, I.iii.129–34)

In this he is similar to most of his playwriting contemporaries, who refer generically to upper-level officers as "captain"—meaning not the rank but a synonym for commander, "one who captains."[18]

Still, it can't be denied the Author had considerable interest in, and knowledge of, military matters. But then, so did every English citizen. We should not forget that during the 1580s and 1590s the nation was at war. Expeditions to the Continent and to Ireland had created thousands of veterans, including Ben Jonson and the future Lord Chamberlain actors Will Kempe, Thomas Pope, and George Bryan.[19] Meanwhile, back at home, thousands more were mobilized for the country's defense. When the Spanish Armada finally attacked in 1588, preparations for invasion had been going on for more than a year. Arms were issued to citizens, and garrisons were manned. Even after the Armada's stunning defeat in a calamitous sea battle, the threat from Spain continued. By 1595 another attack was expected, and the Queen wrote to her generals: "it is not to be doubted that [the Spanish] intend to invade England and Ireland next summer."[20] Over the following three years, record numbers of men were levied and mobilized.[21] It was a time of extraordinary anxiety.

In the popular culture, courtier-soldiers like the Earl of Leicester, the Earl of Essex, and Sir Walter Ralegh became much-discussed and much-admired figures. Their relative merits and tactical philosophies were argued over, obliquely to be sure, in military treatises that were devoured by a worried public. Some of the best-selling titles included Sir Roger Williams's *A Brief Discourse of War* (1590), Sir John Smythe's *Certain Discourses* (1590), William Garrard's *The Art of War* (1591), Matthew Sutcliffe's *The Practice, Proceedings and the Law of Arms* (1593), and Robert Barret's *The Theorike and Practike of Modern Wars* (1598). It should be little wonder the Playwright parodied these tracts, most obviously in Fluellen's obsession with "the disciplines of war," in *Henry V*.[22]

All in all, it seems likely the Author—whoever he was—was an observer of the military, rather than a participant. He does not betray any knowledge beyond that supplied by his sources, his fellow playwrights, and the experience of a common Londoner. For the final word on this subject, I submit a few lines from the Sonnets:

> The painful warrior famoused for fight,
> After a thousand victories once foil'd,
> Is from the book of honour razed quite,
> And all the rest forgot for which he toiled:
> Then happy I, that love and am beloved
> Where I may not remove nor be removed.

(Sonnet 25)

Here, since the Author contrasts himself with the "painful warrior," he confirms he was a soldier only in imagination or, perhaps—if he was the actor Shakespeare—on the stage.

THE SCHOLAR'S EYE

Was the Poet a university man? The proofs that he was usually begin by citing his gargantuan vocabulary, a lexicon more than double the size of any other English writer's. On top of that, it's pointed out that he uses every Tudor rhetorical figure, of which there are approximately two hundred.[23] But does a few years of study at Oxford or Cambridge really explain such linguistic ability? Other writers, like Shaw, Dickens, Melville, and Conrad, managed to develop huge vocabularies and tremendous arsenals of verbal strategies without ever going to college. New words and rhetorical sophistication are normally acquired through reading, and the Author—who can doubt it?—was a sponge when it came to language. Imagine being able to remember, access, and use twice as many words as you normally do—this was the Poet's gift, and all the education in the world couldn't have taught it to him. His lexicon, therefore, does not show great learning so much as great access to word memory. When we remember that the Author's unusual words are not spread evenly throughout his works but are limited to a few plays like *Troilus and Cressida* and *Love's Labor's Lost*,[24] that his normal style consists of familiar terms cunningly arranged, and that he feels free to invent more words than any other writer, the immensity of his word count isn't so startling anyway.

More convincing evidence would be allusions in the Plays and Poems to life at a university. But no such allusions have been found. If the Author was indeed a scholar, his university days didn't make much of an impression on him. There are no Oxford dons or Cambridge masters in the plays, nor any references to them.[25] In fact, the word *university* appears only three times in the whole Canon, and then in vague contexts, such as "the studious universities" (*Two Gentlemen of Verona*) and "my son and my servant spend all at the university" (*Taming of the Shrew*).[26] Academic designations like *bachelor, chancellor, commoner, dean, don, pensioner, proctor, servitor,* or *sizar* (a Cambridge term) are either never used or never used in their academic sense. His scholars, like Hamlet and Horatio, don't reminisce of their days at Wittenberg, and the only memory of academic life that any character articulates is Polonius's boast that he was accounted a good actor in the university and played Julius Caesar (*Hamlet,* III.ii.99–103).

Grammar school, on the other hand, is alluded to repeatedly, though rarely with fondness. Romeo sighs, "Love goes toward love as schoolboys from their books;/But love from love toward school with heavy looks." And Gremio in *The Taming of the Shrew* enthuses, "As willingly as e'er I came from school." The famous Seven Ages of Man speech in *As You Like It* depicts "the whining schoolboy with his satchel/And shining morning face, creeping like snail/Unwillingly to school." "Schoolboys take less delight in their lessons," a character remarks in *Much Ado About Nothing*, "than in finding birds' nests." But the Author must have thought schools were valuable because he has the villainous but comic Jack Cade criticize them in *Henry VI Part Two*. Listing the crimes of his captive, Lord Say, Cade grumbles, "Thou hast most traitorously corrupted the youth of the realm in erecting a grammar school; and whereas, before, our forefathers had no other books but the score and tally, thou hast caused printing to be used, and, contrary to the king his crown and dignity, thou hast built a paper mill. It will be proved to thy face that thou hast men about thee that usually talk of a noun and a verb and such abominable words as no Christian ear can endure to hear" (IV.vii.32–41).

Unlike professors, who never appear as characters in the dramas, schoolmasters are portrayed in *The Comedy of Errors*, *Love's Labor's Lost*, and *The Merry Wives of Windsor*.[27] Significantly, the Author based his pedants on a *commedia dell'arte* stock character who is a university instructor, yet in play after play the Poet reduces him to a schoolmaster, preferring to satirize the teachers of children rather than ivory-tower academics.

As for the grammar school curriculum, the hornbook, from which young students learned their letters, is referred to in *Love's Labor's Lost* and *Richard III*. The *ABC with Catechism* is mentioned in *Two Gentlemen of Verona* and *King John*. When one of the Goths hears a Latin quotation in *Titus Andronicus*, he anachronistically exclaims, "O, 'tis a verse in Horace; I know it well./I read it in the grammar long ago," referring to William Lily's *Shorte Introduction of Grammar*, which was prescribed by royal proclamation for use in every grammar school from 1548 through the seventeenth century. Lily's *Grammar*, as the book is commonly called, contained quotations (some accurate and some not) from Roman classics. The Author seems to be familiar with the 1557 edition because a line from Terence's *Eunuch* is misquoted in *The Taming of the Shrew* as it erroneously appears in that printing of the *Grammar*, not as it exists in Terence's original. The Poet may have read the original but he knew the *Grammar* version better. Holofernes in *Love's Labor's Lost*, Sir Toby in *Twelfth Night*, and Benedick in *Much Ado About Nothing* also quote from Lily's *Grammar*.[28] And, not surprisingly, the parson-schoolmaster Sir

Hugh Evans in *The Merry Wives of Windsor* gives a lesson from the book to young William Page:

> EVANS. William, how many numbers is in nouns?
> WILL. Two.
> . . .
> EVANS. What is lapis, William?
> WILL. A stone.
>
> (*Merry Wives* IV.i.21–32)

Lily writes: "In Nouns be two numbers, the Singular and the Plural. The Singular number speaketh of one: as Lapis, a stone."[29] In short, the Author remembers his early education.

He remembers his Latin poets too. All of the Roman writers he borrows from, in quotation or his own English translation, were part of the typical provincial school curriculum. The most prominent of these was Ovid, many of whose works the Author knew and whose *Metamorphosis*, the Elizabethan classroom favorite, was routinely studied alongside Golding's translation (1567). He also read Virgil, which is to say the first six books of the *Aeneid* as well as Phaer's translation of them; Horace (the odes, epistles, and *Ars Poetica*); Quintilian; the comedies of Terence and Plautus; one or two tragedies of Seneca (though, according to scholars, most of Seneca's plays the Author read in English translations); Juvenal; Cato; Cicero; Livy; Lucan; and probably Julius Caesar.[30] Among modern Latin authors, he's familiar with Erasmus (several works), Mantuan (the *Bucolica*), and the Latin schoolbook versions of *Aesop's Fables*. What's interesting is that the Author doesn't stray far beyond these writers, unlike Jonson who recommends all sorts of Latin works to Drummond—Pliny, Quintilian, Tacitus, Juvenal, Hippocrates—that were not on the Westminster school syllabus (if Jonson indeed went there).[31] This may be what Jonson means when he calls the Poet's Latin "small."

The Author's borrowing from minor figures comes exclusively from school texts and books of Latin adages and fragments that young grammarians were forced to memorize—books like Cullman's *Sententiae Pueriles*, Palingenius's *Zodiacus Vitae*, Mirandula's *Illustrium Poetarum Flores*, and Textor's *Epitheta*. T. W. Baldwin has shown that the Poet translates a fragment of Pacuvius as it is misquoted in the 1573 edition of the *Ad Herennium*, a text that was used to teach rhetoric in the upper levels of grammar school.[32]

Missing from the Canon is any trace of Martial, Catullus, or Silius Italicus. These writers, who were translated and imitated frequently by other Elizabethan poets, were featured prominently in the curricula of Eton and Westminster, making it highly unlikely the Author was a student at either of those institutions or any of the schools that shared their respective curricula. Baldwin demonstrates that the Poet's Latin reading amounts to a modified form of the syllabus of Paul's School, variations of which were used in schools at Ipswich and Worcester. In fact, the Plays and Poems reflect the reading, rhetorical exercises, and elementary logic of the standard grammar school so completely, that Baldwin believes the Author was an excellent student and possibly a tutor or schoolteacher himself. No other dramatist, not even James Shirley, who was a known schoolmaster, puts as much of his early education to poetic use.[33]

At Oxford and Cambridge, young men "sucked the sweets of sweet philosophy" as the servant Tranio describes it in *The Taming of the Shrew*. They devoted themselves to ethics, mathematics, metaphysics, advanced logic and rhetoric, and theology. These subjects were thought to be a good preparation for the professions—law, medicine, and divinity. For an arts degree, the university syllabus involved classical literature and scholastic philosophy, whose core curriculum rested on Aristotle's *Rhetoric*, *Dialectics*, and *Nicomachean Ethics*. For four years, scholars honed their cogitative skills in exercises and disputations on abstract and philosophical subjects often derived from Aristotle. Some examples of genuine disputations, still preserved at Oxford and Cambridge, include whether mental illness is worse than bodily illness, whether there is matter in the sky, whether mothers love their children more than fathers do, whether knowledge is more productive of error than ignorance.[34] Did the Author spend years of his life writing such theses? Most scholars doubt it. Unlike in Marlowe's *Doctor Faustus* and *Edward II*,[35] in the Works there are no hints that their author read Aristotle thoroughly or studied any of the university subjects. He may not even have been able to read Greek.

Greek was taught at some free schools but was required at the two universities.[36] Yet there is no evidence the Author knew the language. Unlike Jonson, he never uses it in his plays. His classical allusions are mostly mythological and could be picked up from reading the other English writers of his time—this was, after all, the Renaissance. John Taylor, the poet and watertaxi-driver, who "avowed his failure to get through the Latin accidence, and his ignorance of all languages but his own," has a greater number of classical allusions in his small body of work than occur in all the Shakespeare plays.[37] When the Author quotes Aristotle in *Troilus and Cressida*, it's the English mistranslation he cites:

> Unlike young men, whom Aristotle thought
> Unfit to hear moral philosophy.
>
> (II.ii.166–67)

The word "moral" comes from the translators; the philosopher wrote "political." The only reference to a Greek source that was not translated into English is in *Titus Andronicus*:

> The Greeks upon advice did bury Ajax
> That slew himself; and wise Laertes' son
> Did graciously plead for his funerals.
>
> (I.i.379–81)

The lines allude to a scene in Sophocles' *Ajax*.[38] But even this source had been translated into Latin, and the turn-of-the-century scholar John Churton Collins showed it was the Latin version that the Poet knew. The line "Grim-visaged war hath smooth'd his wrinkled front," from *Richard III*, is a mistranslation of a line from *Ajax*, and the same line is mistranslated in all three Latin versions of the play the Author might have read.[39] If there are indeed bits of Aeschylus and Euripides in the Plays, Collins believed the Author read them in Latin. But it's also possible there were intermediate sources for some ancient Greek ideas or that the Poet had similar thoughts merely by coincidence. Great tragic writers, it's not unreasonable to believe, might have common sympathies and expressions.

There's no evidence the Author read Plutarch's *Lives* in the original Greek either. Nor Jacques Amyot's 1559 French translation of it. It's certain, however, he knew Sir Thomas North's 1579 translation of Amyot's French. He takes whole passages from North, such as the description of Cleopatra, and converts them into poetry:

> She disdained to set forward otherwise but to take her barge in the river of Cydnus, the poop whereof was of gold, the sails of purple, and the oars of silver, which kept stroke in rowing after the sound of the music of flutes, hautboys, cithers, viols, and such other instruments as they played upon the barge. And now for the person of herself: She was laid under a pavilion of cloth-of-gold of tissue, apparelled and attired like the goddess Venus commonly drawn in picture; and hard by her, on ei-

ther hand of her, pretty fair boys, apparelled as painters do set forth god Cupid, with little fans in their hands, with the which they fanned wind upon her. Her ladies and gentlewomen also, the fairest of them, were apparelled like the nymphs Nereides (which are the mermaids of the waters) and like the Graces, some steering the helm, others tending the tackle and ropes of the barge, out of the which there came a wonderful passing sweet savor of perfumes that perfumed the wharf's side, pestered with innumerable multitudes of people.[40]
[spelling modernized]

In *Antony and Cleopatra*, this becomes:

> The barge she sat in, like a burnish'd throne,
> Burnt on the water. The poop was beaten gold,
> Purple the sails, and so perfumed that
> The winds were love-sick with them; the oars were silver,
> Which to the tune of flutes kept stroke, and made
> The water which they beat to follow faster,
> As amorous of their strokes. For her own person,
> It beggar'd all description: she did lie
> In her pavilion—cloth of gold, of tissue—
> O'er-picturing that Venus where we see
> The fancy outwork nature. On each side her
> Stood pretty dimpled boys, like smiling Cupids,
> With divers-color'd fans, whose wind did seem
> To glow the delicate cheeks which they did cool,
> And what they undid did.
> . . .
> Her gentlewomen, like the Nereides,
> So many mermaids, tended her i' th' eyes,
> And made their bends adornings. At the helm
> A seeming mermaid steers; the silken tackle
> Swell with the touches of those flower-soft hands,
> That yarely frame the office. From the barge
> A strange invisible perfume hits the sense
> Of the adjacent wharfs. The city cast
> Her people out upon her.
>
> (II.ii.191–214)

Elsewhere, the Author retains North's mistakes. In the third act of *Julius Caesar*, Antony reads to the citizenry part of Caesar's will:

> Moreover he hath left you all his walks,
> His private arbours, and new planted orchards,
> On this side Tiber.
>
> (III.ii.247–49)

Plutarch's Greek says "beyond the Tiber." But Amyot's French has "deca la riviere du Tybre"[41] [on this side of the river Tiber], and North follows it: "which he had on this side of the river of Tyber."[42] Where North translates "Lydia" from Amyot's "Lydie" in the sentence "First of all he did establish Cleopatra queene of AEgypt, of Cyprus, of Lydia, and the lower Syria,"[43] Plutarch's original has "Libya" (spelled Lambda-iota-*beta*-upsilon-eta-sigma), not "Lydia." In *Antony and Cleopatra*, the Author follows North, who has followed Amyot:

> Unto her
> He gave the stablishment of Egypt, made her
> Of lower Syria, Cyprus, Lydia,
> Absolute queen.
>
> (III.vi.8–11)

The most obvious measure of a writer's Greek would be his New Testament allusions. The Christian Bible was the principal text for any would-be scholar; it was translated by upper-level grammar school boys as well as by university students. When we look at the Author's references, however, we find they come from the two popular English versions, the Bishop's Bible and the Genevan; he doesn't seem to have been influenced by the original Greek as a university scholar would have been.

Anti-Stratfordians are wrong when they claim the Author knew Greek. But they may have a point when it comes to French. The Poet writes in that language in *Henry V* and *The Merry Wives of Windsor* and scatters Gallic words and phrases throughout the Canon. Some of these phrases (like *adieu* and *pourquoi*) were in the current parlance, but he did not construct whole scenes out of common terms. He must have had some proficiency in French. And we can be relatively sure the French was his—that is, not the work of a francophone collaborator—because the epilogue to *Henry IV Part Two* promises "our humble author will . . . make you merry with fair Katherine of France" and her role in *Henry V* is almost entirely in French.

Yet nothing indicates where Will Shakespeare learned French. The heretics assume one had to attend university to acquire a foreign language and thus rule out nonscholar Shakespeare as a candidate. But, of course, there were other ways to pick up a tongue. For all we know, his schoolmaster taught French in addition to Latin and Greek. Or, Will might have read one or two of the "Teach Yourself French" manuals that were available at the time. Coupled with the Elizabethan training in Latin, which would have made French easier to learn, these books might have been adequate to give him the basic nonidiomatic French evident in the plays. Or he could have studied with one of the countless language tutors in London. They charged a shilling a week and allegedly gave a thorough training in French, Italian, Arabic, Russian, Spanish, Dutch, Turkish, German, or Polish.[44] Still, there is no proof Shakespeare was tutored.

That it would not have been unusual for him to know French can be seen from indirect evidence. In the mid-1590s, as tax records tell us, he lived in Bishopsgate ward, the same ward that was home to "Petty France" (the French district). Bishopsgate was a small section in a city whose total area was less than four square miles, so even if he wasn't habitating among the immigrants, he could hardly have avoided them. By 1604, he was renting rooms from the Mountjoys, a French family that, according to his own court testimony, he had met two years earlier. He was also connected to an émigré milieu through Richard Field, the Stratford-born printer who would have gone to school with Will and whose father knew John Shakespeare. Field was apprenticed to Thomas Vautrollier, a French immigrant, and in the early 1590s married his master's widow, Jacqueline, herself a Frenchwoman. As a printer, he became London's principal typesetter of foreign-language works, particularly French and Italian. Within Shakespeare's own family, Will's son-in-law Thomas Quiney (Judith's husband) knew some French. In 1622, while serving as Stratford's chamberlain, he adorned a ledger with a couplet from a sixteenth-century romance by Mellin de Saint-Gelais. Though he misspelled two words, the fact that he thought some lines of French were an appropriate ornament for an account book shows that one could have had contact with the language even in Stratford.[45]

Another tongue the Author seems to have had is Italian. Two lines of it appear in *The Taming of the Shrew* when Petruchio greets Hortensio with, "*Con tutto il core, ben trovato*" [With all my heart well met], and Hortensio replies, "*Alla nostra casa ben venuto, molto honorato signor mio Petruchio.*" [To our house welcome, my most honored lord Petruchio.] Later in the same play the Poet uses the terms *mi pardonato* [forgive me], *basta* [enough], and *mercatante* [merchant]. In *Love's Labor's Lost*, he quotes a proverb, which he may simply have heard, but which comes directly out of John Florio's learn-to-speak Italian books, the *First* and *Second Fruits* (it's printed in both):

> Venechia, Venechia,
> Che non te vede, che non te prechia
> [Venice, Venice, who has not seen you cannot appreciate you].[46]

A *bona-roba*, he knows, is a courtesan (*Henry IV Part Two*); a *capocchia*, a simpleton (*Troilus and Cressida*); a *cornuto*, a cuckold (*Merry Wives of Windsor*); and *cavalleria*, cavaliers (*Pericles*). *Capriccio, coragio*, and *fico*— caprice, courage, and a fig—bubble up in *All's Well That Ends Well*, *The Tempest*, and *Merry Wives*, respectively. *Via*! [go] occurs in *The Merchant of Venice* and *Merry Wives; alla stoccata* [at the thrust—a fencing term] appears in *Romeo and Juliet*, and *ben venuto* shows up again in *Love's Labor's Lost*. But that's all. This is the total of his written Italian, all familiar or copybook phrases that can be found in the work of other English writers.[47] We can say the same for the dozen or so words of Spanish and pseudo-Spanish he uses; they don't show his knowledge of Spanish so much as the entrance of these words into everyday English.[48]

Had the Author made more use of a book like Florio's *First Fruits*, "wherewith a man in very short space, and with little help, may attain unto the perfection of writing, reading, pronouncing, and speaking of the Italian tongue,"[49] his Italian would certainly have been better, if not as advanced as the book promises. Compare the Poet to Marston, who included eighteen lines of Italian, much more complex and expressive than the Author's, in *Antonia and Mellida*, and to Jonson, who, in *Volpone*, has many more unusual Italian words (like *sforzato, ciarlitani, scartoccios, canaglia, moscadelli, unguento*, and so forth). It seems that Jonson knew the language, yet he told Drummond he understood neither French nor Italian.[50] Might this not be the case with the Author? Virtually every play-maker of the time, even nonuniversity men like Jonson, Dekker, Webster and Kyd, saw fit to include some French, Italian, Spanish, German, Dutch or Flemish in his work. They were trying to appeal to the educated audience members who spoke those languages and to the immigrant populations who had fled the wars on the Continent. Like Petty France, there was an Italian community in London, longing to hear some homegrown phrases in the theatre.

The other evidence that the Playwright knew Italian is that some of his plots seem to come from Italian sources that, as far as we know, had not yet been translated into English. These include Fiorentino's *Il Pecorone* and Masuccio's *Il Novelino* (*The Merchant of Venice*), Cinthio's *Hecatommithi* (*Measure for Measure* and *Othello*), and less certainly, Cinthio's *Epitia* (*Measure*), Gonzaga's *Gl'Ingannati* (*Twelfth Night*), and Bandello's *Ariodante and Genevora* (*Much Ado*). He may have read these in the original, but it's always possible intermediate sources, such as old plays based on these stories, were the Author's real inspiration. For example, the play *Laelia*, based on *Gl'Ingannati*, was performed at Cambridge in 1595 and might be the real source of *Twelfth Night*.[51] It's also possible that translations might have existed in manuscript, like Montemayor's *Diana* (a source for *Two Gentlemen of Verona*), which had been translated from the Spanish as early as 1582, though it remained unpublished for sixteen years.[52] Manuscripts were commonly circulated at this time. Another possibility is that the Author heard the stories from someone who had read them; people bring ideas to writers all the time. "I will get Peter Quince to write a ballad of this dream," exclaims Bottom in *Midsummer*. The published word was not the only means of transmission.

Finally, missing translations of Italian sources might have been published but are now lost. Richard Farmer, the "principal librarian" of Cambridge and master of Emmanuel College, believed such translations were among the books burned by the Puritans during the Civil War. Farmer, in 1767, wrote, "It is scarcely conceivable how industriously the puritanical Zeal of the last age exerted itself in destroying, amongst better things, the innocent amusements of the former. Numberless *Tales* and *Poems* are alluded to in old Books, which are now perhaps nowhere to be found."[53] He goes on to give a tantalizing example. Painter, at the end of the second volume of his *Palace of Pleasure* (1567), appends a teaser, an advertisement for the next volume. He promises that it will boast "such suffrable [*sic*] as the learned Frenchman *François de Belleforest* hath selected, and the choicest done in *Italian*. Some also out of Erizzo, Ser Giovanni Florentino, Parabosco, Cynthio, Straparole, Sansovino, and the best liked out of the Queene of Navarre, and other Authors."[54] Tragically, the third volume is lost or was never published. But it's conceivable that in this lost book the Poet found the plots of *Hamlet*, *The Merchant of Venice*, *Othello*, and *Love's Labor's Lost*. It's known that he found *All's Well That Ends Well* in the earlier volumes of the *Palace of Pleasure*; maybe, somehow, he got hold of the third. In any case, while we must grant him some French, we can't conclude with any confidence that the Author knew Italian or attended university.

MONSIEUR TRAVELER

In Renaissance England, a young gentleman's education was often capped by a trip to the Continent, usually to France or Italy. Just such an excursion, with extended stays in Venice and Milan, is envisioned by readers for the Author. How else to explain his seeming intimacy with the customs, landscape, the very air of Italy? But English playwrights of the period did not have to travel to learn about the birthplace of Petrarch and Machiavelli. Italy came to them.

The Elizabethans were fascinated by Italy. Its culture was studied and its fashions imitated. Undoubtedly, the principal sources of their fascination were the expatriates among them. As early as 1492, Henry VII brought the first Italian humanists to England, and throughout the sixteenth century, merchant ships like those belonging to Antonio in *The Merchant of Venice* docked along the Thames. *The Elephant*, an actual London inn mentioned in *Twelfth Night*, was noted as being commonly filled with Italian visitors.[55] And one could meet immigrants, like the restauranteur Paolo Lucchese, the bookseller Acanio de Renialme, the merchant Nicolo De Gozi, or the physician Theodore Diodati, without ever leaving the city.[56] The first history of Italy in English was published in 1549 (reprinted in 1561), and collections of novellas, on which many plays of the period were based, were devoured by a wide audience.

Commedia dell'arte, Venetian improvised comedy of archetypal characters, was also well known. Troupes toured England as early as 1546 and several times during the 1570s.[57] Thomas Nashe refers to *commedia* in *Pierce Pennilesse* (1592) when he declares English drama superior to the Italian because it is "full of gallant resolution, not consisting like theirs of a Pantaloun, a Whore and a Zanie, but of Emporers, Kings and Princes."[58] Later, Jonson was able to draw on *commedia* without visiting its country of origin.[59] In his *Apologie for Actors*, Thomas Heywood declines to discuss "all the Doctors, Zawnyes, Pantaloones, Harlakeenes in which the French but especially the Italians have been excellent,"[60] indicating his firsthand familiarity with the tradition. Richard Burbage is listed in a "plot," or cue sheet, with an actor playing "Pantaloon," and references to the main characters of *commedia* can be found in many plays of the era. To choose one instance, in John Day's play *The Travailes of*

Three English Brothers (1607) the actor Will Kempe is imagined preparing an improvised *commedia* performance with an Italian "Harlekeen." The Harlekeen insists that "we must have an Amorado that must make me cornuto. . . . Then we must have a Magnifico that must take up the matter betwixt me and my wife."[61]

As we would expect if their Author never saw the country he was writing about, the plays give few specifics to create their Italian settings. Instead they rely on atmosphere to evoke not the real locales—the real plague-haunted, island city of Venice, for example, with its dank green canals and labyrinths of dark, narrow alleyways—but rather, in Harley Granville Barker's phrase, "a Venice that lived in the Elizabethan mind."[62] An Italy, moreover, very much like England in summer. The Poet's contemporaries festoon their plays with just as much, if not more, observable details. There is more Venetian local color in Ben Jonson's *Volpone*, for instance, than in either *The Merchant of Venice* or *Othello*. The Author has heard of gondolas and the Rialto, observes Murray J. Levith in *Shakespeare's Italian Settings and Plays*, "but Jonson knows the ships in St. Marks, the Grand Canal, the Arsenal, the monastery of San Spirito, and that Jews loaned money for house furnishings."[63]

Levith notes that the Poet never mentions the sights that were most obvious to contemporary visitors. Verona is "old" in *Taming of the Shrew;* it's "fair" and has "streets" and "walls" in *Romeo and Juliet*, but the Author doesn't remark upon its ancient Roman amphitheatre, nor does he mention the city's encircling wall of brick, built in the 1530s, which impressed the travelogue writer Fynes Moryson.[64] The same goes for the wall's triumphal gates. In *All's Well That Ends Well*, nine scenes are set in Florence, yet none of the city's physical characteristics are referred to; there is no river Arno, no Ponte Vecchio, no Duomo. The Duke is nowhere described as a Medici.[65] Similarly, Mantua is a place to be from or to go to, but what the city looks like is never described. Pisa, twice in *Taming*, is called "renowned for its grave citizens," as if the Poet's eye, in its fine frenzy rolling, somehow failed to notice the Leaning Tower. Also missing from the Canon is Venice's Arsenal, a building which, in the mid-sixteenth century, William Thomas considered the city's most notable. Fifty or so years later, Moryson and Thomas Coryat were very impressed with it too.[66] In fact, the Author doesn't mention a single Italian building, bridge, or square.[67]

The great scholar E. K. Chambers remarked, in regard to Venice, the Author "shows familiarity with some minute points of local topography," and the notion was picked up by Oxfordians Charlton Ogburn, Tom

Bethell, and Joseph Sobran.[68] But what "local topography" are they talking about? Canals? Islands? Bridges? The Author mentions none of them. (Are we to believe a writer—any writer—who had been to Venice could set two plays there without mentioning canals?) The only example of landscape Ogburn and Sobran cite is a dubious one first proposed by the nineteenth-century German commentator Karl Elze:

> The name of Gobbo, which he has bestowed on the clown [in *The Merchant of Venice*], reminds us vividly of the Gobbo di Rialto, a stone figure which serves as a supporter of the granite pillar of about a man's height, from which the laws of the Republic were proclaimed.[69]

But the word "gobbo" was Italian for hunchback.[70] The Author did not have to go to Italy to discover it; it was even collected in John Florio's 1598 Italian dictionary, *World of Words* (page 152) as meaning "crookbacked." Among the Italians living in London, he may have met a man nicknamed "Gobbo."[71] Maybe he got the name from *commedia dell'arte*; the hunchbacked "Pulcinello" character, the forerunner of the English "Punch," could have been called Gobbo in an improvised performance. Or, naturally, the Author might have heard of the statue from someone who had seen it. Take your pick. (The name is spelled "Iobbe" in the first quarto and first folio editions of *Merchant*, so the Author may never have written "Gobbo" at all; the name he intended may have been "Job.")

If the Poet ever did tour Italy, he paid little attention to geography. In *The Two Gentlemen of Verona*, the Duke of Milan advises Thurio and Proteus,

> I pray you stand not to discourse,
> But mount you presently and meet with me
> Upon the rising of the mountain foot,
> That lead toward Mantua, whither they are fled.
>
> (V.ii.44–47)

But the way to Mantua from Milan is flat, not mountainous. In the same play, Proteus and Panthino are both worried about losing the tide for their voyage to Milan, even though Verona is situated too far above sea level to be affected by tides. In *The Taming of the Shrew*'s Padua, Lucentio muses upon his absent servant:

> If, Biondello, thou wert come ashore,
> We could at once put us in readiness

And take a lodging fit to entertain
Such friends as time in Padua shall beget.

(I.i.42–45)

These lines make no sense unless the Author envisions inland Padua with
a seacoast. Lucentio thinks Biondello is rowing from an anchored ship,
not stepping off one of the small canal boats that can, in reality, dock at
Padua. Otherwise, why does he think he needs to wait for him? Why is
Biondello dawdling in the canal? In any case, the way from Pisa to Padua
is overland. In *The Tempest*, the Author gives Milan a seacoast too. Prospero tells his daughter how they were placed on a leaky raft and aban-
doned at sea, a practice even then associated with pirates:

In few, they hurried us aboard a bark,
Bore us some leagues to sea, where they prepared
A rotten carcass of a butt, not rigg'd,
Nor tackle, sail, nor mast, the very rats
Instinctively have quit it. There they hoist us,
To cry to th' sea that roar'd to us.

(I.ii.144–49)

But Milan is not near any river that can carry a "bark." Even if it were,
Prospero doesn't mention the long journey through a maze of canals and
rivers (changing boats along the way) just to get to the Mediterranean.
By "some leagues to sea" the Author must mean "some leagues *out* to sea"
or else the usurpers left Prospero and his daughter to die at the beach.
Not a very smart plan. Milan is again a port in *The Two Gentlemen of
Verona*:

PROTEUS. But now he parted hence to embark for Milan.
SPEED. Twenty to one then he is shipp'd already.

(I.i.71–72)

And when Speed departs, Proteus bids him farewell with,

Go, go, be gone, to save your ship from wrack,
Which cannot perish having thee aboard,
Being destin'd to a drier death on shore.

(I.i.148–50)

Yet the normal route from Verona to Milan, like Pisa to Padua, is by land. And even if one opted for the much longer and more complicated journey down the Adige and up the Po, fighting the current, and then through forty miles of canals, it would be a real trick to die in a shipwreck.

In 1908, Sir Edward Sullivan believed he could explain why landlocked cities are ports in the plays. He claimed to discover waterways that connected the cities during the 1500s. Probably he was looking at German maps of the period that view Italy from the Alps and inaccurately show a maze of rivers[72] (Figure 5). In fact, there is no archaeological evidence these waterways ever existed. Surely after only four hundred years there would be some trace of them; the one from Verona to Milan would have stretched at least eighty miles. Given the violent history of Italy during the Renaissance, and the efforts of the city states to defend themselves from one another (like Verona's wall), such canals are absurd. Yet, hilariously, as late as 1997, Joseph Sobran argued that knowledge of these waterways was proof the Author had been to Italy!

Levith catalogues other gaps. For example, wine cellars were public gathering places in the Italy of the time, not, as play after play assumes, alehouses. Similarly, Antonio's patronage of Bassanio in *The Merchant of Venice* is a practice that was typical in England but doesn't jibe with Italian custom.[73] The Author shows little knowledge of Venice's government or laws. In *Othello*, he seems to have no idea how the Doge and Senate interrelated. Unlike in *Merchant*, the Doge did not preside over Venetian courts of law, nor did magnificoes serve as judges.[74] Venetian Jews were "not allowed to buy any lands, houses, or [have] stable inheritances" despite the evidence of the play, and they were required to live in a "ghetto," which the Author never mentions.[75] The Poet invents the law that Portia cites at the play's climax, the statute which declares that for plotting against the life of a Venetian citizen the punishment was death and the confiscation of goods. No such law existed. Nor was there a Jewish gaberdine, like the one Shylock talks about; the Author invented that too.

To be sure, he gets some things right. The "special officers of the night," mentioned in the first act of *Othello*, did exist. The name Bellario in *Merchant* is a correct Paduan name, although the Bentivolii in *Taming of the Shrew* were not from Pisa as in the play, but from Bologna; they ruled that city in the sixteenth century. Not surprisingly, the Poet had heard about gondolas and Venetian magnificoes, and he had seen "twiggen" Chianti bottles, which were imported from Tuscany. In *Merchant*, the custom of offering pigeons as gifts is accurate. He would have observed it among émigrés. Flocks of Englishmen were attending

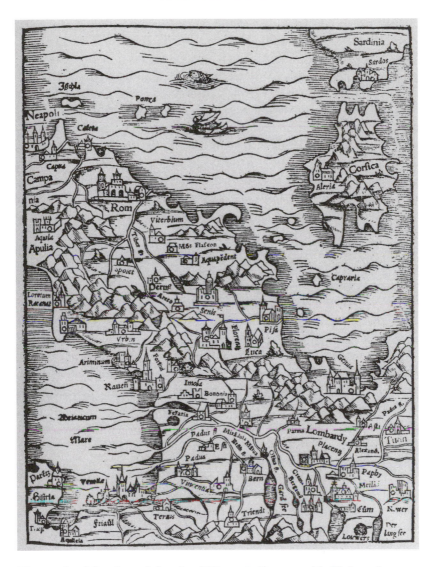

Figure 5. Map from Sebastian Münster's *Cosmographia Universale* (1575). General Research Division, the New York Public Library, Astor, Lenox, and Tilden Foundations.

the University of Padua, so he wouldn't have had to go there to hear of it; Greene mentions Padua's "famous University" in *Mamilia* (1583).[76] Likewise, Milan's St. Gregory's Well was regularly mentioned by other Elizabethan writers. Twentieth-century scholar Ernesto Grillo tells us that Bergamo was famous for sail making and, if so, the news might have reached England. Belmont is accurately described as being twenty miles from Venice, but there are several places named Montabello, Levith reminds us, and no one knows which one the Author had in mind.[77] He did not have to go to Italy to see Correggio's painting *Io and Jupiter*, which is described by the lord in *Taming*'s Induction; a copy was on display at Belvoir Castle (a place, I might add, where the actor William Shakespeare could have been called upon to perform). The inscription on Giulio Romano's Mantuan tomb, which the Author alludes to in *The Winter's Tale*, was available to him in the 1550 edition of Vasari's *Lives of Seventy Excellent Painters, Sculptors and Architects*.[78] The Latin inscription would likely catch his eye in a book otherwise in Italian, though he probably came across it in some intermediary source.

He seems to be aware of the ferry to Venice when he mentions the "traject" in *Merchant*. The quarto version of the play has "tranect," and editors plausibly argue this is a misprint for "traject," an anglicization of "traghetto" (ferry). Portia tells her servant,

> Now, Balthasar,
> As I have ever found thee honest-true,
> So let me find thee still. Take this same letter,
> And use thou all th' endeavor of a man
> In speed to Padua. See thou render this
> Into my cousin's hands, Doctor Bellario,
> And look what notes and garments he doth give thee,
> Bring them, I pray thee, with imagin'd speed
> Unto the traject, to the common ferry
> Which trades to Venice. Waste no time in words
> But get thee gone. I shall be there before thee.
>
> (III.iv.45–55)

It's unclear if the Author thinks the ferry runs from the mainland to the city (there's no evidence he knows Venice sits on a group of islands), or if he thinks the ferry crosses a river, like those that traversed the Thames ("traghetto" is what Italian immigrants would have called the English watertaxi berths). But he does seem to know that a boat to the city existed, even if he's really thinking of London.

It's perhaps telling that of the twelve plays with Italian or Roman settings, readers "sense" Italy in only three—*Taming, Merchant,* and *Othello.* In these the Author made his greatest efforts at local color and atmosphere. Even Grillo, who believed the Author visited Italy, concluded he must have done so after penning his early plays. In *Two Gentlemen of Verona* and *Romeo and Juliet*, Grillo writes, "we find little that encourages us to believe the poet had actually seen the locality where the development of the action takes place."[79] But even for the three "Italian" plays, if we change the names of characters and places, we can see how little of the country is really in them. And, as many readers observe, the Italian people are completely absent; the Author populates Italy with Englishmen.

Regardless of who wrote the Plays, it's likely that Robert Armin portrayed Feste in *Twelfth Night* and the Clown in *Othello*. Armin was the actor in the Lord Chamberlain's and later in the King's Men who took on the fools' parts. He was also, believe it or not, a "good Italian scholar."[80] In addition to writing comic plays and books of humor, he published translations from Italian. So it's not surprising to find "the Lady of Strachy," an anglicization of an Italian idiom for a haughty woman, in *Twelfth Night*, or the knowledge that Neapolitans have nasal accents in *Othello*.[81] Armin might have suggested them. Though of course they could just as easily have found their way to England some other way). Armin might have suggested plots too and could be responsible for the mystery of the untranslated sources, at least after 1599 when he joined the Lord Chamberlain's Men.

With scholars on the stage, immigrants in the pubs, and travelers returning at the piers, it's no surprise that the Author knows what little he does about Italy. No long voyage to the Peninsula was required.

CHAPTER 5
Lawyer's Fingers

If the average reader suspects that the Author had an exceptional education, served in war, and sojourned in Italy, readers with special knowledge suspect even more. The Poet, it is claimed, is an expert in hunting, angling, falconry, horsemanship, medicine, classical mythology, folklore, the Bible, natural history, gardening, agriculture, music, heraldry, precious stones, typography, and more. "What happens," according to Paul Clarkson and Clyde Warren, "is that a sincere and otherwise sound scholar absorbs the entire learning of his particular pet subject. . . . He then reads into Shakespeare's plays a gloss as subtle and unconscious as it is encyclopedic—a gloss which is at most suggested but rarely justified by the text. The same literary technique will undoubtedly enable antiquarians of the future to demonstrate that Rudyard Kipling was a schoolteacher, a soldier, a deep-sea fisherman, a railroad man, a diplomatist, an engineer, a naturalist, an expert automobile mechanic, and a profound Chaucerian scholar—although we know he was none of these."[1]

The Author's familiarity with law, though, seems to be genuine. Edmund Malone, an eighteenth-century scholar and himself a lawyer, ruminated that the Poet's "knowledge and application of legal terms seems . . . not merely such as might have been acquired by the casual observation of his all-comprehending mind; it has the appearance of technical skill; and he is so fond of displaying it on all occasions."[2] Even in nonlegalistically oriented plays, Malone noticed, plays like *All's Well That Ends Well* (as opposed to, say, the courtroom-climaxed *Merchant of Venice*), the Author's mind turns to legalisms. Two centuries later, W. Nicholas Knight declared the same for the Sonnets: "The sonnets indicate that . . . [the Author] had acquired a knowledge of the varied legal terminology

pertaining to inheritance laws, arrest and court procedure, but most obviously the accoutrements accompanying legal documents, such as bonds,
mortgages, writs, wills, compacts, articles, Chancery forms, covenants,
and fair copies of the same embossed with seals, printed in fair style and
proper hand. They also indicate his preoccupation with inheritance, wills,
usury, increase, fear of loss, suits, court cases . . . etc."[3]

The Author's wide use of legalisms convinced many in the nineteenth
century that the Plays must have been written by a lawyer. It became the
fulcrum of the case for the Elizabethan jurist Sir Francis Bacon. Mark
Twain believed, "the man who wrote the plays was limitlessly familiar
with the laws, and law-courts, and law proceedings, and lawyer-talk, and
lawyer-ways. . . . [A] man can't handle glibly and easily and comfortably
and successfully the *argot* of a trade at which he has not personally served.
He will make mistakes; he will not, and can not, get the trade-phrasings
precisely and exactly right: and the moment he departs, by even a shade,
from a common trade-form, the reader who has served that trade will
know the writer *hasn't*."[4]

Twain is wrong, of course. A lawyer-poet might misconstrue legal
jargon as badly as anyone, and he might even do it intentionally in the
service of better poetry. But what about Twain's assertion? Does the Author really make no mistakes? One thinks immediately of that travesty
of judicial procedure, the trial scene in *The Merchant of Venice*. Only
after the dramatic court battle does Portia, the judge, reveal the following:

> It is enacted in the laws of Venice,
> If it be proved against an alien,
> That by direct or indirect attempts
> He seek the life of any citizen,
> The party 'gainst the which he doth contrive
> Shall seize one half his goods; the other half
> Comes to the privy coffer of the state,
> And the offender's life lies in the mercy
> Of the Duke only.
>
> (IV.ii.347–56)

If this law existed, as it does in the imaginary world of the play, it should,
by all logic, have been cited at the outset of the hearing. On its authority, Shylock should have been warned not to proceed further and judg-

ment found in favor of Antonio. It makes better theatre for Portia to bring up the statute after the exciting courtroom fireworks, when it's time to punish the villain, but it's ludicrous legal procedure—even in the Author's nonrealistic Venice.

The Author makes other mistakes too. For example, only in the play's created world can a creditor not take less than is due him; Shylock, Portia insists, cannot take *less* than a pound of flesh.[5] In addition, the play turns on the fact that the contract does not mention blood, yet the grant of something implies whatever is unavoidable in the obtaining of it.[6] If you are awarded your ex-husband's TV in a divorce settlement, it's implied that you may enter his house to take it.

Still, it was not the Author's jurisprudence, which might be altered for dramatic effect, that Twain and others found so persuasive; it was his use of legal terminology. Yet the Poet makes mistakes in that too. The Canadian lawyer R. F. Fuller found some in Sonnet 46:

> Mine eye and heart are at a mortal war,
> How to divide the conquest of thy sight:
> Mine eye my heart thy picture's sight would bar,
> My heart mine eye the freedom of that right.
> My heart doth plead that thou in him dost lie
> (A closet never pierc'd with crystal eyes),
> But the defendant doth that plea deny,
> And says in him thy fair appearance lies.
> To 'cide this title is impanelled
> A quest of thoughts, all tenants to the heart,
> And by their verdict is determined
> The clear eye's moiety and the dear heart's part—
> As thus: mine eye's due is thy outward part,
> And my heart's right thy inward love of heart.

Fuller comments that the Author calls the allegation of the heart the "plea," instead of the "declaration." Also, he represents the case as a property action, a dispute over "title" to the "sight" of the beloved, even though what's sought is exclusive viewing rights, not real estate; such an action should never involve tenants or moieties, it should be a civil case. Meanwhile, the jury consists of the "tenants of the heart," but these tenants cannot be jurors since their landlord is the plaintiff![7] In *Henry VI Part Three*, as Clarkson and Warren noticed, the term *entail* is misused. The king declares to York,

> I here entail
> The crown to thee and to thine heirs for ever,
> Conditionally that here thou take an oath
> To cease this civil war, and whilst I live
> To honor me as thy king and sovereign.
>
> (I.i.194–98)

Henry's queen spits these words back at him:

> To entail him and his heirs unto the crown,
> What is it, but to make thy sepulchre . . . ?
>
> (I.i.235–36)

But something can be entailed only when it is actually awarded, and York does not receive the crown *in possession*. The crown is not "entailed" to him as an estate would be; he has merely been named its inheritor.[8] In short, the Author's use of legal terms is not always perfect, as Mark Twain was led to believe.

In the history plays, legal phraseology is often derived from the Author's sources. For example, in Act Two of *Henry IV Part One*, Mortimer, Glendower, and Hotspur partition England as if legally partitioning a manor between joint tenants. This does not demonstrate a knowledge of law, though, because the Author lifts the passage from his source in Holinshed's *Chronicles*. In *Henry VIII*, Act Three Scene Two, when the Duke of Suffolk addresses Wolsey about *praemunire* (the offense of asserting papal jurisdiction in England), the Poet again takes the passage from Holinshed.

Over the past hundred and fifty years or so, lawyers and judges have used their special expertise to try to determine whether the Author had a legal education. Their conclusions have varied from "profound legal scholar" to "no real knowledge." Few, however, have compared the Poet's legal allusions to those of other playwrights of the time. Two who did were Clarkson and Warren, who spent eleven years researching references to English law in eighteen Elizabethan dramatists, including the Author. They conclude that "about half of [the Author's] fellows employed on the average more legalisms than he did—some of them a great many more. For example, the sixteen plays of Ben Jonson (whose apprentice years were spent in laying bricks, and certainly not in copying deeds and drafting pleadings) have a total of over five hundred references from all fields of the law. This surpasses [the Author's] total from more than twice as many plays. Not only do half of the playwrights employ legalisms more freely than [the Author] but most of them also exceed him in the detail and complexity of their legal problems and allusions, and with few exceptions display a degree of accuracy at least no lower than his."[9] Similarly, Irish judge Sir Dunbar Plunket Barton noticed that the Author's legal allusions were less technical and less numerous than Jonson's, Dekker's, Peele's, and Nashe's, none of whom (that we know) studied law.[10] In addition, he found the Author's figurative use of legal terms was hardly exceptional. Take the phrase "fee-simple"—the absolute and perpetual estate in land descending from ancestor to heirs unless sold or willed otherwise. The Poet makes metaphorical use of the term:

> An I were so apt to quarrel as thou art, any
> man should buy the fee-simple of my life for an
> hour and a quarter.
>
> (*Romeo and Juliet*, III.i.31–33)

But so do Lyly, Nashe, Marston, Heywood, Middleton, Beaumont, and Webster. "A good evidence to prove the fee-simple of your daughter's folly" says a character in Lyly's *Mother Bombie*; Beaumont's *Love's Cure* contains the line "the pillage of/the night is only mine, mine own fee-simple. . . ." Or look at the verb *enfeoff*, meaning to convey an estate. The Author's Henry IV grouses that his predecessor, Richard II, has "Enfeoff'd himself to popularity," and Robert Greene's Serlbie in *Friar Bacon and Friar Bungay* vows to "infeofe fair Margret in all." Jonson uses the noun forms *feoffment* (the estate enfeoffed) and *feoffee* (the receiver) four times each in *The Devil Is an Ass*, while Chapman includes *feoffments* in a list of legal terms in *All Fools*. Middleton uses "infeoffments" inaccurately in *A Fair Quarrel* to describe an estate left by will.[11] And Middleton was a lawyer! So much for Mark Twain.

Among sonneteers, nonlawyers Barnabe Barnes and Michael Drayton are fond of legal imagery. Barnes writes in *Parthenophil and Parthenophe* (1593),

> Ay me! She was and is his bail, I wot,
> But when the mortgage should have cured the sore
> She passed it off by deed of gift before.
>
> (Sonnet 8)

And when, through thy default, I thee did summon
Into the Court of Steadfast Love, then cried,
"As it was promised, here stands his Heart's bail
And if in bonds to thee my love be tied,
Then by those bonds take Forfeit of the Sale."

(Sonnet 11)

Those eyes (thy beauty's tenants!) pay due tears
For occupation of mine heart, thy freehold
For tenure of Love's service!

(Sonnet 11)

Drayton's cycle to a woman named *Idea* (1599) uses courtroom metaphors:

The verdict on the view
Do quit the dead and me not accessory;
Well, well! I fear it will be moved of you!
The evidence so great a proof doth carry.

(Sonnet 51)

The anonymous author of *Zepheria* (1594) sees love as a lawsuit:

How often hath my pen (mine heart's solicitor!)
Instructed thee in breviat of my case!
. . .
How have my sonnets (faithful counselors!)
Thee, without ceasing, moved for Day of Hearing!
. . .
How have I stood at bar of thine own conscience;
When in Requesting Court my suit I brought![12]

Where the Author's allusions surpass those of his contemporaries, Barton observed, is in their "quality and aptness," rather than in their quantity or technicality.[13] He was a better poet, if not a better jurist. After comparing the Author to his contemporaries, Clarkson and Warren state "categorically" that the internal evidence from the Works is "wholly insufficient" to prove he was a lawyer, worked in a law office, or had training in the law.[14] Fuller believed the Author must have apprenticed with a conveyancer in order to gain his knowledge of real property law, the

85

kind of law he seems to know best (he uses sixty terms from it).[15] But it was in reference to real property, specifically, that Clarkson and Warren compared the Author to other writers. Were they all conveyancers?

There are several reasons why legal expressions were part of the common idiom of the English Renaissance stage, even for writers without a background in law. First of all, it was a litigious time. For the Elizabethans, law took the place of professional sports as the most popular public amusement. Local courts met every two weeks, and even the uneducated crammed into the galleries, following the action of each case like a tennis match. "At a time when there were few places of recreation in town," writer O. Hood Phillips explains, "people found attending the courts and watching judicial procedure a dramatic and diverting pastime."[16] They were also quick to become litigants. "Lawyers," reports Nashe in *Pierce Pennilesse His Supplication to the Divell*, "cannot devise which way in the world to beg, they are so troubled with brabblements and suits every term, of yeomen and gentlemen that fall out for nothing."[17] The appetite for litigation created a backlog of drawn out cases, and the resulting "law's delay" moved theologians like Roger Hutchinson to pray, "would God the King's Majesty, by the assent of his Parliament, would make some statute that all suits should be determined and judged within the compass of a year, or half a year if their value were under a hundred pound."[18] People even told time—calendar time—by the terms when the law courts were in session: Hilary (23 January–21 February), Easter (20 April–15 May), Trinity (31 May–14 June), and Michaelmas (9 October–28 November).

Dramatists had a special reason to stuff their plays with legalese: They had a close relationship with the legal societies known as the Inns of Court. Plays were routinely performed at the Inns (the diarist John Manningham saw a 1602 production of *Twelfth Night* at one of them), and several playwrights, including Lodge, Beaumont, Marston, Middleton, and John Ford, were members. Throughout the period, the Inns of Court were used as gentlemen's clubs as well as colleges for the study of law, and they became the center of literary activity and associations in London. Jonson dedicated his *Every Man in His Humour* and *Every Man Out of His Humour* to the Inns, and, in 1633, Thomas Heywood wrote a legalistically phrased introduction to Marlowe's *Jew of Malta*, addressed to "My Worthy Friend Master Thomas Hammon, of Gray's Inn."[19] Neither Jonson nor Heywood were themselves members or lawyers, but both had friends who were.

Of the thirteen or fourteen Inns of Court, only three are mentioned in the Works: Middle Temple, Clement's Inn, and Gray's Inn. Not surprisingly, these are the three with traceable ties to William Shakespeare. Thomas Greene, who rented rooms from Shakespeare at New Place and in his diary refers to the actor as his "cosen," was a member of Middle Temple, the same Inn where Manningham saw *Twelfth Night*. In the 1590s, he sponsored the membership of John Marston, the future playwright. Greene's brother John, who is mentioned in Greene's diary as speaking to Shakespeare and who became a trustee of Shakespeare's Blackfriars property in 1618, was of Clement's Inn. Gray's Inn was where *The Comedy of Errors* was performed in 1594, and since that play belonged to Shakespeare's acting company, and he is listed as a payee for performances in 1594, we can assume he acted in it—even if he didn't write it.

Besides contact with members of the Inns of Court, Shakespeare had a personal means to learn about law: his own and his family's involvement in litigation. From 1568 to 1569, Will's father served as Bailiff of Stratford, among whose duties was to preside as a judge at the fortnightly court of record. Later he was elected High Alderman, and he continued as a justice of the peace.[20] Watching his father preside, young Will could not have helped but become familiar with the terminology of law and contracts. In Stratford, let me pause to emphasize, the head of government was also the chief judge. This may explain why heads of government, mysteriously, act in a judicial capacity throughout the plays.

Near the end of 1576, some kind of calamity befell John Shakespeare. Suddenly he stops attending town council meetings and the family suffers financial troubles. Whatever the cause, John and Mary began selling their assets in the late 1570s and mortgaged some land to Mary's brother-in-law Edmund Lambert. According to later court papers, John claimed that when the mortgage came due in 1580, he brought the money to Lambert's home in Burton-on-the-Heath, but Lambert refused it, saying John could have the land back only when all of his debts to Lambert were paid. John agreed. But in 1587, Lambert died and the land in question passed to his son John. John Lambert did not acknowledge his father's verbal agreement and claimed the land had been *sold* to his father, not mortgaged. This inspired the lawsuit at Queen's Bench in Westminster in 1589 to which William Shakespeare's name was attached. On 24 November 1597, the case was reopened in Chancery. Even though the new suit was nominally brought by John and Mary Shakespeare against John Lambert, William's presence in London makes it reasonable to assume that John and Mary's son William brought the new suit in his parent's name. It would finally be settled in 1599 out of court, with the land lost. As it happens, knowledge of conveyances, recoveries, and indentures evidenced in the Author's early plays is consistent with the *Shakespeare v.*

Lambert court case. Legal references in *Hamlet* also pertain to this case,[21] as do the terms in Sonnet 134:

> So now I have confess'd that he is thine,
> And I myself am mortgag'd to thy will,
> Myself I'll forfeit, so that other mine
> Thou wilt restore to be my comfort still:
> But thou wilt not, nor he will not be free,
> For thou art covetous, and he is kind;
> He learn'd but surety-like to write for me
> Under that bond that him as fast doth bind.
> The statute of thy beauty thou wilt take,
> Thou usurer, that put'st forth all to use,
> And sue a friend came debtor for my sake,
> So him I lose through my unkind abuse.
> Him have I lost, thou hast both him and me,
> He pays the whole, and yet am I not free.

Notice *mortgage, forfeit, restore, surety, underwrite, bond, statute, sue, debtor,* and even *usurer*—Edmund Lambert became a usurer when he refused the offer of the mortgage payment.[22]

In 1602, Shakespeare was involved with conveyancing when he sued to confirm his purchase of New Place. The previous owner, William Underhill, had been poisoned by his teenage son Fulke soon after he sold the house to Shakespeare in 1597. When Fulke was hanged for the crime two years later, Shakespeare's right to the house remained insecure. The new heir, Hercules Underhill, was a minor, but upon his coming-of-age, he might have challenged the sale as an unjust swindle of his rightful inheritance. So as soon as Hercules turned twenty-one, Shakespeare preemptively sued him and obtained a clear grant of the estate. This experience could have taught the actor some property and criminal law, if, unlike other men of his class, he didn't already know it.

There is no guarantee, of course, that he had much contact with his own lawsuits (attorneys might have handled them) or was interested in his father's court cases (those that John oversaw and those that he brought), but his connection to the law tallies with the Poet's use of it. Like William Shakespeare, the Author was no lawyer. His knowledge was similar to other nonspecialists', even if his dazzling poetic gifts far outshone theirs.

CHAPTER 6
The Courtier's Tongue

For most anti-Stratfordians, the Author's empathetic portraits of princes and earls, coupled with his buffoonish caricatures of servants and artisans, prove he was a nobleman. He identifies with royalty and nobility, they observe, and has contempt for the lower classes. He does not enter the souls of characters from the lowest castes with nearly the same sensibility he reserves for those from the highest, and this attitude, this pattern of empathy, is said to amount to evidence that the Author was an aristocrat. The problem is, nearly every playwright of the time shares the pattern. In most Elizabethan and Jacobean dramas, the gentry and aristocracy are fully developed individuals at the center of the action, while the lower-class characters are clowns with names like Spigot and Milkpail, as in Heywood's *A Woman Killed with Kindness*. It was a convention of their theatre. Marlowe did not write about shoemakers, Webster about tailors, or Chapman about farmers. The middle-class sons of bricklayers and saddlers depicted the strivings of kings and foreign dukes. Like Sophocles, who was also middle class, or Chekhov, who identified with wealthy landowners, they were aristocratic in sympathy.

They also shared a faith in the social order, a fear of revolution and upheaval, and a general disdain for social climbers. The Author has apparent contempt for ambitious stewards like Malvolio in *Twelfth Night*, but Ben Jonson is even more satirical in *The Poetaster*, where the undeserving would-be poets Pantalabus and Crispinus boast of their status as gentleman. And yet no poet climbed higher or more shamelessly than Jonson, a member of the bricklayer's guild who became King James's court poet. To argue, as some heretics do, that William Shakespeare would not ridicule social aspirants being one himself is, frankly, poor psychology. People often despise those who are most like themselves. On the other hand, there's no guarantee that Shakespeare thought of himself as aspiring. He may have believed to his core that membership in the gentry was rightfully his by birth, given his father's position and his grandfather's heritage as a scion of Arden. Once again we see the impossibility of reading biography from the plays.

The Author's diction is the basis for another argument. Joseph Sobran asserts that his "habitual language is the idiom of the courtier."[1] But we can say the same of Marlowe, Chapman, Daniel, Marston, Webster, Middleton, Beaumont, or Fletcher. It was Fletcher whose dialogue was especially admired by aristocratic theatre-goers who saw in it the epitome of the way they would like to speak.[2] One did not have to be a courtier to imitate courtly language. In the *Arte of English Poesie* (1589), Puttenham advises the "maker or Poet" to use the language "spoken in the king's Court, or in the good towns and cities within the land" by men "civil and graciously behavioured and bred," defining it further as "the usual speech of the Court, and that of London."[3] So for a poet to have the diction of a courtier was not unusual; it was the normal dialect of the city. If there were really any noticeable difference between the "habitual language" of the Author and that of other playwrights, it would be easy to tell if he wrote *Edward III* or *Arden of Faversham* or the *Elegy by W. S.* or any of the other works doubtfully attributed to "Shakespeare"; all we would have to do is look for the "idiom of the courtier." But the styles of Elizabethan authors are all very similar. We may also observe that the Author did not always have his courtier's tongue. Early plays like *The Comedy of Errors* or *The Taming of the Shrew* demonstrate little of the high tone or refined speech of later dramas; it's hard to believe a nobleman penned either of them.

Still, if there is no such thing as a nobleman's vocabulary, there is indeed a nobleman's imagery, casting the unfamiliar thought or feeling in the familiar terms of aristocratic experience. Does the Author think like that? It seems rather the reverse, that he generally depicts the lives of the nobility in the imagery of artisans. Troilus and Ulysses speak the language of woodcutters: "my heart, as wedg'd with a sigh, would rive in twain" (I.i.34–55), says Troilus; "Blunt wedges rive hard knots" (I.iii.316), muses Ulysses. Macbeth pictures his insomnia as a handicraft problem, when he longs for "sleep that knits up the ravell'd sleave of care" (II.ii.34). The minister Polonius thinks in terms of barrel-making in his advice to Laertes to "grapple [tried friends] unto thy soul with hoops of steel" (*Hamlet*, I.iii.63). C. L. Barber and Richard Wheeler find it "striking that in many of the Sonnets, even as [the Author] expresses his adulation of aristocratic heritage, he does so in prudential monetary and legal terms of middle-class provenance, terms used in upright dealing—or sharp practice."[4] Dennis Kay notices the same thing: "The speaker [of the Sonnets] inhabits a bourgeois world of debts, loans, mortagages, bonds, contracts, accounts, surpluses, audits, interest, credit, repayment and usury."[5]

The real question is, what does the Author know about aristocratic life? Social historian Muriel St. Clare Byrne looked into this question and came to this conclusion: not much. At least, not at first. In *Romeo and Juliet*, for example, Lord Capulet's behavior is "untrue to the facts of contemporary noble life. . . . [The Author] may label Capulet the head of a noble household, who can treat Paris, 'a young Nobleman, Kinsman to the Prince,' as his equal, and a proper match for his daughter; but when it comes to a scene like Act IV Scene iv, which shows the home life of this supposed nobleman, . . . it is quite certain that an Elizabethan nobleman, with his retinue of anything from twenty to eighty gentlemen officers, and from a hundred to five hundred yeoman servants, did not come into personal contact with Antony and Potpan, Peter and Angelica, and did not himself have to issue orders for the quenching of fires and the turning up of tables. In these scenes, Capulet is brother to Dekker's jolly shoemaker, Simon Eyre, not to Lord Burghley."[6] But Byrne goes on to say that the Author's "personal knowledge of the life and detail of a noble household grew with the years."[7] Old Capulet would not have been able to tell his grooms where to find drier logs for the hearth, but Leonato in *Much Ado About Nothing* (a later play) could "pass very credibly," in Byrne's opinion, as a noble gentleman who could "receive the Prince in his house."[8] By the time *Twelfth Night* was written, the Author had learned even more; Olivia's household, with its protocols for receiving guests, its officious steward at his mistress's elbow, and its literate gentlewoman housekeeper, represents an accurate picture of an Elizabethan manor.

He knows less about life at the palace. For Byrne, the "etiquette and ceremonial complications of regal life find but little reflection in the plays. What [the Author] either did not know, or else deliberately rejected for dramatic purposes, was the circumstance and order of life in a royal household."[9] She finds it "surprising . . . that he should so entirely neglect the dramatic opportunities offered by the intimate-formal routine of Court life, had he been familiar with it. *Henry VIII*, in which we must allow for the collaboration of Fletcher, is the only play which exploits it in any way. . . . Court life in the plays is definitely a homely affair in comparison with Court life at Whitehall."[10] To reach his mother's closet, for example, Hamlet "could not have progressed so far through antechambers and presence chambers without some announcement from the grooms of the Chamber, the gentlemen-ushers, and the gentlemen of the Privy Chamber, let alone the guard!"[11] Nor should messengers "burst into the royal presence without being announced by gentlemen-ushers. But they rush in gaily in *Cymbeline* (II.ii), in *Hamlet* (IV.vii), in *Antony and Cleopatra* (II.v), in *Richard III* (II.iv), and in *Henry V* (II.iv), when no particular dramatic purpose save economy is thereby served. In *Richard II*, Aumerle—a man already suspect—rushes wildly into the presence (V.iii), to be pursued to the door a moment later, first by his father and then by his mother, both of whom shout and clamour for admission until the king unlocks the door. The reasonable stage version of actuality can be seen in *Henry VIII* (III.i), where a gentleman enters to Queen Katherine to crave admission for Wolsey and Cardinal Campeius."[12] When it comes to murdering King Duncan, Macbeth and his wife would have found it "extraordinarily difficult" to "get rid of their own ladies and gentlemen-in-waiting and their own grooms, without first going through the ceremony of going to bed."[13] Had he been familiar with a nobleman's nightly preparations, the Author could have dismissed them in a few lines. But they are never alluded to. "It is all very well," Byrne continues, "for Lady Macbeth to tell her husband,

> Get on your night-gown, lest occasion all us,
> And show us to be watchers;

but actually the nightgown—which was a dressing gown or robe—would have been in the care of the Yeoman of the Wardrobe, and when required would have been handed to a gentleman-in-waiting who would have helped his lord to put it on. Macbeth would probably have had no idea where to find his nightgown for himself."[14]

Of course, Professor Byrne's caveats do not prove the Author knew nothing of court life. He may have altered what he knew for theatrical purposes. But the point is, based on the internal evidence of the plays, we cannot conclude he was an aristocrat.

～

Indisputably, the Author was familiar with sports practiced by the nobility. His specific idiosyncratic images from falconry, hunting, archery, tennis, fencing, and bowls suggest he had some experience with all of these pastimes. But none of them were strictly aristocratic activities. "In the sixteenth century," writes a Victorian scholar, "tennis courts were common in England, and the establishment of such places was countenanced by the example of royalty."[15] Archery was encouraged for every young man, regardless of class, because it was thought important for the defense of the country.[16] Fencing was even more popular, prompting Tudor writer Roger Ascham to declare in 1545 that there were masters to teach it "almost in every town."[17] Naturally, actors were especially steeped in the sport and even Richard Tarlton, the famous comedian, achieved the rank of master.[18]

Of hunting, military historian J. W. Fortescue observes, "His knowledge of deer was considerable, but his experience of the chase of the deer, with hounds only, seems not to have been great. . . . [O]f harbouring [tracking] and the true refinements of the art of venery, which might have supplied him with many images, he says nothing. On the other hand, he knew all about driving deer into enclosures from which they could not escape."[19] He's more familiar, in other words, with the ways of quiet, strategic poaching. Fortescue points out the multiple images from poaching, such as bribing the keepers of a deer park:

> 'Tis gold
> Which buys admittance (oft it doth), yea, and makes
> Diana's rangers false themselves, yield up
> Their deer to th' stand o'th' stealer
>
> (*Cymbeline*, II.iii.67–70)

and the problems of hunting after dark:

> When night-dogs run, all sorts of deer are chas'd
>
> (*Merry Wives*, V.v.238)

and "the delight of outwitting the custodian of the park after a successful foray"[20]:

> What, hast not thou full often struck a doe,
> And borne her cleanly by the keeper's nose?
>
> (*Titus Andronicus*, II.i.93–94)

The last is spoken incongruously by a Gothic prince who, presumably, would never have occasion to poach since he owned his own forests. Probably, therefore, this is a glimpse of the Author's experience rather than the character's. In any case, as contemporary sources like Gervase Markham's *Countrey Contentments* (1611) indicate, hunting with hounds was not a sport exclusive to the nobility in Elizabethan England any more than it is in present-day Kentucky.[21] The diarist John Manningham observed in 1602, "A nobleman on horseback with a rabble of footmen about him is but like a huntsman with a kennel of hounds after him,"[22] clearly showing that a hunter and a nobleman were not the same thing.

Oxfordian Charlton Ogburn argues that since public bowling alleys were proscribed by repeated acts of Parliament, bowling—a game similar to Italy's bocci or France's petanque—was a sport of the landed gentry. To historians, though, the fact that "repeated" acts of Parliament were needed is evidence these acts were ineffective. This is substantiated by contemporary documents like Gosson's *Schoole of Abuse* (1579):

> Common bowling alleys are privy moths, that eat up the credit of many idle citizens, whose gain at home are not able to weigh down their losses abroad, whose shops are so far from maintaining their play, that their wives and children cry out for bread and go to bed supperless oft in the year.[23]

[spelling modernized]

John Earle says much the same thing in 1628 in *Micro-cosmographie*. Though played by gentlemen like Sir Francis Drake, who wished to finish a game even when he heard the Spanish Armada was in the Channel, bowls was also played and gambled on by ordinary citizens. Among playwrights, Spurgeon remarks that Dekker, a nonuniversity man much less an aristocrat, also had "a definite knowledge of the game."[24]

As for the sport of falconry, or hawking, which reached its height of popularity in the late 1500s and early 1600s, according to Henry Thew Stephenson in *The Elizabethan People*, "It was practiced at the time by everyone who could afford the luxury, and it was considered to be, beyond all others, the proper sport for a country gentleman." The latter "found life hard if it had to be lived without a hawk."[25] This is confirmed by Master Stephen, the comic country squire in Ben Jonson's *Every Man in His Humour*: "I have bought me a hawk and a hood and bells and all, I lack nothing but a book to keep it by. . . . Why, you know an a man have not skill in the hawking and hunting language nowadays, I'll not give a rush for him" (I.i.34–39).[26] It was the kind of sport a man of property, like John Shakespeare before his decline, would have likely pursued. We know it was practiced in his vicinity because a Puritan survey of 1586 describes the vicar of Grafton, near Stratford, as "an old priest" whose "chiefest trade is to cure hawks that are hurt or diseased, for which purpose many do usually repair to him."[27] Since there were few noblemen in the area, his customers must have been non-noblemen.

Gerald Lascelles comments in *Shakespeare's England*, "So great a hold had falconry taken upon the minds of country folk in Elizabethan times that its technical terms were habitual to ordinary conversation."[28] Many writers of the era use its language, including Spenser, Heywood, and Drayton—none of whom were born into the gentry. But the Author's references are so numerous and specific that he seems to have had real experience of the sport. Interestingly, his images often come from the training and care of the birds, activities handled in wealthy households by the falconer and his assistants, the falconer's boys.[29] It's the backstage aspects of falconry and hunting that he seems to be most familiar with, a falconer's point of view rather than his master's.

If Edward de Vere, the Earl of Oxford, wrote the Works, one sport we would expect to be alluded to with the specificity of experience would be tilting. The earl was a celebrated tilter and the winner of two of the three tournaments in which he competed.[30] The courtier Sir Philip Sidney dedicates two sonnets to the sport in his *Astrophel and Stella* (1591). Speaking from the tilter's saddle, he describes his pride, "Having this day my horse, my hand, my lance/Guided so well, that I obtained the prize" and, on another day, how being distracted by the sight of his love: "Nor trumpets sound I heard, nor friendly cries" and his adversary bested him.[31] Yet the Author's references to the sport are few, and those are almost all conventional, such as "Break a lance and run a-tilt at Death" (*Henry VI Part One* III.ii.50–51) or "Man but a rush against Othello's breast" (*Othello* V.ii.270)—if this latter is indeed jousting and not spearing. The most specific one is an observation from a spectator's point of view:

> as a puisne [inexperienced] tilter, that spurs his horse but on one side, breaks his staff like a noble goose.
>
> (*As You Like It*, III.iv.43–44)

The same play contains the Author's only allusion to the quintain, a target in tilting, and one can almost imagine he had recently seen a tilt when he wrote the play. The Poet preferred falconry and bowls.

Even so, we can't prove he never tilted; we can't prove something from an absence of evidence—that's the Oxfordians' game. What we can deduce with certainty is that the Author found some sports more useful to his poetry than others, and these he almost certainly played at least once.

He was also familiar with rustic children's games like nine men's morris, filliping the toad, dun is in the mire, and base; it's doubtful an earl would have even known these existed. In a similar vein, the Author makes seventeen references to the butcher's trade.[32] His King Henry VI, for example, oddly has studied the scene outside an abattoir and recalls it when he shudders at the fate of Duke Humphrey of Gloucester:

> And as the butcher takes away the calf,
> And binds the wretch, and beats it when it strays,
> Bearing it to the bloody slaughter-house,
> Even so remorseless have they borne him hence;
> And as the dam runs lowing up and down,
> Looking the way her harmless young one went,
> And can do nought but wail her darling's loss,
> Even so myself bewails good Gloucester's case.
>
> (*Henry VI Part Two*, III.i.210–17)

Surrounded by servants at all times, it would have been difficult for a nobleman to acquire that kind of knowledge; it would have been much easier for a commoner.

∽

In *Love's Labor's Lost*, the Author seems to have an insider's knowledge of a foreign court—specifically, a meeting at Nerac in 1578 between Henri of Navarre and his then-estranged wife, Marguerite de Valois. He knows their dispute involved lands in the province of Aquitaine; he knows Marguerite traveled with her coquettish maids of honour; he's aware that the political diplomacy, as well as the parties and entertainments, mostly occurred in the park, outside the king's residence; and he even knows one of the queen's favorite stories: how a relative of one of her maids of honour was rejected by a lover and died of a broken heart.[33] How could he know all these things unless he traveled in court circles?

One possible answer derives from a source now lost, a source like the one advertised at the end of volume two of Painter's *Palace of Pleasure*, "the best liked out of the Queene of Navarre." The large number of women's roles and the lightness of the play's tone have led many scholars to believe it was originally written for a boys' company of actors and adapted by the Author for adult players. Perhaps he did not write the original. Another possibility is that he got the story from a French expatriate, of which there were plenty living in London. For a Frenchman, the meeting at Nerac was an extremely significant event which, for a time, ended the civil wars. All of the details known to the Author would have been familiar to many French men and women who were adults in 1578.

The names of characters in the play, such as Biron, Longueville, Dumain, and Boyet did not come from 1578, but rather from the early 1590s when England aided Henri against the Spanish. The Earl of Essex, the commander of the English forces, banqueted with Navarre, Longueville, and Biron in September 1591 (for which he was rebuked by Queen Elizabeth for temporarily abandoning his troops).[34] The Duc de Longueville was a principal supporter of Henri, and Marshal Armand de Biron was the supreme military commander of France. An enemy of Henri in 1578, the latter was not at Nerac. As for the others, Antoine Boyet was the French finance minister, and Charles Duc de Mayenne was an opponent of Henri, but he made peace with the king in 1595.[35] To learn these names the Author might not have even needed a French expatriate. He might have picked them up from news pamphlets or heard them at St. Paul's Cathedral, the general meeting place of Londoners and the site of the book market. John Chamberlain, the commoner letter-writer who provides much of what we know about Elizabeth's court, told his correspondent in Paris not to bother recounting political news because "Paul's is so furnished that it affords whatsoever is stirring in France."[36]

It did not afford everything, though. In *Henry V*, the king asks the herald, "What is thy name? I know thy quality." And the herald replies, "Montjoy." What the Author doesn't seem to know is that *montjoy* was a herald's official designation, not a personal name. It's the kind of mistake the Stratford actor might be especially prone to since he is blindly following Holinshed and copying his source's mistake. For an earl or courtier, however, an error like that would be easy to spot.

In *Love's Labor's Lost*, one character calls another a "Monarcho." That was the name of a figure at Elizabeth's court in the 1570s. But the Author did not have to be a courtier to know of him. Monarcho seems to have been an icon of Elizabethan pop culture. Francis Meres writes in 1598, "Popular applause doth nourish some, neither do they gape after any other thing, but vain praise and glory—as in our age . . . *Monarcho* that lived about the Court."[37]

～

William Cecil, Lord Burghley, had several points in common with the character of Polonius, the scheming adviser to Claudius in *Hamlet*. As Lord Treasurer, Burghley held an analogous position in Elizabeth's court, becoming her chief minister and the Machiavellian power broker behind the throne. In his private life, he wrote a list of precepts for his son Robert, published in 1619, that is similar to Polonius's famous advice ("Neither a borrower nor a lender be"), and he set spies on his son Thomas when the latter visited Paris, just as Polonius does to Laertes. In letters, Burghley sometimes expressed himself in long elaborate circuitous sentences like those that inspire Queen Gertrude to chide, "More matter, less art" (*Hamlet*, II.ii.95). He even promoted the interests of fishermen in Parliament, arguing for Wednesday to be a compulsory fish day, while Polonius is fond of angling metaphors.[38]

Assuming Polonius was based on Burghley, would the Author have had to have been a court insider to learn these things? Almost certainly not. As the most powerful figure in England after Elizabeth, Burghley was the center of a great deal of public interest. Commoner John Chamberlain, for example, knows all the details of Burghley's estate at his death: "Of his private wealth there is but £11,000 come to light, and that all in silver. . . . And his lands seem not so great as was thought, for Master Secretary [Burghley's son, Robert Cecil] says his own part will not rise to £1600 a year upon the rack."[39] Burghley was lampooned by Spenser in *The Faerie Queene* as the "rugged forehead" and by Nashe in *Pierce Pennilesse*. And even after he was dead, he was the subject of less-than-flattering anecdotes in John Manningham's diary. Sir Robert Cecil figures prominently in both Chamberlain's letters and Manningham's memoranda, and one can imagine he was especially voluble on the subject of his father and the source of much public information. While there is no specific proof that Burghley's writing of precepts or sending of spies was common gossip, these are the kinds of things Chamberlain and Manningham knew.

We should not forget that the common people had a vested interest in the careers of courtiers. Their lives and livelihoods were affected daily by the shifting winds of royal favor. They owed their allegiance to one or another noble lord and so, as Coriolanus scornfully observes of the Roman citizenry, they gossiped about their betters:

> They'll sit by th' fire, and presume to know
> What's done i' th' Capitol; who's like to rise,
> Who thrives, and who declines; side factions, and give out
> Conjectural marriages, making parties strong,

And feebling such as stand not in their liking
Below their cobbled shoes.

(I.i.191–96)

Possibly, the Author learned things about Burghley from someone who was indeed a courtier. It's not as though the nobility never spoke to poets. Chapman dedicates his *Charles Duke of Byron* to the brother of Elizabeth's spymaster: "My honourable and constant friend Sir Thomas Walsingham, Knight, and to my much loved from his birth, the right toward and worthy gentleman his son, Thomas Walsingham, Esquire." In a metropolitan population of 200,000 on less than four square miles of land, contact between classes was unavoidable. Unlike today, social separation was not expressed by physical and spatial separation. "The parish was more like a microcosm of the city as a whole than a social quarter," writes literary historian Emrys Jones.[40] One had contact with the lowest-born but also the highest. And, if the Author were an actor, his access would be even greater. Players at this time were simultaneously disreputable, base, scorned, and on intimate terms with the aristocracy—just like prostitutes. In 1619, William, Earl of Pembroke, wrote to Lord Doncaster in Germany to say how being "tender-hearted he could not endure" to see a play at Court "so soon after the loss of my old acquaintance Burbage."[41] Burbage had been dead for two months. Three years earlier, Thomasina Ostler, the widow of actor William Ostler and John Heminges' daughter, won a verdict of £250 against Walter Ralegh Jr., the son of Sir Walter, for insult and slander.[42] The actor George Bryan, listed in the First Folio as having performed in the plays, is recorded as being a Groom of the Royal Chamber by the time of Elizabeth's funeral in 1603. Shakespeare and his fellows would assume that title the following year. The high-born John Davies of Hereford wrote of players in *The Scourge of Folly*,

for some Crowns

Spent on a supper, any man may be
Acquainted with them, from their Kings to Clowns.

(Epigram 180)

In short, the Author would have had ample opportunity to hear gossip about Burghley, especially if he were an actor.

There is also the possibility of coincidence. Ministers are often garrulous and fathers often bombard their sons with axiomatic advice. The use of spies may simply have struck the Poet as something any overprotective parent would do if he could afford it and knew how to hire them. The Author may have had no idea that Burghley actually did this.

~

What Joseph Sobran calls the Author's "feudal preoccupation with kinship and lineage" is really the Author's preoccupation with Holinshed. It's from Holinshed the Poet copies his brain-numbing litanies of titles and geneology so prevalent in the history plays. For example, Richard Duke of York's detailed incantation of his family tree in *Henry VI Part Two*, to choose a representative passage, was purloined from the Chronicles:

> [Edmund Mortimer's] eldest sister, Anne,
> My mother, being heir unto the crown,
> Married Richard Earl of Cambridge, who was
> To Edmund Langley, Edward the Third's fifth son.
> By her I claim the kingdom. She was heir
> To Roger Earl of March, who was the son
> Of Edmund Mortimer, who married Philippe,
> Sole daughter unto Lionel Duke of Clarence;
> So, if the issue of the elder son
> Succeed before the younger, I am King.
>
> (II.ii.43–52)

Holinshed has,

> And the said Anne coupled in matrimony to Richard earl of Cambridge, the son of Edmund of Langley, the fifth son of Edward the third, and had issue Richard Plantagenet commonly called duke of York. . . . To the which Richard duke of York, as son to Anne, daughter to Roger Mortimer earl of March, son and heir of the said Philip, daughter and heir of the said Lionell, the third son of king Edward the third the right, title, dignity royal, and estate of the crowns of the realms of England and France . . . belongeth afore any issue of the said John of Gaunt, the fourth son of the same king Edward.[43]

[spelling modernized]

What the heretics claim as evidence of a courtier's mind is really just evidence of theft. If the Author was indeed an earl or a duke, he was content to rely on Holinshed, a commoner, rather than display his own obsession with heritage or knowledge of medieval history.

Finally, we should ask if a nobleman wrote the following exchange in which Valeria describes Coriolanus' son:

> I saw him run after a gilded butterfly, and when he caught it,
>   he let it go again, and after it again, and over and over he
>   comes, and up again; catch'd it again: or whether his fall en-
>   rag'd him, or how 'twas, he did so set his teeth and tear it. O,
>   I warrant how he mammock'd it! [tore it to pieces]
> VOLUMINIA. One [of his] father's moods.
> VALERIA. Indeed la, 'tis a noble child.
>
> (*Coriolanus*, I.iii.60–67)

Would a courtier imply that the essence of nobility was moody cruelty? Or is it more likely that the Author was a witness to the impulsive whims and contemptuous violence of his social superiors? The Poet cast a distrustful eye on mobs and democracy, but he had no romantic illusions about those above him either.

CHAPTER 7
The Sonneteer

In the late 1590s the unscrupulous publisher William Jaggard decided to capitalize on the name "Shakespeare." Somehow he had come across two of the Author's early sonnets—poems that would later be printed, in slightly different versions, as numbers 138 and 144 in *Shakespeares Sonnets* (1609).[1] Jaggard bundled these sonnets with three speeches from *Love's Labor's Lost* (already in print) and added poems by Christopher Marlowe, Bartholomew Griffin, Richard Barnfield, and other poets still unidentified. The resulting collection he labeled *The Passionate Pilgrim by W. Shakespeare*. No one knows its date of publication; the only surviving copy of what may be the first edition is missing its cover. But copies of the second edition are still extant and these bear the date of 1599. Here's the rub. This is the version of Sonnet 138 that Jaggard published:

> When my love swears that she is made of truth,
> I do believe her (though I know she lies)
> That she might think me some untutor'd youth
> Unskillful in the world's false forgeries.
> Thus vainly thinking that she thinks me young,
> Although I know my years be past the best,
> I smiling credit her false-speaking tongue,
> Outfacing faults in love with love's ill rest.
> But wherefore says my love that she is young?
> And wherefore say not I that I am old?
> O, love's best habit's in a soothing tongue,
> And age in love loves not to have years told.

> Therefore I'll lie with love, and love with me,
> Since that our faults in love thus smother'd be.

At the time it appeared, William Shakespeare was thirty-five years old.

In a way we've reached the epicenter of the Authorship Question. This is the one piece of evidence that actually contradicts Shakespeare's candidacy. (When I'm asked what is the best anti-Stratfordian argument, I think of Sonnet 138.) Were this the only sonnet in which the Author refers to his advanced age, we could easily dismiss it as an aberrational experiment in fiction, a youthful exercise in projecting one's point of view into the mind of an old man; however, there are other sonnets (published in 1609) in which the Poet describes himself as aged in appearance:

> But when my glass shows me myself indeed,
> Beated and chopp'd with tann'd antiquity
>
> (Sonnet 62)

> Against my love shall be as I am now
> With Time's injurious hand crush'd and o'erworn;
>
> (Sonnet 63)

> In me thou seest the glowing of such fire
> That on the ashes of his youth doth lie
>
> (Sonnet 73)

"Why dost thou pine within and suffer dearth," the speaker of Sonnet 146 asks of his soul and refers to his body as a "fading mansion." Meanwhile, the morbid and melancholy Sonnets 71, 72, and 74 intimate the Poet may soon be dead. In a time when plagues were common and any illness might be fatal, one did not have to be sixty—or even twenty—to fear the end was near or to imagine one's death, but as these sonnets are part of a group with 73, a sonnet that begins "That time of year thou mayst in me behold/When yellow leaves or none or few do hang," we can legitimately presume their speaker's mortal thoughts are inspired by his actual aging.[2] Thus, since Shakespeare was only thirty-five (or younger, given the dates these poems are thought to have been composed), either he didn't write the Sonnets or he thought of himself as old while still a young man. Byron certainly felt that way when he wrote, "My days are in the yellow leaf; . . . /The worm, the canker and the grief/Are mine alone!" in *On This Day I Complete My Thirty-Sixth Year* (1824).[3] A third possibility—and this is more likely than it sounds—is that he adopted the fictional persona of a haggard elderly man for the above poems.

Such a contrivance is not at all uncommon. T. S. Eliot imagines himself as aged in several of his youthful poems, like "The Love Song of J. Alfred Prufrock" ("I grow old . . . I grow old . . . /I shall wear the bottoms of my trousers rolled") and "Gerontion" ("Here I am, an old man in a dry month"). In the Author's own time, Richard Barnfield makes use of the convention in *The Affectionate Shepheard* (1594), a poem that may have greatly influenced the Sonnets:

> Behold my gray head, full of silver hairs,
> My wrinkled skin, deep furrows in my face.[4]

Barnfield was twenty.

Masks are hard to maintain, however. Sonnet 17's "Be scorn'd, like old men of less truth than tongue" seems to imply the speaker is not yet himself an old man. In other sonnets, he doesn't seem much older than the Fair Youth, the young man of high social rank who is the subject, and usually the addressee, of the poems numbered 1 through 126. For example, the speaker is unsure who will die first. "If thou survive my well-contented day," he writes in Sonnet 32, "When that churl Death my bones with dust shall cover. . . ." And Sonnet 81 begins, "Or I shall live your epitaph to make,/Or you survive when I in earth am rotten. . . ." If—and this is not a small if—these two sonnets were addressed to a healthy nonsuicidal man in his early twenties, it's reasonable to suppose their author was in his thirties; were he any older, he would probably assume that he would be the first to die. The key dramatic event of the sequence, the "theft" of the speaker's mistress by the young man, also implies the two men are close in age. In nine sonnets devoted to the situation, he suspects the infidelity (144), forgives his friend (34, 35, 40), blames the woman (41), rationalizes that since the friend and he are one, "she loves but me alone" (42), begs her to leave the friend and take him back (133, 134), and reminds the young man—years later—of his suffering "in [the friend's] crime" (120), but he mentions their age discrepancy only once, when he chides his friend's "years" and "straying youth" for causing the friend to wrong him in Sonnet 41. He never sees age as a factor in the woman's choice, never laments that she might desire a younger lover, as a man in his forties naturally would if his rival were in his twenties. In Sonnet 22, the speaker expects to be around when the youth ages:

My glass shall not persuade me I am old,
So long as youth and thou are of one date,
But when in thee time's furrows I behold,
Then look I death my days should expiate.

At the other extreme, when the Author refers to his "pupil pen" (Sonnet 16), he seems to be a poet at the beginning of his career, with a long life ahead of him. Ultimately, the speaker's age is mysterious.

One would think that the Sonnets would readily yield up a consistent or at least *stable* portrait. After all, unlike the plays, they're written in the first person; they seem to convey the Author's private emotions and ideas rather than those of a character. But the Sonnets aren't diary entries.[5] Though their profound intimacy suggests a rooting in actual experiences, they are also, as Helen Vendler has shown, highly structured works of art,[6] and we have no way of knowing where experience leaves off and imagination begins. We can deduce some characteristics of the fictional speaker, but we don't know which qualities, if any, also belong to the Author. All we can describe is the persona.

So let's describe the persona.

First of all, his name is Will (as he tells us outright in Sonnet 136). He "toils" by day (27, 28) in a trade that has ruined his reputation ("Thence comes it that my name receives a brand") and, because fortune "did not better for [his] life provide than public means which public manners breeds," he sees this occupation as the root cause of his unspecified "harmful deeds" (111). He is "poor," "despis'd" (37), an "outcast," and sometimes he's "in disgrace with fortune and men's eyes" (29), feeling "bewailed guilt" (36) and the sting of "fortune's dearest spite" (37). Barred from "public honour and proud titles" (25), the "earth can yield him but a common grave" (81). He has no friends, and those he did have are dead and buried, and he prays for their souls (29, 30, 31). Though he contrasts himself with "the rich" (52), he does own a horse (50, 51) and jewels (48), and he can afford to buy the Fair Youth a commonplace book, a small book of blank pages for private thoughts (77). Sonnets 78 through 86, which express anxiety concerning a Rival Poet, make clear the young man is the speaker's patron. "I have frequent been with unknown minds,/And given to time your own dear-purchas'd right," he admits in Sonnet 117—*dear-purchas'd* being the key phrase. From Sonnet 152, we can deduce he's probably married because he tells his mistress, "In loving thee thou know'st I am forsworn." Having sworn marriage vows, he has now broken his pledge.

Except for the speaker's age, this account sounds suspiciously like William Shakespeare. The latter's profession of acting and playwriting sorts well with the disreputable "public means" and we know he had a patron in the young, handsome Henry Writhosley, Earl of Southampton, to whom he dedicated *Venus and Adonis* and *The Rape of Lucrece*. A man with Shakespeare's obvious desire for social status who was a mere actor, a "base fellow" as players were generally regarded, would also likely feel disgraced. In his own hometown, plays were so little respected that the Stratford borough council passed an ordinance in December 1602 forbidding their performance.[7] An apocryphal anecdote, a joke really, in John Manningham's diary from March 1602[8] indicates Shakespeare had a personal reputation he might have been ashamed of, as well:

> Upon a time when Burbage played Rich[ard] 3, there was a Citizen grew so far in liking with him, that before she went from the play she appointed him to come that night unto her by the name of Ri[chard] the 3rd. Shakespeare, overhearing their conclusion, went before, was entertained, and at his game ere Burbage came. Then message being brought that Richard the 3[r]d was at the door, Shakespeare caused return to be made that William the Conqueror was before Rich[ard] the 3rd. Shakespeare's name William. ([From] Mr. Touse.)[9]

[spelling modernized]

(Though it's tempting to believe the original punchline was "William the Conquerer *came* before Richard III," the verb *to come* had not yet acquired its sexual connotation.) From this note we can see the kind of bawdy world Shakespeare was assumed to be part of (and, for all we know, *was* part of). Shakespeare's personal shame probably extended to his lack of education, the same shortcoming confessed in Sonnet 78 when the speaker contrasts himself with other "learned" poets before he concludes,

> But thou art all my art, and dost advance
> As high as learning my rude ignorance.

Yet anti-Stratfordians insist the speaker is a nobleman. They point to such lines as "Shall Time's best jewel from Time's chest lie hid?" (65) or

"As on the finger of a throned queen/The basest jewel will be well esteem'd" (96) as evidence of a courtier's experience, forgetting that Shakespeare performed several times a year before the throned queen and that
his will attests he owned jewels. When it comes to Sonnet 91, they read
the poem as if the speaker possesses everything he names:

> Some glory in their birth, some in their skill,
> Some in their wealth, some in their body's force,
> Some in their garments, though new-fangled ill,
> Some in their hawks and hounds, some in their horse;
> And every humor hath its adjunct pleasure,
> Wherein it finds a joy above the rest,
> But these particulars are not my measure,
> All these I better in one general best.
> Thy love is better than high birth to me,
> Richer than wealth, prouder than garments' cost,
> Of more delight than hawks or horses be;
> And having thee, of all men's pride I boast:
> Wretched in this alone, that thou mayst take
> All this away, and me most wretched make.

Clearly the Sonneteer does not have ill new-fangled garments so we
should question whether he has high birth or wealth either. He may have
hawks and horses since the comparison is to the amount of delight rather
than the actual possessing of them, but the last three lines call even this
into question. He would be "most wretched" because all he has is his
friend's love, an idea reiterated in other sonnets. At best what we can say
is, he may or may not himself have the things that other men take pride
in.

Only Sonnet 125 can be said to use a courtier's imagery:

> Were't aught to me I bore the canopy,
> With my extern the outward honoring,
> Or laid great bases for eternity,
> Which proves more short than waste or ruining?
> Have I not seen dwellers on form and favor
> Lose all, and more, by paying too much rent,
> For compound sweet forgoing simple savor,
> Pitiful thrivers, in their gazing spent?
> No, let me be obsequious in thy heart,

And take thou my oblation, poor but free,
Which is not mix'd with seconds, knows no art,
But mutual render, only me for thee.
   Hence, thou suborn'd informer, a true soul
When most impeach'd stands least in thy control.

That he has seen "dwellers on form and favor" suggests he has witnessed a courtier's milieu, but the whole thrust of the sonnet's argument is that he is not one of the "dwellers," and he casts their fawning in very uncourtier-like, middle-class terms of rent and compound interest. The Earl of Oxford's partisans have assumed the canopy in the first line was the golden one Oxford allegedly carried over Queen Elizabeth's head as she walked up the nave of St. Paul's on 24 November 1588, but there's no evidence he ever carried a canopy. And aside from the fact that Master Shakespeare could have borne canopies in stage productions or as a royal groom, it's unclear whether the speaker has literally borne a canopy at all since he has certainly not literally "laid great bases." To most readers, the first lines mean "Would it be any credit to me if I bore *your* canopy, honoring you only in outward appearance?" In other words, he is explaining why he has *not* borne canopies. From the context it seems the speaker is defending himself against accusations by the "suborned informer" that he doesn't really love his patron/friend. The speaker's defense is, why should I make a show of my devotion? Why should I bear canopies, or lay great bases, or flatter to artificially demonstrate my affection? My only offering is my pure guileless love.

   For a lyric that points away from a noble Poet with less subtlety, we need only look to Sonnet 143. Did an earl write this?

Lo as a careful housewife runs to catch
One of her feathered creatures broke away,
Sets down her babe and makes all swift dispatch
In pursuit of the thing she would have stay;
Whilst her neglected child holds here in chase,
Cries to catch her whose busy care is bent
To follow that which flies before her face,
Not prizing her poor infant's discontent . . .

                                        (Sonnet 143)

It's the most specific image in the Sonnets and it's a domestic scene from a commoner's experience, not a courtier's. Or consider Sonnet 25:

> Let those who are in favor with their stars
> Of public honor and proud titles boast,
> Whilst I whom fortune of such triumph bars
> Unlook'd for joy in that I honor most.

An earl would always have his proud title of earl, and noblemen usually had more than one.[10] Oxford was also the Lord Great Chamberlain of England, and another candidate, William Stanley, the Earl of Derby, was "King of the Isle of Man." Fortune did not bar either of these men from "proud titles." Elsewhere, the Sonneteer tells us "The earth can yield me but a common grave" (81), and, rather than be praised untruthfully, he vows "My name be buried where my body is" (72). The latter is an impossibility for an earl, though a likelihood for a poet whose only chance at immortality is his verse. Indeed this is the sense of the rest of the sonnet:

> My name be buried where my body is,
> And live no more to shame nor me nor you;
>> For I am shamed by that which I bring forth
>> And so should you, to love things nothing worth.

As for the "common grave," the Earl of Oxford was, in fact, buried without a monument, but he could hardly have anticipated this indignity during his lifetime. Finally, we know the speaker's patron occupied a more elevated rung on the social ladder than the Poet. In Sonnet 36 the Author laments,

> I may not evermore acknowledge thee
> . . .
> Nor thou with public kindness honor me.

Only those of higher social rank could "honor"; it is the Fair Youth who might be a nobleman. Their discrepancy in social status is perhaps most overtly expressed in Sonnet 37:

> As a decrepit father takes delight
> To see his active child do deeds of youth,
> So I, made lame by Fortune's dearest spite,
> Take all my comfort of thy worth and truth.
> For whether beauty, birth, or wealth, or wit,

Or any of these all, or all, or more,
Intitled in thy parts do crowned sit,
I make my love ingrafted to this store:
So then I am not lame, poor, nor despis'd,
Whilst that this shadow doth such substance give,
That I in thy abundance am suffic'd,
And by a part of all thy glory live.

By attaching himself to his beloved's beauty, birth, wealth, and wit, the speaker confesses, he relieves his own poverty, ostracism, and ill-fortune.

Let me pause to point out that the Poet's lameness here is metaphorical. He is not physically lame, like the decrepit father, but mysteriously hobbled by Fortune's dearest (worst) spite. Michael Wood, assuming Shakespeare's authorship, has recently suggested that the actor may be alluding to the death of his son.[11] The two other references to lameness in the Sonnets are equally figurative. In Sonnet 89, the Poet makes the following hypothetical:

Say thou didst forsake me for some fault,
And I will comment upon that offense;
Speak of my lameness, and I straight will halt,
Against thy reasons making no defense.

If the Author were actually lame, then the third line would be meaningless. He does not normally halt, but he would do so to prove the young friend's assertion, and he would not defend himself by arguing that he is *not* lame. In Sonnet 66, "strength by limping sway disabled" is something the Poet is "tired" of "beholding"; it is not something he himself claims to have experienced. The speaker is no more lame than he is a nobleman.

For a true courtier's viewpoint we can consult Sidney's Astrophel, the speaker of *Astrophel and Stella*. His is a world of tournaments, court intrigue, and international politics, a world in which conversations are of matters of state:

Whether the Turkish new-moon minded be
To fill his horns this year on Christian coast
How Poles' right king means, without leave of host,
To warm with ill-made fire cold Moscovy;
If French can yet three parts in one agree;
What now the Dutch in their full diets boast

. . .
How Ulster likes of that same golden bit,
Wherewith my father once made it half tame
If in the Scottish Court be welt'ring yet;
These questions busy wits to me do frame.
                    (*Astrophel and Stella*, Sonnet 30)[12]

Reflecting the Elizabethan fashion that a courtier should disdain poetry, he denies he's looking for immortality from his verse:

In truth I swear, I wish not there should be
Graved in my epitaph a Poet's name.
                    (*Astrophel and Stella*, Sonnet 90)[13]

Military glory was the only kind of fame an aristocratic knight was supposed to crave.

Some heretics are willing to concede the speaker's traits don't match a nobleman's. So they turn their attention to the man behind the poems, the Sonneteer himself. How, they ask, could the Poet address the socially superior Fair Youth as intimately as he does if he were not himself a nobleman? In the poems, the speaker assumes the roles of close friend, admiring poet, devoted servant, surrogate father, jealous lover. Sometimes he addresses the youth with the emotionally distant "thou," sometimes with the more personal "you."[14] In early numbered sonnets, he urges the young man to marry and reproduce ("You had a father, let your son say so"); later, he criticizes his friend's fondness for praise and sexual "vices." It would have been highly improper and impudent for a commoner to address his superior with such familiarity. Therefore, the deniers argue, despite the poetic disguise of the "poor, despised" speaker, the Poet must have been, in reality, his young friend's social equal. But, of course, there are holes in this logic. First of all, friendships between the classes were not unheard of. Francis Bacon became a close associate of the Earl of Essex, and openly referred to the lord as his "friend," when Bacon was no more than a gentleman.[15] Second, as I implied before, the relationship with the idealized youth might be wholly imaginary, even if the fictionalized character was inspired by a real person. Or the relationship may be an artistic composite of several acquaintances which the Poet has creatively combined to make one imaginary whole.[16] But let's say there was indeed only one young patron/friend. Did the Sonneteer show him all the poems? Sonnet 71 implies he did not:

Nay, if you read this line, remember not
The hand that writ it . . .

If you read this line. The Poet could have kept to himself those sonnets that might have given offense, especially if the intimacy with his sponsor was imagined. On the other hand, maybe the intimacy was real and their relationship was unusual. It's not hard to believe two men could develop the complicated personal bond depicted in the Sonnets, in spite of their social differences.

The nature of that bond is yet another bone of contention in the Authorship Debate. Many heretics insist the relationship is homosexual. And certainly the speaker is physically attracted to the young man, as he tells us in Sonnet 20:

A woman's face with Nature's own hand painted
Hast thou, the master mistress of my passion;
A woman's gentle heart but not acquainted
With shifting change as is false women's fashion;
An eye more bright than theirs, less false in rolling,
Gilding the object whereupon it gazeth;
A man in hue all hues in his controlling,
Which steals men's eyes and women's souls amazeth.
And for a woman wert thou first created,
Till Nature as she wrough thee fell a-doting,
And my addition me of thee defeated,
By adding one thing to my purpose nothing.
   But since she prick'd thee out for women's pleasure,
   Mine be thy love, and thy love's use their treasure.

His attraction is to the youth's *feminine* beauty. He finds him "lovely" to the extent he looks like a woman. And that visual appeal is what the Poet writes about most. As Helen Vendler describes it, "The infatuation of the speaker with the young man is so entirely an infatuation of the eye—which makes a fetish of the beloved's countenance rather than of his entire body—that gazing is the infatuation's chief and perhaps best and only form of intercourse."[17] The Sonnets give us hints however that, over time, the relationship became physical.[18] On occasion, the Poet seems to employ the common Elizabethan euphemism of *nothing* for female sex organs. The Author's most familiar use of this slang is this exchange in *Hamlet*:

OPHELIA. I think nothing, my lord.
HAMLET. That's a fair thought to lie between maids' legs.
OPHELIA. What is, my lord?
HAMLET. Nothing.

(III.ii.117–21)

He employs it again in Sonnet 20 (above) and in Sonnet 136 ("For nothing hold me . . ."). And perhaps again here:

> Never believe, though in my nature reign'd
> All frailties that besiege all kinds of blood,
> That it could so preposterously be stain'd,
> To leave for nothing all thy sum of good,
> For nothing this wide universe I call,
> Save thou, my rose, in it thou art my all.

(Sonnet 109)

"I would not leave you for a woman," he is saying, if the pun is intended. (The second "*nothing*," though, is ostensibly *not* a pun.) We should also bear in mind that the sonnets to the young man are similar in tone and imagery to other writers' sonnets to women.[19] The speaker's love is apparently identical in kind. It is an affection beyond that of mere friendship or of a poet for a patron, even though at this time the language of patronage was highly eroticized.[20] It is also beyond that of nonsexual Platonic love; if the relationship were really only a "marriage of true minds," the speaker would not be obsessed with his beloved's beauty.

Still, the Sonnets are less homoerotic than other Elizabethan lyrics. The speaker never expresses a wish to kiss his beloved "boy" as Richard Barnfield's Affectionate Shepherd does his:

> O would to God (so I might have my fee)
> My lips were honey, and thy mouth a bee,
> Thou shouldst then suck my sweet and my fair flower
> That now is ripe, and full of honey berries:
> Then would I lead thee to my pleasant bower
> Filled full of grapes, of mulberries and cherries.

(Stanza XVI)

As with Shakespeare, there is nothing in what we know of Barnfield's life to suggest he was anything but a heterosexual married man. His poetry goes beyond what is known of his biography, but—like with Shake-speare—that does not prove he didn't write it. Marlowe is another cre-ator of homoerotica which is much more overt than the Author's. In *Hero and Leander*, the god Neptune plays wantonly with the swimming Lean-der:

> He watched his arms, and as they opened wide,
> At every stroke, betwixt them would he slide,
> And steal a kiss, and then run out a dance,
> And as he turn'd, cast many a lustful glance
> And throw him gaudy toys to please his eye,
> And dive into the water and there pry
> Upon his breast, his thighs, and every limb,
> And up again, and close behind him swim,
> And talk of love.
>
> (II.183–91)

The Author's speaker reserves his lust for the dark-haired adulterous woman who is his mistress. His love for her is a "fever" (147), a "mad-ness" (140), "lust in action" (129), "flesh . . . rising at [her] name" (151). He longs to "kiss the tender inward of [her] hand" (128) and to be kissed by her (143). Unlike with the young man, there is no question his love for her is physical. At least one sonnet leaves no doubt that their rela-tionship has been consummated. In Sonnet 152, he tells her she is "twice forsworn" in swearing love to him because she has broken her "bed-vow."

Does this mean the speaker is bisexual? Applied to the time of the Son-nets, the term is meaningless. Sexuality was not tied to identity for the Elizabethans. People didn't think of themselves as gay or straight. Ho-mosexual acts were considered behaviors that anyone might engage in, and they were forbidden by church and state as "buggery" and "sodomy." Like today, some men and women were predominantly homosexual in their desires, but few were exclusively homosexual in practice. This is not the case, however, in the Sonnets. What we can say about the Author's speaker is, he is sexually attracted to the feminine, regardless of whether he found it in a woman or an androgynous young man. But it is the woman for whom he feels uncontrollable lust. He is primarily hetero-sexual, his *desire* is heterosexual, even as he loves both the Fair Youth and the Dark Lady.

CHAPTER 8

Footprints in the Garden

When we examine the Plays and Poems closely, when we compare them to their sources and to the works of other writers, when we recognize that the Author's Latin (and lack of Greek) is consistent with a grammar school education, and that what seems like specialized legal and military knowledge was no more than the idiom of his time, it becomes clear that the Poet was not a courtier, nor a lawyer, nor a scholar, nor a soldier. He could have been William Shakespeare. And because he could have been, and because the external evidence—the Folio epistles, the Stratford monument, the posthumous references—all tell us he *was*, we are obligated, as historians, to conclude this was the case.

What about internal evidence? Are there traces of the actor in the Writings?

The first place to look might be Sonnet 136, in which the Author explicitly says, "my name is *Will*." This declaration comes at the end of the two so-called "Will sonnets" (135 and 136), in which the Poet puns on his name eighteen times:

135

Whoever hath her wish, thou hast thy *Will*,
And *Will* to boot, and *Will* in overplus;
More than enough am I that vex thee still,
To thy sweet will making addition thus.
Wilt thou, whose will is large and spacious,
Not once vouchsafe to hide my will in thine?
Shall will in others seem right gracious,

And in my will no fair acceptance shine?
The sea, all water, yet receives rain still,
And in abundance addeth to his store,
So thou being rich in *Will* add to thy *Will*
One will of mine to make thy large *Will* more.
   Let no unkind, no fair beseechers kill;
   Think all but one, and me in that one *Will*.

136

If thy soul check thee that I come so near,
Swear to thy blind soul that I was thy *Will*,
And will, thy soul knows, is admitted there;
Thus far for love my love-suit, sweet, fulfill.
Will will fulfill the treasure of thy love,
Ay, fill it full with wills, and my will one.
In things of great receipt with ease we prove
Among a number one is reckon'd none:
Then in the number let me pass untold,
Though in thy store's account I one must be,
For nothing hold me, so it please thee hold
That nothing me, a something sweet to thee.
   Make but my name thy move, and love that still,
   And then thou lovest me, for my name is *Will*.

That Shakespeare was known as Will is confirmed by Thomas Heywood in *The Hierarchie of Blessed Angels* (1635). Enumerating poets' nicknames, he writes that Marlowe was known as Kit, and Heywood himself was Tom to his friends. As for the Author,

> Mellifluous *Shake-speare*, whose inchanting Quill
> Commanded Mirth or Passion, was but Will.

Of course, it's possible that in the Will sonnets the Poet is playing upon his front man's name, or that he intended the persona of the whole sequence to be his front man. But such a game would mean the Sonnets are not autobiographical, as they seem, but libelous fiction. Remember: "William Shakespeare" was not an assumed name—it belonged to a real person, and anyone reading the Sonnets, including his wife, would think he had committed adultery. A poet risking his own marriage and reputation is one thing; risking someone else's, someone very much alive who is acting as your agent, is another. The whole idea is, frankly, bizarre. The simpler and more natural inference is that Shakespeare was the Author.

The dedications of *Venus and Adonis* (1593) and *The Rape of Lucrece* (1594), both printed by Richard Field of Stratford-upon-Avon, also point to the actor. The earlier one reads as follows:

TO THE RIGHT HONORABLE HENRY WRIOTHESLEY,
Earl of Southampton, and Baron of Titchfield.

Right Honorable, I know not how I shall offend in dedicating my unpolished lines to your Lordship, nor how the world will censure me for choosing so strong a prop to support so weak a burden, only if your Honor seem but pleased, I account myself highly praised, and vow to take advantage of all idle hours, till I have honored you with some graver labor. But if the first heir of my invention prove deformed, I shall be sorry it had so noble a godfather: and never after ear so barren a land, for fear it yield me still so bad a harvest. I leave it to your honorable survey, and your Honor to your heart's content, which I wish may always answer your own wish and the world's hopeful expectation.

Your Honor's in all duty,
WILLIAM SHAKESPEARE

[spelling modernized]

We can see from the first sentence that the Author is of a lower social rank than Wriothesley and doesn't know him very well. His first thought is of his fear of giving offense. If the poem is liked, he promises to do better next time. If it isn't, he shall never write again—a hyperbolic threat at first glance, but since he only wrote one more narrative poem after this one, perhaps the second effort, *Lucrece*, was not well received by its patron. The words "first heir" mystify some commentators because the Author had probably written several plays by 1593. But *Venus and Adonis* is his first published work, his first serious production; plays may have been trifles to the young Poet. And since at this time none of his dramatic works had been published, they could not have survived him as his "heirs."

Compare the *Venus* dedication with the one for *Lucrece*:

TO THE RIGHT HONORABLE, HENRY WRIOTHESLEY,
Earl of Southampton and Baron of Titchfield

The love I dedicate to your Lordship is without end: whereof this pamphlet without beginning is but a superfluous moiety. The warrant I have of your honorable disposition, not the worth of my untutored lines, makes it assured of acceptance. What I have done is yours, what I have to do is yours, being part in all I have, devoted yours. Were my worth greater, my duty would show greater, meantime, as it is, it is bound to your Lordship; to whom I wish long life still lengthened with all happiness.

Your Lordship's in all duty,

William Shakespeare

The relationship between Wriothesley and Shakespeare has changed. In the first dedication, the two men haven't met, but by the second the Poet is speaking of love. The tone here is more personal, and skeptics today find it too personal for an actor addressing an earl. Only someone of equal social rank, they claim, could address a nobleman in such an intimate way. No one at the time, however, is known to have remarked upon the dedication at all, so perhaps the skeptics are deluding themselves about what was appropriate in the Elizabethan era. Besides, is the epistle really that intimate? Yes, the Poet speaks of love and devotion, but his enthusiasm sounds like a dog's for its master; the obsequiousness of the first dedication is still there. Its language is the idiom of patronage, which, as I've said, was unusually amorous; benefactors were commonly showered with protestations of eternal love. He is now duty-bound to Southampton, he has a "warrant" of the earl's "disposition," which probably means he has received money for the first poem. By "untutored lines" he seems to mean "unlearned"; he's downplaying his poetry as imperfect because of his lack of education. The phrase is of a piece with "pupil pen" and "rude ignorance" from the Sonnets. And, most important, it jibes with what we know of Shakespeare.

If someone else is the Author, then, these dedications, like the Stratford monument, represent an elaborate and unnecessary hoax. Writing from the point of view of a commoner, portraying a change in the relationship between poet and patron, throwing in an agricultural image (since the alleged author comes from the country), making a reference to his lack of education—for what? Dedications were not mandatory, and if the Author thought his books would be naked without them, why not write ordinary ones?

These introductions are not the only connection between Southampton and Shakespeare. In 1604, a letter from the courtier Sir Walter Cope to Burghley's son Robert Cecil reveals,

> Burbage is come, and says there is no new play that the Queen [James's wife Anna] has not seen; but they have revived an old one called Love's Labour Lost, which for wit and mirth he says will please her exceedingly. And this is appointed to be played to-morrow night at my Lord of Southampton's.[1]

"Burbage" was probably Richard's brother Cuthbert, who was a main profit-sharer in the King's Men and was in service to Cope. Here we see Shakespeare's company performing one of the Author's plays before Southampton and the Queen. Probably they had played at "my Lord of Southampton's" before; Titchfield, the earl's residence, was equipped with a hall, designated for theatrical performances, called the "Play-house room."[2]

More direct evidence of Shakespeare's hand can be found in the dramas. As we've seen, "Bardolphe" and "Fluellen"—the names of characters in *Henry V*—turn up, along with John Shakespeare, on a list (dated 25 September 1592) of nine Stratford citizens who have been absent from church.[3] On other Stratford documents are "Bates," "Court," and "Williams"—the surnames of the soldiers in *Henry V*'s night scene.[4] The full name of Stratford denizen Stephen Sly is mentioned in the Induction to *The Taming of the Shrew* (Ind.ii.93). In the same scene, the tinker who is made to think he's a lord—Christopher Sly—begs those around him to "Ask Marian Hacket, the fat alewife of Wincot, if she know me not" (Ind.ii.21–2). Wincot was a hamlet four miles from Stratford. In 1591, there was a family named Hacket living there. (A baptism is recorded in the local parish register.) How could anyone know that Hackets lived in Wincot unless they had been there?[5]

Two Stratford names are present in the Works in disguised forms. The first appears in *Cymbeline*, when the British princess Imogen dresses as a boy and pretends to the invading Romans that the headless body of her step-brother Cloten belonged to a man she claims to have served:

> This was my master,
> A very valiant Britain, and a good,
> That here by mountaineers lies slain. Alas,

There is no more such masters. I may wander
From east to occident, cry out for service,
Try many, all good; serve truly; never
Find such another master.
LUCIUS.   . . . Say his name, good friend.
IMOGEN.   Richard du Champ.

(IV.ii.368–73, 376–77)

"Richard Field" in French. Field was disposed to this kind of punning on his name. He printed several works between 1596 and 1600 under the name Ricardo del Campo (Italian for "Richard Field"). Not only did he produce *Venus and Adonis* and *The Rape of Lucrece*, in 1601 he printed the Author's poem *The Phoenix and the Turtle* in a collection titled *Love's Martyr*, and he was also responsible for printing many of the Poet's sources.

The other Stratford pun is hiding in Sonnet 145:

Those lips that Love's own hand did make
Breath'd forth the sound that said "I hate"
To me that languish'd for her sake;
But when she saw my woeful state,
Straight in her heart did mercy come,
Chiding that tongue that, ever sweet,
Was us'd in giving gentle doom,
And taught it thus anew to greet:
"I hate" she alter'd with an end
That followed it as gentle day
Doth follow night, who like a fiend
From heaven to hell is flown away:
   "I hate" from hate away she threw,
   And sav'd my life, saying "not you."

Hate away and *Hathaway* were pronounced very similarly in Warwickshire; the dialect rendered both as *het-away*. The "Warwickshire *a*"—as it's sometimes called—accounts for the otherwise grating pun in *The Taming of the Shrew*, where Petruchio tells Katherine:

For I am he am born to tame you, Kate,
And bring you from a wild Kate to a Kate

Conformable as other household Kates.

(II.i.276–78)

Kate and *cat* were both pronounced like *ket* in Warwickshire. Surely it's not a coincidence that the Author climaxes his sonnet with "hate away" and Shakespeare's wife was Anne Hathaway. Surely it's not a coincidence that, stylistically, this is one of the earliest sonnets. And surely it's not a coincidence that this is the only lyric in the Dark Lady sequence in which the pronoun "you" is used; in the others, he addresses his mistress with the literary "thou." It's not for nothing this poem is called the Anne Hathaway Sonnet.

Anne's cousin Frances married Davy Jones, the head of a group of amateur mummers in Stratford. He and his troupe were paid by the borough council for performing a "pastime at Whitsuntide," a week before Shakespeare's daughter Susanna was born in 1582.[6] Such a presentation, a custom specific to rural English villages, is incongruously remembered by the princess Perdita in *The Winter's Tale*:

> Come, take your flow'rs.
> Methinks I play now as I have seen them do
> In Whitsun pastorals.

(IV.iv.132–34)

Stratford pops up again in a coincidence involving colors of cloth. In *A Midsummer Night's Dream*, Bottom ponders what beard to play Pyramus in: "your orange-tawnie beard, your purple in graine beard" (I.ii.94–5). Just as these two colors are found side by side in the play, they appear side by side in a Stratford inventory of 1596: "orange tawnye brode cloth," "violet in grayne."[7]

Hamlet's famous philosophical reflection, "There's a divinity which shapes our ends,/Rough-hew them how we will" (V.ii.10–11), applies specifically to the cutting and shaping of wool-skewers, important implements in John Shakespeare's trade. The raw materials of gloving and whittawering—calfskin, sheepskin, lambskin, fox skin, dog skin, deerskin, and cheveril (kid skin)—abound in the plays. Researcher Edgar Fripp points out, "[The Author] knew that 'neat's-leather' was used for shoes, sheep's leather for a bridle . . . and he comments humorously on the capacity of tanned leather to keep out water. . . . On account of its softness and flexibility cheveril was used in the making of the finer quality of gloves. [The Author] speaks of a 'wit of cheveril, that stretches from an inch to an ell broad' [*Romeo and Juliet*]. This is technical language borrowed from his father's business. He mentions also . . . 'a cheveril glove, . . . how quickly the wrong side may be turned outward' [*Twelfth Night*]."[8] John's other business, wool dealing, is featured in *The Winter's Tale*. "Let me see," cogitates a slow-witted shepherd, "every 'leven wether tods, every tod yields pound and odd shilling: fifteen hundred shorn, what comes the wool to?" (IV.iii.32–34). Every eleven sheep, in other words, yield a tod (twenty-eight pounds) of wool, and every tod sells for a pound and one shilling (twenty-one shillings). Twenty-one shillings was, in fact, the price of a tod of wool at Stratford in the sixteenth century, as documents attest.[9]

Caroline Spurgeon expresses surprise that while the Author uses imagery from a number of trades, including that of blacksmith, butcher, potter, tailor, weaver, glover, printer, and dyer, the craft he mines the most for his metaphors is carpentry. Screwing, nailing, riveting, hooping a barrel with metal ribs; the use of wedges; the tendency of wood to warp; the use of hammers, mallets, handsaws, files, and vices; the small, deep hole an augur makes—all find their way into his poetry. But if we think of the Author as Shakespeare, his knowledge becomes less mysterious. In 1599 Shakespeare and his fellows showed off carpentry skills when they tore down the Theatre, built by James Burbage in 1576, and reconstructed it on the South Bank of the Thames, calling it the Globe. As for barrel-making, or coopering, it was vital in Stratford where the principal commercial activity was brewing. It shouldn't surprise us he's familiar with it.

That the Globe was located next to a bear-baiting arena may account for the Author's many images from that "sport." Spurgeon could not find a single similar image in any other Elizabethan dramatist's work.[10] It is bear-baiting, a gory spectacle in which a bear fights with a pack of dogs and bets are placed on which dog will fight the longest, that provides the Author's most personally characteristic metaphors, his poetic fingerprint.[11]

Spurgeon finds the Author's knowledge of sewing and mending "somewhat unusual," and she credits it to his observation of women.[12] She may be right, but it's also possible that stitching costumes as an actor would teach him about making an old cloak into a new jerkin, knitting up raveled sleeves, patching, trimming, and basting. His male characters use as many sewing and mending metaphors as his females do, which suggests he did not associate this activity solely with women. Jesting with Don Pedro in *Much Ado About Nothing*, Benedick teases his friend with a metaphor from dressmaking: "The body of your discourse is sometime guarded with fragments, and the guards are but slightly basted on neither" (I.i.285–87). *Guards* meant ornaments, and *fragments*, little odds and ends. You trim your conversation with not-very-clever bits of wit, he is saying, and they are only lightly sewn on (*basted*) to the subject you are talking about.

The fact that Shakespeare lived with a headdress-weaver, or tiremaker, accounts for the references to tiremaking in the late plays. Falstaff, in *The Merry Wives of Windsor*, tells Mistress Ford,

> Thou hast the right arched beauty of the brow that becomes the ship-tire, the tire-valiant, or any tire of Venetian admittance.
>
> (III.iii.56–58)

In *Pericles*, Gower speaks of weaving "the sleided silk" (IV.cho.21), a phrase from the aspect of the craft that involved the making and working of gold and silver thread. And *The Winter's Tale* conjures "golden quoifs and stomachers" (IV.iv.224), the former being a cheaper variety of headdress. *Antony and Cleopatra* contains the technical terms "cloth of gold, of tissue" but, as we've seen, he filched these, word for word, from North's translation of Plutarch.

We would expect to find traces of the Warwickshire dialect in the Works, and we do. Words like *ballow*, North Midlands for cudgel; *batlet*, a short staff for beating clothes in the wash; *gallow*, meaning to frighten; *geck*, meaning fool; *honey-stalks*, specific in the region to clover flowers; *mobled*, meaning muffled; *pash*, the local onomatopoetic for "to smash"; *potch*, to thrust; *tarre*, to incite; and *vails*, peaks or tips, all show up in the Canon.[13] *Wappered*, meaning tired or jaded, is a Cotswold dialect word that appears in *Timon of Athens* and *The Two Noble Kinsmen*.[14] In *Antony and Cleopatra*, Scarus's simile of "the breeze upon her, like a cow in June" makes little sense until it's understood that *breeze* means stinging gadfly in Warwickshire. Describing a sea battle, Scarus says,

> Yon ribaudred nag of Egypt
> (Whom leprosy o'ertake!) i' th' midst o' th' fight,
> When vantage like a pair of twins appear'd,
> Both as the same, or rather ours the elder—
> The breeze upon her, like a cow in June—

Hoists sails and flies.

(III.x.10–15)

Cleopatra's vessel fled the scene, even though she had the advantage, like a cow retreating from a gadfly. *Dey* in Stratford meant dairy, which explains Constable Dull's statement that Jacquenetta is "allow'd for the dey-woman" (*Love's Labor's Lost*, I.ii.131): she's a milkmaid. In Warwickshire, she would use a sye bowl to skim the milk, which explains the line "thy head stands so tickle on thy shoulders that a milkmaid, if she be in love, may sigh it off" (*Measure for Measure*, I.ii.172–74).[15] *Contain yourself* in *Taming of the Shrew*, *Timon of Athens*, and *Troilus and Cressida* was noted by George Wilkes, in the nineteenth century, to be a very common Warwickshire phrase for "restrain yourself."[16] Overall, according to Appleton Morgan in his *Study of the Warwickshire Dialect* (1899), every one of the Author's plays includes regional words and phrases, especially *Hamlet* and *Henry V* (34 each), *The Winter's Tale* and *Henry VI Part Two* (21 each), and *Troilus and Cressida* (20).

Does any of this mean William Shakespeare wrote the plays? Yes and no. It means he didn't *not* write them. What we know about Shakespeare is consistent with the Author.

∼

If the only things we know about Shakespeare's personality are that he was honest (both Jonson and Chettle say so) and had an air of nobility ("indeed gentle," "gentle Shakespeare," "swan of Avon"), at least we know what he looked like. Though scholars are reluctant to say so, the Chandos portrait in the London's National Portrait Gallery is almost certainly an authentic likeness (Figure 6). It was either painted from life, or it's a copy of a painting from life. How can we be sure? Because it was used as a model for the Droeshout engraving in the First Folio. The engraver Martin Droeshout was fifteen when Shakespeare died and at most twenty-two when he made his engraving. He must have used a portrait, cameo, miniature, or someone's description to base his image on. The oddities of his work point to his using some other picture and copying it badly. The hair doesn't balance at the sides, the head is too large for the body, the mouth is not directly under the nose, the left eye is larger and lower than the right, and the neck rises out of the starched collar at an angle that's humanly impossible unless it were very long and curved like a waterfowl's, giving new meaning to the epithet "swan of Avon." All of these curiosities are explained by the Chandos portrait. The strange hair on the left side of the engraving is an attempt to recreate the bushy curls in

Figure 6. The Chandos Portrait of William Shakespeare attributed to John Taylor. National Portrait Gallery, London.

the portrait which balance naturally with the bushy mane on the right. The mouth's displacement is the result of drawing the mouth and nose separately, as one who is copying is apt to do. In the painting, one eye is slightly larger and lower than the other but not grotesquely so (few people have perfectly symmetrical faces); the discrepancy became exaggerated as they were copied. The head and neck, which rise out of the body naturally, became disproportionate when Droeshout derived them from the portrait and replaced the Elizabethan turned-down collar with a Jacobean starched collar and doublet. He removed the earring (if indeed it was there to begin with) and gave the subject a haircut and a shave (you can still see the beard stubble in the engraving). He made the head more bulbous, less egg-shaped, and mimicked the shadows under the eyes (which result from the overhead light source) in such a way that they look like eye-bags. One detail Droeshout ignored is the tan line from the subject's hat. The skin above his hatline is lighter and his long curly hair has been pushed down by his headwear. This is a man who spent some time outdoors—like an actor. As for the shave, I suspect in his later years, Shakespeare wore his whiskers as the engraving and the monument portray, in a Jacobean manner, and Shakespeare's friends informed the engraver and sculptor of this.

Shakespeare's real portrait, though, is in his Works. "Look how the father's face lives in his issue," Jonson remarked to those readers who had known the man. "The race of Shakespeare's mind, and manners, brightly shines in his well-turned and true-filed lines." Dozens, perhaps hundreds, of people—including "our James"—were still alive who had witnessed for themselves the race of Shakespeare's mind, and they would know instantly if Jonson were lying, if he were playing a joke on posterity by claiming the man with "small Latin and less Greek" was reflected in the plays. He would never have mentioned the "father's face" at all if he didn't think others would recognize it too. He was writing for an audience of his own time, the early 1620s, not for readers generations hence when all who knew Shakespeare were dead and buried.

Thanks to Jonson, we know Shakespeare's personality was perceivable in his plays. The man and the Author were almost certainly one. (Almost? Well, yes. We can't be *absolutely* certain, but then we can't be absolutely certain about the Earth revolving around the sun either: only the evidence tells us that it's so.)

Making the case for Shakespeare is not difficult, but it's not sufficient either. It's not enough to show why Shakespeare was the Author; it's also necessary to dismantle the cases for the major rival claimants—especially the most popular alternative candidate, the seventeenth Earl of Oxford. "Eliminate the impossible," advised Sherlock Holmes, "and whatever remains, *however improbable*, must be the truth."[17] If the other candidates' claims can be shown to be impossible, then whatever improbability remains, however bizarre, must be true—even the remarkable improbability that a glover's son from Stratford was the greatest literary genius of all time.

PART TWO

~

The Men Who Didn't

CHAPTER 9
Suspects

Most Authorship candidates aren't worth refuting. If someone honestly believes Queen Elizabeth, or Henry VII's adviser Cardinal Wolsey, or the translator John Florio's father, wrote the Canon of Shakespeare—well, there's no arguing with crazy people. But even the loopiest theories are born of the same basic flaw in reasoning. Instead of looking at all the evidence and piecing it together like a puzzle—or a brontosaur—a single item of data is used to determine the Author's identity, a single bone decides the shape of the whole skeleton. Other bones are either ignored or arranged in such a way as to construct the preordained outcome—a stegosaur, let's say.

Take the case for Roger Manners, fifth Earl of Rutland.

At some point, a Shakespeare denier was touring Belvoir Castle, the ancestral residence of the earls of Rutland. Surveying the artifacts in the Elizabethan Salon, he chanced to look up at the ceiling, and what should he behold but a fresco of Correggio's *Jupiter and Io*, transposed magnificently from a copy of the original in Milan. Just that morning, he had been rereading the Induction of *The Taming of the Shrew*, in which a nameless lord offers to show the drunken tinker Christopher Sly a "picture":

> We'll show thee Io as she was a maid,
> And how she was beguil'd and surprised,
> As lively painted as the deed was done.

(Ind.ii.54–56)

Aha! thinks the denier. Only the Earl of Rutland could have seen this painting, so Rutland must have been the Author! It doesn't occur to him

129

that Correggio's might not be the only "picture" of Io, or that someone else might have seen the Belvoir ceiling—someone like one of the players who are enlisted by the lord to help trick Christopher Sly. Armed with his one piece of "evidence," his single bone, the heretic begins to investigate his candidate. And lo and behold he discovers some amazing coincidences.

Rutland had a brother named Oliver whom he bickered with throughout his life and ultimately dispossessed—just as the character Oliver dispossesses his brother Orlando in *As You Like It*. In the mid-1590s, Rutland toured Italy and attended the University of Padua, the same institution Lucentio is enrolling in *The Taming of the Shrew*. While he was there, two of his fellow students had the common Danish last names of Rosenkrans and Gyldenstjerne—the same names as Hamlet's schoolfellows. In 1597, Rutland sailed with the Earl of Essex on the latter's military expedition to the Azores. On that voyage, according to Rutlanders, he would have learned what the Author knew about sea battles and seafaring. He joined Essex a second time on the campaign in Ireland from April to June 1599. His return from this latter excursion seems to have been occasioned by a case of swollen legs—in other words, like the anti-Stratfordian vision of the Sonneteer, he may have been lame. Just as he got back, the Author wrote *Henry V*—the first play in the Canon, according to Rutlanders, that shows real knowledge of warfare. At this time he was said to have gone to plays "every day"[1] with the Earl of Southampton—the same Earl of Southampton who was the dedicatee of the Author's narrative poems and the probable subject of the Sonnets. In 1601, the year the Poet entered his gloomy period, producing *Hamlet*, *Othello*, *Lear*, *Macbeth* and the tragicomic problem comedies, Rutland was imprisoned in the Tower of London for his role in the Essex Rebellion. He was released the following spring. In 1603, he was sent by King James to Denmark to represent the crown at the christening of the newly born Danish heir. Rutlanders believe this explains the revisions the Author made to *Hamlet* between the publications of the 1603 and 1604 quartos. Names in the 1603 *Hamlet* like Geruth, Corambis, and Montano are changed to the more Scandinavian Gertrude, Polonius (Plönnies), and Reynaldo (Ranald). The anonymous Gentleman in the first quarto became the Danish Osric in the second. Danish words like *Danskers* (how Danes refer to themselves) and *crants* (floral wreaths) appear in the 1604 edition, but nowhere else in the Plays and Poems. The second quarto also includes bits of local color like the Danish king's Swiss guards and the court's drunken feasts, where toasts were punctuated by pistol fire. Rutland died in 1612, which explains why his front man, William Shakespeare, stopped writing plays around that time. At the earl's death, the library at Belvoir contained many of the books the Author made use of, a coincidence that *could* be explained by identifying the earl as the Poet.

So what's wrong with Rutland? The first problem is his age. He was born in October of 1576, which means he was only fifteen when Robert Greene quotes a line from *Henry VI Part Three*. He was sixteen and a half when *Venus and Adonis* was published, seventeen when *Titus Andronicus* was printed, and twenty at the publication of *Richard II*, *Richard III*, and *Romeo and Juliet*. Before he turned twenty-two, the Author had written at least sixteen plays (those praised by Meres), two narrative poems, and some of the Sonnets. Rutland would have had to have been an exceptional child prodigy to turn out those masterpieces—a fact which would have been noted in the extensive writings of the man responsible for his upbringing, Sir Francis Bacon.[2] Not only was he too young, he was out of the country, traveling in Europe and studying at Padua in late 1595 and all of 1596. In 1597 he was with Essex, fighting with the Spanish navy in the North Atlantic. There simply isn't time for him to have written all the works that Meres mentions. There isn't even any evidence he was a poet.

What about Denmark? Do the changes in the 1604 quarto mean the Author must have visited Denmark in 1603? Actually, they probably reflect a vogue of interest in the country inspired by the new play-loving Queen, James I's wife, Anna of Denmark. Any playwright would have been wise to learn a bit about Scandinavia and add a few homey touches to his composition. It's hard to say for certain if this is what happened, though, because the 1603 quarto is not a first draft of the play but a "bad quarto," possibly a memorial reconstruction, badly remembered by the contract player who acted the part of Marcellus (which is recalled perfectly) and sold to a publisher. No one knows what the earlier versions of *Hamlet* were like.

The same kind of specious logic the Rutlanders indulge in is practiced by the advocates for other fringe candidates. Partisans for Robert Devereux, the Earl of Essex, observe the earl had a close, mentor-like relationship with the Earl of Southampton, and the Author of the Sonnets had a close, mentor-like relationship with Southampton. Therefore, they conclude, Essex was the Author. In his book *Shakespeare: The Mystery*, George Elliott Sweet reasons that since the Author was the most "myriad-minded" person of the time, and Queen Elizabeth was the most "myriad-minded" person of the time, Queen Elizabeth was the Author. On such false foundations, the heretics begin to build their dinosaurs. Having had their road-to-Damascus revelation, they hunt for clues that bolster their vision. They scour the Works and contemporary documents for secret codes and reflections of events in their candidate's life. Invariably, because anything can mean anything when you take it out of context, they find the bones of their hero.

SIR FRANCIS BACON

The early anti-Stratfordians preferred Bacon. Like the supporters of Queen Elizabeth, they fell prey to their own bad syllogism: Since Bacon was the most brilliant man of the time, and Shakespeare was the most brilliant man of the time, Bacon must be Shakespeare. In philosophy this is called "begging the question"—mistaking a subjective definition for a logical proof. The reality, of course, is that both men were brilliant, though in very different ways.

Born in 1561, Francis was the youngest son of Nicholas Bacon, a man who had risen from an abbot's shepherd to Lord Keeper of the Great Seal, a high government office. Francis's uncle, through his mother, was the powerful Lord Burghley. It was because of Burghley that Bacon became the personal lawyer to the Queen, enjoying, in the words of Bacon's most recent biographers, "uncommon access to her presence."[3] But Burghley also thwarted his nephew's ambitions. The Lord Treasurer and his son Sir Robert Cecil ensured that Bacon held no official post in the government or the legal hierarchy during Elizabeth's reign, despite his obvious qualifications.

At age fifteen, Bacon had graduated from Cambridge and been admitted to Gray's Inn to study law. By age twenty he was a member of Parliament, and a year later a barrister. Around 1588 he became a protégé of the Earl of Essex and a contact man in Essex's intelligence service. When the earl became annoyed with the Queen's physician, a Spanish convert from Judaism named Dr. Roderigo Lopez, and accused him of spying for Spain and conspiring to poison Elizabeth (this was in 1594), Bacon prepared the charges which led to Lopez's execution. He was a loyal servant to the earl, and throughout the 1590s, a grateful Essex tried to win his loyal servant the solicitor-generalship. But even the earl could not advance Bacon's career. The Queen herself had to approve all appointments, and on advice from Burghley and his son Sir Robert

Cecil, she refused Essex's suit. By the end of the decade, Bacon considered himself in "disgrace"[4] because of Elizabeth's apparent lack of faith in him.

To make matters worse, in 1598, he was arrested for debt. Always profligate, Bacon consistently spent more than he took in no matter what his income. His brother Anthony helped him borrow more money, and he was quickly cleared of his obligations, but his personal finances were now public knowledge.

Part of his spending may have been to pay hush money to anyone who knew of his liaisons with male lovers and male prostitutes. Bacon seems to have been exclusively homosexual. When he married at the age of forty-five, it was clearly not for lust or love. His new bride was a barely pubescent heiress who was all of fourteen; he had had his eye on her fortune since she was eleven.

The most painful episode in Bacon's career came when he was asked by the Queen to prosecute his own patron. During Essex's ill-fated 1599 campaign to put down the rebels in Ireland, the earl had fallen out of favor with his sovereign when, against her wishes, he appointed Southampton to the position of General of the Horse (the commander of the cavalry) and then, on his own initiative, Essex began negotiating with the enemy. His star fell further when he suddenly returned to England, after the Queen had specifically forbidden him to do so. He famously marched straight into her bedchamber while she was in her nightgown, a shocking breach of etiquette. Pacing back and forth before his *déshabillée* monarch, he vented his frustration with her and her advisers for micromanaging his conduct of the war. A few days later he was placed under house arrest for insubordination. A hearing was held the following June at which the Privy Council stripped him of all his offices of state and continued his house arrest. One of his prosecutors was Bacon. The future philosopher, feeling his loyalty to the Queen superseded his loyalty to Essex, participated without reluctance. But in the ensuing months, Bacon tried to persuade Elizabeth to return the earl to favor, though his efforts were to no avail. In December of 1600, despite Essex's pleas, the Queen punished him further. She did not renew his farm of the tariffs on sweet wines (the import duties had been going to his coffers), so now Essex was heading for bankruptcy. Desperate, he convened his allies—including Southampton—and laid out plans to seize the Queen and force her to change her government. On February 8, 1601, three hundred armed men assembled in the courtyard of the earl's residence, Essex House. When four emissaries from the royal Court—the Lord Keeper of the Great Seal, the Comptroller of the Queen's Household, the Lord Chief Justice, and the Earl of Worcester—arrived at the scene, the revolutionaries took them prisoner, placing them under guard in the library. The earl and his followers then marched into the walled city of London, where Essex believed he could rally more supporters and where he tried to convince the head of the city's militia to let his men have muskets. He was disappointed in both. In addition, this maneuver cost the earl precious minutes. By the time his band decided to move on toward the palace, their adversaries were ready for them. A proclamation was read that denounced Essex as a traitor and promised that anyone assisting him would be hanged. On learning of it, many of the three hundred men slinked away and joined packs of bystanders so as not to be seen with him. Realizing which way the wind was blowing, Essex tried to leave the city, but the gate was blocked by a group of soldiers. After a standoff, gunfire erupted, halberds and pikestaffs swung and stabbed, and there were several dead and wounded on both sides. The rebels scattered. Essex, Southampton, and about thirty supporters fled to the river, where they scrambled onto boats without regard to who owned them. Frantically, they rowed for their lives back to Essex House, which was on the Thames about three-eighths of a mile upriver. When they reached the mansion, just ahead of their pursuers, they learned that their hostages had been freed. They had no bargaining chips now and could only fight. For the next several hours, while Essex House was laid siege, men on both sides died in the melee. Finally, at about 10 P.M., the earl surrendered. He and his followers were conveyed to the Tower of London, where they awaited their interrogations and trials.[5]

Assigned to prosecute Essex and Southampton were Attorney General Sir Edward Coke and Francis Bacon. History tells us that despite having been a member of the earl's inner circle, it was Bacon who argued the case more effectively and who was most responsible for the sentences of death. (Southampton's punishment was commuted to life in prison; he remained in the Tower until April 1603.)

With the accession of James I, Bacon's career took dramatic leaps forward. In 1603, he was knighted. Because he was a busy and vocal member of Parliament, pressing for union with Scotland, he was made Solicitor-General in 1607. In 1613, he became Attorney General; in 1616, a Privy Councillor, and the next year Lord Keeper of the Great Seal, as his father had been. He was elevated to Lord Chancellor, the high judge of the Court of Chancery, in 1618, and created Baron Verulam the same year. In 1621, he became Viscount St. Albans and was given a seat in the House of Lords. All the while he continued to advise the king, participate in Parliament, and mastermind his own rise as well as that of George Villiers, the future Duke of Buckingham. He also engineered the falls of the Earl of Somerset, once the king's favorite, and Sir Walter Ralegh. Then in 1621, the same year he became a viscount, Bacon's own career came crashing down when he was convicted of taking bribes. All of his government responsibilities were removed from him, and he was banished from the House of Lords.

After his disgrace, he spent the last five years of his life writing, revising, and translating into Latin his numerous works on science, law, history, politics, and philosophy, including his utopian work of fiction, *The New Atlantis*. Ironically, Bacon is most famous for his critique of inductive reasoning; he complained that people are too quick to make generalizations, to base their knowledge on limited examples, individual experiences, and personal tastes—exactly what the supporters of his Authorship do when they assume that only college-educated courtiers could have written in the Author's high tone because it seems to them that that should be the case.

Bacon's life provides his partisans with plenty of glimpses of the Author. His cousin, the hunchbacked and duplicitous Sir Robert Cecil, was, by their lights, the original for Richard III; Dr. Lopez, the model for Shylock; Burghley, the basis for Polonius; and the rash half-mad Essex, the inspiration for Hamlet.[6] Bacon's sense of disgrace in the late 1590s is supposedly recorded in the Sonnets, as is his homosexuality. Certainly, he was interested in the stage; at Gray's Inn, he arranged for masques—ornate allegorical playlets—to be performed in 1588, 1594, 1613, and 1615.[7] And he even claimed in a 1603 letter to be a "concealed poet"; we know he authored at least some of the entertainments he produced. But finding biographical connections is not the principal means of argument for Baconians. More important to them are similarities in thought, diction, and phraseology—so-called parallelisms. For example, in his aphoristic philosophical essays Bacon wrote, "be so true to thyself, as thou be not false to others,"[8] advice not unlike Polonius's

> This above all: to thine own self be true,
> And it must follow, as the night the day,
> Thou canst not be false to any man.

(Hamlet, I.iii.78–80)

Bacon states in another essay that "chiefly, the mold of a man's fortune is in his own hands,"[9] which is the same idea as Cassius' line in *Julius Caesar*: "Men at some time are masters of their fates" (I.ii.134). In his *Sylva Sylvarum* (1627), also known as *Natural History*, Bacon observes that "marigolds . . . and indeed most flowers do open and spread their leaves abroad when the sun shineth . . . and . . . close them, or gather them inward . . . towards night,"[10] just as the Author notices "the marigold, that goes to bed wi' th' sun,/and with him rises weeping" (*The Winter's Tale*, IV.iv.105–6). And so on. Many of the parallelisms are proverbial expressions, shared by most writers of the period, but three-fourths of the common sayings Bacon jotted down in his notebooks (152 out of 203) were quoted or alluded to in the Author's plays,[11] an astonishing coincidence that, like Rutland's library, could be explained if the viscount were the Poet.

So why not Bacon?

One reason is vocabulary. Assuming Bacon was the Author, J. M. Robertson ponders "how it could come about that the same man, repeatedly using in his nondramatic writings such familiar terms as *atheism, theology, theological, knowledges, illumination, renovation, magnify, magnitude, amplitude, deficience, proficience, tacit, transitory, signature, . . . analogy, medium, mystical, imposture, commonplace, recede, . . . deduce, mediocrity, immersed, benign, righteousness, alloy, generate, magnet, superlative*—and many hundreds more, equally common—could contrive to write (as the Baconians hold) thirty-seven plays, covering a productive period of some twenty years, without once using any of them dramatically? How should he chance to avoid, in all his playwriting, the use of two such common idioms as 'at a stand' and 'at a stay,' when they came to him quite naturally in his other writings? . . . How, after writing often of 'politiques' in his avowed works, should he always write 'politicians' in his alleged plays, when other dramatists (e.g., Ben Jonson) used 'politiques'? Using the metaphor of 'oblation' so frequently in his signed works, how could he abstain from using it once in his plays? . . . How should it be possible for him to write of 'vicissitude' seven times in one essay and never once in thirty-seven plays?"[12] The Baconians answer that it *was* possible. A writer's artistic vocabulary usually differs from his philosophical one. But there is no answer for Bacon's different renderings of the same word—"politiques" instead of "politicians," or "submiss" instead of the Author's "submissive," or "militar" instead of the Poet's "military." These are two different writers.

Author John Michell points out another problem with Bacon. At the public trial of the Earl of Essex, one of the proofs that the earl intended to overthrow the Queen was that he was "often present" at plays portraying the usurpation of Richard II, and "with great applause, giving countenance and liking to the same."[13] Essex, Bacon's longtime patron, would almost certainly have known his protégé's secret and could have answered the charge that he saw nothing wrong with enjoying a play that was written by the Lord Prosecutor himself![14] But even if Essex was in the dark, someone in the galleries would have known Bacon was the Author and, at some point, would have exposed the lawyer's grave hypocrisy and judicial malpractice. With the potential scandal in mind, it's unthinkable Bacon would have allowed the play-going argument to be introduced at all.

Fourteen years later, in 1615, Bacon was prosecuting a man who criticized forced payments to the Crown. "Benevolences," as these taxes were called, amounted to extortion, the man declared, and were reminiscent of the tyrannies of Richard II. Bacon replied, "For your comparison with Richard II, I see you follow the example of them that brought him upon the stage and into print in Queen Elizabeth's time"[15]—a retort that, like the charge against Essex, exposes Bacon to scandal if he himself was one of those who wrote a play about the deposed king.

Nonetheless, Bacon was indeed a "concealed poet." Manuscripts of a first draft and final copy of an interlude performed before Queen Elizabeth on 17 November 1595 survive in Bacon's handwriting, yet at the time they were attributed to "Mr. Cuffe, servant to the Earl of Essex."[16] Henry Cuffe was another follower of the earl, one who lost his head after the Essex Rebellion. The interlude itself, a series of orations praising the Queen, is composed in a stilted, carefully wrought language, bearing no relation to the writing style of the Author.

What has been called "the best evidence for Bacon"[17] turns out not to be evidence at all. In 1597, Joseph Hall in his *Satires* ridiculed a writer whom he referred to by the pseudonym "Labeo," the name of a bad poet—Attius Labeo—who lived during the reign of Nero and made a ridiculous translation of *The Iliad*:

> For shame write better *Labeo*, or write none
> Or better write, or *Labeo* write alone.
> Nay, call the *Cynick* but a witty fool,
> Thence to abjure his handsome drinking bowl:

Because the thirsty swain with hollow hand
Conveyed the stream to wet his dry weasand.
Write they that can, tho they that cannot do:
But who knows that, but they that do not know.[18]

A year later, in an appendix to *Pigmalions Image*, John Marston seemed to identify Labeo as the Author. He wrote,

So Labeo did complain his love was stone,
Obdurate, flinty, so relentless none[19]

which is a paraphrase of lines 199 and 200 of *Venus and Adonis*:

Art thou obdurate, flinty, hard as steel?
Nay, more than flint, for stone at rain relenteth.

Also in 1598, Marston responded to Hall's *Satires* with *Satires* of his own. He defended some of the disguised writers he assumed Hall had attacked, but he made no further mention of Labeo. Baconian Walter Bagley, however, believes Labeo was alluded to in the line

What, not *mediocria firma* from thy spite?[20]

Mediocria firma ("the middle way is surest") was Bacon's family motto. If Bacon was Labeo, and Labeo wrote *Venus and Adonis*, then Bacon is the Author. But there's a problem. Although it's possible (though not likely) that "mediocria firma" was intended to refer to Bacon, only wishful thinking connects it to Labeo. So Bagley's evidence is imaginary. In addition, Hall specified in Book VI of his *Satires* that Labeo was a writer of "heroic" and romantic poetry, who imitated Sir Philip Sidney and who would

filch whole pages at a clap for need
From honest Petrarch, clad in English weed.[21]

Probably Hall had Samuel Daniel or Michael Drayton in mind.[22] Daniel had written the heroic *Civil Wars* and the Sidney-inspired *Delia*, while Drayton had stolen from Petrarch for his sonnet cycle, *Idea's Mirror*. Whoever it was, it wasn't the Author.

As for parallelisms, Professor Steven May sums up their basic short-coming. "Elizabethan poets" he writes, "drew upon a broad, common range of motifs, rhetorical devices, allusions, and adages, so that, given the relative abundance of [the Author's] verse, it would be surprising indeed to find a contemporary poet whose themes and phrasing did not correspond at some point and in some way with a passage or two by the Bard."[23] For example, "all the world's a stage" was an observation shared by Lodge, Chapman, Marston, Nashe, Rowley, Jonson, Webster, Beaumont and Fletcher, Massinger, Sir Thomas Browne, Bacon, and of course the Author. Many alleged parallels, though, are simply common expressions that can be found in any other writer, even today. Joseph Sobran cites *fertile soil*, *high degree*, *speedy haste* as well as the associations of *reaps* and *harvest*, *harvest* and *toil*, and *bees* and *honey* in a poem by the Earl of Oxford and in the Author's Works.[24] He then claims the number of parallel commonplaces is significant, but of course it's not. Given the enormous sample size of the Poet's output, one can find plenty of ordinary expressions. It's the uncommon ones that count. So even though three-quarters of Bacon's favorite maxims can be found in the Plays and Poems, it's not evidence; there are, after all, only so many English proverbs.[25] There is also the problem of pla-giarism, which in the days before copyright laws was rampant. All Eliz-abethan writers stole from common sources and from each other, consciously and sometimes unconsciously. John Ford seems to have borrowed quite a bit from the Author, whereas the Author borrowed from Marlowe. Since Bacon's parallel passages all postdate the publi-cation or performance of the allegedly similar passages in the Canon, it's quite possible Bacon saw and read the work of the Author and was influenced by it.

I hesitate to mention the oddest aspects of the Baconian case—the cryptograms, the ciphers, the secret codes that, it is claimed, the philoso-pher incorporated into his poetry in order to reveal his authorship to fu-ture generations. These have been discredited—most effectively in *The Shakespearean Ciphers Examined*, by William and Elizabeth Friedman—so I won't browbeat them here; nor will I comment at all on their concealed messages (which no one has been able to decode independently) such as that Bacon was the rightful king of England, being the son of Queen Eliz-abeth and the Earl of Leicester, whom she married in secret, and that, in addition to the Canon of Shakespeare, he wrote the works of Marlowe, Peele, Greene, Spenser, Jonson, Robert Burton, Montaigne, and Cer-vantes.[26] Some things speak for themselves.

GROUP THEORIES

Inevitably, dissatisfaction with Bacon as a candidate led some heretics to modify their position. If Bacon's lack of military experience bothered them, they simply envisioned a collaborator like Sir Walter Ralegh, who had the necessary expertise. If his connections to the theatrical world seemed tenuous, they added a professional playwright, like Marlowe or Jonson. One of the first of these Groupists was Delia Bacon. Her imagined coterie included Ralegh, Bacon, Spenser, Sidney, Lord Buckhurst, Lord Paget, and the Earl of Oxford. By 1881, Appleton Morgan granted Shakespeare a copyist role but felt the writing was all done by noblemen—Southampton, Ralegh, Essex, Rutland, the Earl of Montgomery, and Bacon. Thomas W. White, in *Our English Homer* (1892), could make do without any noblemen, except for Bacon; his team had Greene, Peele, Daniel, Marlowe, Shakespeare, Nashe, and Lodge, with Bacon serving as the general editor. W. G. Ziegler, three years later, made do without Bacon, attributing the plays to Marlowe, Ralegh, Rutland, and others. In 1931, Gilbert Slater was the first, but not the last, to include the Countess of Pembroke in a group. And Wallace McCook Cunningham perhaps holds the record for the largest group, pairing Bacon with seventy others, including naval hero Sir Francis Drake and Henry VIII's Chancellor, Sir Thomas More.

Thomas W. White's title is significant. Around the turn of the twentieth century, it was believed that the lyrics of Homer were actually the creations of many different poets, and the same was believed of the Author. Even orthodox Stratfordian scholars held that large chunks of the Canon were the work of other men. Today, however, because of stylistic analyses performed during the past hundred years, both oeuvres have been vindicated as the productions, for the most part, of single individuals.

Given the Canon's enormous lexicon, it may seem logical that many hands created the Work, and indeed some of the plays, like *Two Noble Kinsmen* and *Pericles*, are collaborations while others (probably) are revisions of other men's plays. But the vast bulk of material bears the stamp of one man. We know this for several reasons. First of all, the Author repeatedly returns to the same source books, most famously Holinshed's *Chronicles* (1587 edition), Ovid's *Metamorphoses* (Golding's translation), and North's *Plutarch's Lives*. In four different plays (*Love's Labor's Lost*, *Romeo and Juliet*, *Richard II*, and *Henry IV Part Two*), he refers to the contemporary ballad "King Cophetua and the Beggar Maid." Did a group pass these volumes around? It seems unlikely. Furthermore, in the Plays and Poems there is a striking consistency of image and idea. The Author returns again and again to the same idiosyncratic phrases and associations. For example, as Spurgeon shows, he connects *eyes* and *vaults*.[27] Consider:

> And I will kiss [Death's] detestable bones,
> And put my *eyeballs* in thy *vaulty* brows
>
> (*King John*, III.iv.29–30)

and

> Startles mine *eyes*, and makes me more amaz'd
> Than had I seen the *vaulty* top of heaven
>
> (*King John*, V.ii.51–52)

and

> Hath nature given them *eyes*
> To see this *vaulted* arch and the rich crop
> Of sea and land
>
> (*Cymbeline*, I.vi.33–35)

and

> I'll say yon grey is not the morning's *eye*,
> 'Tis but the pale reflex of Cynthia's brow;
> Nor that is not the lark whose notes do beat
> The *vaulty* heaven so high above our heads
>
> (*Romeo and Juliet*. III.v.19–22)

and

> Had I your tongues and *eyes*, I'ld use them so
> That heaven's *vault* should crack
>
> (*King Lear*, V.iii.259–60)

and even in *Timon of Athens* appears the phrase "when our vaults have wept" (II.ii.159). *Eye* leads to *vault*, which he further seems to associate with the sky. The sun is the eye of the sky under the brow of heaven. Likewise, dogs, candy, and flattery are associated in *Henry IV Part One*:

141

> Why, what a candy deal of courtesy
> This fawning greyhound then did proffer me
>
> (I.iii.251–52)

in *Antony and Cleopatra*,

>   The hearts
> That spaniel'd me at heels, to whom I gave
> Their wishes, do discandy, melt their sweets
> On blossoming Caesar
>
> (IV.xii.20–23)

in *Julius Caesar*,

> With that which melteth fools—I mean sweet words,
> Low-crooked curtsies, and base spaniel fawning
>
> (III.i.42–43)

in *Hamlet*,

> No, let the candied tongue lick absurd pomp,
> And crook the pregnant hinges of the knee
> Where thrift may follow fawning
>
> (III.ii.60–62)

and elsewhere.[28] From play to play, the Author makes reference to the same pool of adages—the superstition, for instance, that he who is born to be hanged can never drown. In *Two Gentlemen of Verona*, Proteus tells Valentine's servant,

> Go, go, be gone, to save your ship from wrack,
> Which cannot perish having thee aboard,
> Being destin'd to a drier death on shore.
>
> (I.i.148–50)

In *Henry VI Part Two*, the queen says,

> The pretty-vaulting sea refus'd to drown me,
> Knowing that thou wouldst have me drown'd on shore,
> With tears as salt as sea, through thy unkindness.
>
> (III.ii.94–96)

And even a late play like *The Tempest* has Gonzalo hope the Boatswain's presence will prevent a shipwreck:

> I have great comfort from this fellow. Methinks he hath no
>   drowning mark upon him, his complexion is perfect gallows.
>   Stand fast, good Fate, to his hanging.

(I.i.28–31)

This particular adage is used by countless other writers; its *repeated* use is what marks it as evidence of a single mind. Finally, the Author's writing style is unlike anyone else's. It's basically monosyllabic ("To be or not to be . . ."), but it employs a vast vocabulary, combining words from wildly disparate areas of knowledge and experience ("I have sounded the very base-string of humility"; "he draweth out the thread of his verbosity"; "Patch grief with proverbs"). The Author has a fondness for puns and wordplay ("the bawdy hand of the dial is upon the prick of noon"), for unusual compound adjectives ("honor-flaw'd," "sin-concealing," "dark-working"), and for double epithets—two words of similar meaning joined by a conjunction ("book and volume of the brain," "knotted and combined locks," "rash and unbridled boy"). His many neologisms—invented words—usually have Anglo-Saxon roots ("enskyed," "empoison," "unrecalling"); Bacon's neologisms, in contrast, were Latinate ("instauration") or Greek ("euthanasia"). In the Author's poetry, nouns can become verbs ("but if you mouth it"), and word order is often inverted ("bawd I'll turn" instead of *I'll turn bawd*). Similes are usually extended ("As an unperfect actor on the stage,/Who with his fear is put besides his part"), and personifications, his favorite kind of metaphor, tend to "animate the inanimate," in critic Alfred Harbage's phrase, to give movement to the unmoving ("my sword weeps for the poor king's death"). Harbage has noticed that the human personifications ("the pitiful eye of tender day") are associated with the good, while subhuman ones ("the jaws of darkness to devour it up") are associated with evil.[29] Overall, it's a style in which word-pictures and metaphorical language constantly move us beyond the immediate dramatic situation to the realm of imagination.

There was only one Author. Suggesting otherwise raises some rather uncomfortable questions. For starters, how did the proposed group operate—like a quilting bee, with all the writers sitting around a single table? Or did they each write from different locations and their work was somehow spliced together? With more Authors involved in the conspiracy, including several prominent citizens, how was it possible to maintain the secret for so long? The greater the number of conspirators, the greater the probability of exposure. Seeing the folly of their theories, most (but not all) proponents of a group Authorship returned to championing individual candidates.

WILLIAM STANLEY, SIXTH EARL OF DERBY

An archivist named James Greenstreet first proposed Derby in 1891. He discovered two letters concerning the earl, sent by a Jesuit spy with the name or pseudonym of George Fenner. Fenner was reporting on the possibility of persuading certain English noblemen to join in a plot against the Queen. Both of his letters were dated 30 June 1599, and both were intercepted by the counterespionage service of the Privy Council. In both, one of which he was sending to Antwerp and the other to Venice, he scribbled, "Th'erle of Derby is busyed only in penning comedies for the common players."[30] Whether the earl was really a playwright or whether Fenner was speaking in code is unknown, but Greenstreet was convinced that Derby was a writer—and not just a writer but the Author.

Greenstreet's candidate, William Stanley, was born in 1561, the second son of Henry, Lord Strange, the future fourth Earl of Derby. After a childhood passed at the family estates in Warwickshire and Lancashire, William matriculated at age eleven, along with his elder brother Ferdinando, at St. John's College, Oxford. Ten years later, his studies completed, he traveled abroad with his tutor, Richard Lloyd. Together they toured the continent for five years, visiting France and Spain and probably, although there is no record of it, Italy, Greece, and the Holy Land. In Spain, according to one story, he fought a duel and escaped the country disguised as a friar. What's more certain is that he returned home in 1587. From that point, according to Derbyites, he may have been involved with his brother's acting troupe, Lord Strange's Men, a company that many of the later Lord Chamberlain's Men belonged to. In September 1592, William was appointed governor of the Isle of Man. He served as the island's chief judge and top administrator for fourteen months, during which time his father died and his brother became the fifth Earl. Two months after Ferdinando's accession, William returned to London. He would not be an earl's brother for long, though. On April 16, 1594, Ferdinando died under mysterious circumstances—he may have been poisoned—and William became the sixth Earl of Derby. One would think his new responsibilities would be enough to keep him occupied for at least six months, but in August he became a member of Lincoln's Inn, probably using it not as a law school but as a social club where he could mingle with others interested in legal questions. The following January (1595), he married Elizabeth Vere, the daughter of the Earl of Oxford. At the wedding celebration, the Lord Chamberlain's Men may have performed *A Midsummer Night's Dream* for the first time.[31] When the new reign began in 1603, Derby became a Privy Councillor and, later, Lord Lieutenant of Lancashire and Cheshire, reporting on the training and condition of troops to be sent to Ireland. In 1612, he was awarded the kingship of the Isle of Man, a title that had been in his family for generations and was now restored to him. By 1627, he retired into a life of privacy, living on £1000 a year. He died in 1642 at the age of eighty-one.

As an anti-Stratfordian suspect, Derby is just about perfect. Noble-blooded, Oxford-educated, well-traveled, he even studied law, had military knowledge, liked hunting and hawking, had Catholic sympathies, knew foreign courts, loved the theatre,[32] and possibly had contact with William Shakespeare, if the actor was one of Lord Strange's players. Certainly, he had the right first name for the "Will" sonnets and the right initials for poems signed "W. S." None of Derby's plays, if he wrote any, survive in his own name, and only a few of his letters are extant, so there's no inconvenient paper trail that can be compared to the Works.

If Derby was indeed a writer, then perhaps Spenser is referring to him in his poem *Colin Clouts Come Home Againe,* under the pseudonym of "Aetion":

> And there though last not least is *Aetion,*
> A gentler shepheard may no where be found:
> Whose *Muse* full of high thoughts invention,
> Doth like himselfe Heroically sound.[33]

These lines immediately follow praise for the recently deceased Ferdinando Stanley and his mourning wife, Alice (called "Amytas" and "Amarillis" in the poem), and they precede praise for "Astrofell" (Sir Philip Sidney) and "Cynthia" (Queen Elizabeth). It's possible, therefore, that "Aetion" was Derby, especially if Spenser knew that the earl's heroic poetry was similar to his bombastic way of expressing himself. Furthermore, "Aetion" means man of the eagle, and there's an eagle on the crest of the Stanley coat of arms. But wait. It's also possible that "Aetion" refers to Shakespeare. If Shakespeare had been one of Ferdinando's players,

Spenser could be thinking of the Poet immediately after his patron. The words "like himselfe" would then refer not to his way of speaking but to his name. Derbyites put these two interpretations together and claim that since Spenser could be alluding to Derby, and could be alluding to Shakespeare, he must be alluding to both. A very strange bit of reasoning. A just-as-likely "Aetion" is William Warner, whom Francis Meres cites as one of the best writers of heroic poetry and whose surname contains "war." Another possibility, if Spenser was grouping high-ranking courtier poets together and if he wrote a lot of martial poetry that is now lost, is the Earl of Essex. "Aetion" proves nothing.

Like all Authorship heretics, Derby's partisans imagine people from their claimant's life are reflected in the plays. Derby's tutor, Richard Lloyd, is seen as the model for the pedant Holofernes in *Love's Labor's Lost*; his friend, the astrologer John Dee, is claimed to be the original for Prospero in *The Tempest*; his steward, William Farrington, inspired *Twelfth Night*'s Malvolio. In fact, in *Love's Labor's Lost*, the Author does lampoon a book by Richard Lloyd: *A brief discourse of the most renowned acts and right valiant conquests of those puissant Princes called the Nine Worthies* . . . (1584). Lloyd's line, "A lion which sitting in a chair hent a battle-axe in his paw argent" becomes "your lion, that holds his pole-axe sitting on a close-stool" in the Author's play. So, perhaps, Lloyd *was* one of the models for the pedant Holofernes. But this proves nothing either. Lloyd's book was published so anyone could have used it as a source. Especially Shakespeare. As an actor working with former members of Lord Strange's Men, Shakespeare would have had ample opportunities to hear of Richard Lloyd and his book. If he was himself one of Ferdinando's players, he probably included the parody to amuse his patron or even his patron's brother.

The alleged evidence isn't evidence at all. Nothing recommends Derby as the Author, and two things speak against him. The first is that he died in 1642. If, when his front man died, he stopped writing plays under the name of William Shakespeare, why didn't he switch to another name? Where are the plays and poems from the last thirty years of his life? If he retired, as Derbyites assume, why didn't he, in secret, edit the First Folio for publication? The other point is that he had his own company of players, the Earl of Derby's Men. They seemed to have been formed soon after Stanley became an earl, presenting plays at Norwich by September 1594. They performed Heywood's *Edward IV* and the anonymous play *The Trial of Chivalry* among others, and they acted before the Queen in 1600 and 1601. According to a mention of them, they were still in existence in 1618.[34] So why did Derby continue to write plays for his brother's old company (now the Lord Chamberlain's) and not for his own? He could just as easily have written anonymous works for the players he was financially contributing to.

Still, it's a wonder Derby is not the favorite Authorship claimant. He fits the mold of what the heretics say they're looking for in every way. But perhaps too little is known about his personality, so he doesn't capture the imagination as a Bacon or an Oxford does. To trade Shakespeare for Derby is to exchange one unknown for another, and part of the appeal of an alternative Author is that it's someone with a dashing figure and a distinctive voice separate from his poetry.

CHRISTOPHER MARLOWE

Believers in Marlowe's candidacy have a conception of the Author different from that of the Baconians, Oxfordians, Derbyites, and Rutlanders. For them, the Poet was not a nobleman, lawyer, or soldier; he was a divinity student and a spy.

Marlowe was born in Canterbury, home to the famous cathedral, in 1564, three months before Shakespeare. Though ostensibly from the same class, Marlowe grew up in somewhat meaner circumstances than did the alderman's son. His debt-ridden father was a shoemaker and did not own multiple houses and great tracts of farmland as Shakespeare's father did. It was a scholarship to the King's School—a university preparatory school, attached to Canterbury Cathedral—that first offered Marlowe, at age fourteen, prospects beyond the life of a tradesman.

Prior to his enrollment, there is no record of his attending grammar school, but we can assume he did, given his later academic accomplishments. In 1581 he entered Cambridge on another scholarship. There, he studied divinity for the next six years,[35] but his education was interrupted by several long absences. When the university withheld his degree because the dons had heard a rumor that he had been sneaking off to the Jesuit seminary at Rheims, France,[36] the Privy Council sent a letter explaining that Marlowe had been out of the country in service to the government. Apparently, he had been posing as a Catholic convert in order to spy on the Rheims seminarians. At the urging of the highest ministers in the government, Marlowe was awarded his M.A. But he did not enter the Anglican priesthood. Marlowe continued his work as a government agent and began his illustrious career as a playwright and poet. Before his death in 1593 he penned seven plays, including *The Jew of Malta*, *Doctor Faustus*, and *Edward II*, two major poems—*Hero and Leander* and *The Passionate Shepheard to His Love*—and translations of Lucan's *Pharsalia* and Ovid's *Elegies*.

Sir Thomas Walsingham, whose cousin Francis headed the secret service, became the young playwright's patron soon after his graduation from Cambridge. Marlowe also enjoyed the friendship of Sir Walter Ralegh, the astronomer and mathematician Thomas Hariot, the Earl of Northumberland (called the "Wizard Earl" because of his interest in the occult), and other members of Ralegh's freethinking philosophical circle, known to its enemies as the "School of Atheism." These associations, Marlovians, like A. D. Wraight believe, are reflected throughout the plays and poems of the Author.

In 1589, Marlowe was attacked in the street by William Bradley, an innkeeper's son, who recognized him as a friend of the poet Thomas Watson, Bradley's sworn enemy. Marlowe fended off his assailant with rapier and dagger until Watson arrived on the scene. Onlookers claimed that upon seeing Watson, the hotheaded Bradley left his fight with Marlowe to engage the newcomer. A few minutes later, Bradley was dead and Watson's sword was dripping with his blood. The two poets were arrested, and Marlowe spent two weeks in Newgate Prison. (Watson was released five months later on a verdict of "self-defense.")[37] Marlovians insist this incident inspired the swordfight in the third act of *Romeo and Juliet*, even though its particulars are different.[38]

The playwright was arrested again in January 1592 in the English-occupied city of Vlissingen, or Flushing, in Holland. This time the charge was "coining." He had induced a goldsmith to make and pass off a counterfeit Dutch shilling. Both men, the goldsmith and Marlowe, were denounced by Richard Baines, a government informer who was Marlowe's "chamber-fellow," and all three were shipped back to London. After another brief stay in prison, say his supporters, Marlowe was qualified to write the line in Sonnet 74, "when that fell arrest/Without all bail shall carry me away . . ."

By May he was a free man again. We know this because he was bound over to the constables of Shoreditch at that time in order to "keep the peace."[39]

Later in 1592, the poet was home in Canterbury and quarreled with William Corkine, a tailor and part-time musician. The two men decided to fight a duel—a duel, in the Marlovian imagination, similar to the one between Hamlet and Laertes. Unlike the fictional contest, though, the weapons of choice were "staff and dagger," and neither participant was killed. Marlowe and Corkine were hauled before the local judge and accused of disturbing the peace. Subsequently, they sued each other for assault, but by the time their case came to court, the men protested they were now reconciled and had become fast friends (like Hamlet and Laertes, who exchange forgiveness as they lay dying). Corkine's son, in fact, later set Marlowe's *Passionate Shepheard* to music.[40]

A more deadly fracas occurred on 30 May 1593. At a house in the London suburb of Deptford, Marlowe was stabbed through the eye with a dagger. What exactly happened may never be known, but an official version of the event was approved by the coroner's inquest. Four men—"Christopher Morley," Ingram Frizer, Nicholas Skeres, and Robert Poley—all gentlemen, had met at the house of Eleanor Bull, a widow, around ten in the morning. For a few hours, they conferred together in a room until they were served dinner. After dinner they "were in a quiet sort" for a while, and then they walked in the garden until six o'clock. At that time, they returned to the room and called for their supper. When they had finished eating, an altercation erupted between Marlowe and Frizer over the bill, the "reckoning." Marlowe was lying on a bed at the time, and Frizer was seated at the table between Skeres and Poley, facing away from the bed. Suddenly, Marlowe leapt up, grabbed Frizer's dagger, which was in a scabbard behind its owner's back, and gave Frizer two wounds in the head. Trapped between the two other men, Frizer struggled with Marlowe for the weapon and, "in defense of his life," stabbed Marlowe over the right eyelid, killing him instantly.[41]

That's the official version. Left out of the coroner's report was any further identification of the men and what they talked about as they strolled Mistress Bull's garden. Poley, Skeres, and Frizer were, like Marlowe, secret agents. As Charles Nicholl has shown in his acclaimed study of Elizabethan espionage, *The Reckoning* (1992), Poley was a longtime operative of the Cecils (Burghley and Sir Robert); Skeres served the Earl of Essex; and Frizer worked for Sir Thomas Walsingham, who was Marlowe's patron, though perhaps all of them were really employed by the Cecils.[42] Their discussion that day undoubtedly centered on recent developments in the world of espionage.

On the night of May 5th, a libellous 53-line poem had been tacked up on the wall of the Dutch churchyard in London. It accused Dutch, French, and Italian immigrants of a variety of crimes and called for violence against them. And it did so with allusions to three plays by Christopher Marlowe. By May 12th, Marlowe's former roommate, the playwright Thomas Kyd, had been arrested for the libel and tortured. Under interrogation, Kyd was informed that a heretical manuscript, three pages long, had been found among his papers, a manuscript denying Christ's divinity. It was a "fragment of a disputation," as Kyd later described it, copied out of an old book in an italic hand. Kyd affirmed that the document belonged to Marlowe and must have been "shuffled" with his own papers when they were writing together in the same chamber. Meanwhile, an informer's report against an agitator named Richard Cholmeley (pronounced "Chumley") was delivered to the government. Among its allegations was that Cholmeley

> saith & verily believeth that one Marlowe is able to show more sound reasons for atheism than any divine in England is able to prove divinity, & that Marlowe told him he had read the atheist lecture to Sir Walter Ralegh & others.[43]

With evidence mounting against him, Marlowe was apprehended on May 18th at Scadbury, Thomas Walsingham's estate, where the poet was living. Two days later, he appeared before the Privy Council for questioning. But Marlowe was not detained; he was set free on bail and ordered to report to the Council daily. Someone highly placed, probably the Cecils, may have intervened on his behalf. Why he did not report to the Council on the day he was murdered is one of the mysteries surrounding his death. On May 27th, his old chamber-fellow Richard Baines had sent a sworn statement to the authorities, listing the blasphemies he had heard Marlowe utter. These included that "Moses was but a juggler," that is, a sham magician, "that the first beginning of religion was to keep men in awe," "that Christ was a bastard and his mother dishonest," "that St. John the Evangelist was bedfellow to Christ," "that he used him as the sinners of Sodom," and "that all they that love not tobacco and boys are fools." All of these accusations and the previous month's events would have been under discussion in Mistress Bull's garden.

Did that discussion lead to Marlowe's murder? Did the poet-spy say something that led the others to decide he couldn't leave the house alive? We don't know.

Whatever transpired, it was probably not the story the coroner was told at the inquest. That version of events seems concocted to win a verdict of self-defense for Frizer and to keep Skeres and Poley uninvolved. Still, something like the men's testimony might have happened. An argument over the "sum of pence" could have escalated, provoking Frizer to pull a knife; Marlowe seems to have had that effect on people.

In any case, the official version won out. Frizer spent a month in jail and was then pardoned by the Queen.

Enter the Marlovians. In 1895, W. G. Ziegler suggested that Marlowe's murder was not a mystery at all. He proposed, in the introduction to his novel *It Was Marlowe*, that Marlowe survived his supposed death and went on to write the plays of Shakespeare with Ralegh, Rutland, and others. After the discovery of the inquest report in 1925, Gilbert Slater conjectured the entire episode in Deptford was staged, that another man's body—perhaps a sailor's—was substituted in Marlowe's place while the poet fled the country unseen; he then returned having assumed a new identity and became one of Slater's *Seven Shakespeares*. In 1955, Calvin Hoffman elaborated on the scenario, asserting that Marlowe lived the rest of his life abroad, writing plays that found their way back to England and into the repertory of the Lord Chamberlain's Men. He attributed the whole Shakespeare Canon to Marlowe in his book *The Murder of the Man Who Was Shakespeare*. More recent Marlovians claim that once in exile Marlowe wrote the Sonnets, the bulk of which express his longing for his patron/lover, Sir Thomas Walsingham.[44]

Is there any validity in these theories? Could the Marlovians be right? Well, they correctly point out that Poley, Skeres, and Frizer were informers, swindlers, and con men—not assassins. A political murder, if that's what it was, could be more efficiently carried out by professionals; a slit throat in a dark alley and no one's the wiser. But the inference they draw from these facts is not the simple one—that the murder was unplanned. They conclude there was no murder at all, or rather that a different, unknown man was killed.

Other facts speak against this theory. First of all, there was no extradition at this time, so all one had to do to make Marlowe disappear was get him to the Continent under an assumed name. The staged murder would have been superfluous.[45] Second, Marlowe's body was not hastily buried in the night as Marlovians assume. The inquest was not conducted until 1 June, roughly thirty-six hours after the murder. There was plenty of time for anyone who knew Marlowe to have seen the body; sixteen jurors in addition to the coroner viewed the corpse. The conspirators were taking a mighty chance that their fraud would not be discovered on 31 May or 1 June, before the playwright was buried in the churchyard across the street. At the ceremony, one of the pallbearers was the publisher Edward Blount, who tells us as much in his dedication of *Hero and Leander* in 1598:

> We think not ourselves discharged of the duty we owe to our friend when we have brought the breathless body to the earth. For albeit the eye there taketh his ever-farewell of that beloved object, yet the impression of the man that hath been dear unto us, living an afterlife in our memory, there putteth us in mind of further obsequies due unto the deceased.[46]

[spelling modernized]

Marlowe was dead. And no one, anywhere, reports seeing him alive after 30 May 1593.

But let's say the Marlovians are right. Let's say another man died in Deptford, and Marlowe was whisked off in the night to France or Italy, and by some magic he got his plays and poems back to a front man in London. That front man was not William Shakespeare.

Simply put, Marlowe doesn't write like "Shakespeare." His vocabulary is smaller and less encyclopedic.[47] His language is less imaginative, less metaphorical. He doesn't revel in puns and wordplay. In addition, he lacks the Author's sense of humor; Marlowe is rarely funny. At the centers of his plays are megalomaniacal antiheroes whose ambitions are larger, and whose cynicism is more misanthropic, than any characters in Shakespeare. Spurgeon shows that the quality of his imagery is different too. With the Author, images from "nature (especially the weather, plants and gardening), animals (especially birds), . . . the body in health and sickness, indoor life, fire, light, food and cooking, easily come first; whereas with Marlowe, images drawn from books, especially the classics, and from the sun, moon, planets and heavens far outnumber all others."[48] He makes few allusions to the behaviors of insects, birds, reptiles, fish, and other fauna, suggesting he did not observe the natural world as closely as the Author did.

Beyond style is the question of sources. For Marlowe to write the Canon in exile, he would have needed access to all the sources the Author used, which were published in the 1590s and early 1600s. Few of those works are likely to have made it across the Channel.

The only aspect of the Marlovian case that holds any water is in parallel passages. Aside from common phrases, the Author stole, parodied, quoted, or used as a template, numerous lines from Marlowe's plays and poems. "These arms of mine shall be thy . . . sepulchure" (*Henry VI Part*

Two/Jew of Malta), "the moon sleeps with Endymion" (*Merchant of Venice*/Marlowe's translation of Ovid's *Elegies*), "pampered jades of Asia" (*Henry IV Part Two/Tamburlaine Part Two*), and so forth. He knew his rival's compositions well. And he knew something of Marlowe's death. In *As You Like It*, he ascribes a line from *Hero and Leander* to a poet who has died:

> Dead shepherd, now I find thy saw of might,
> "Who ever lov'd that lov'd not at first sight?"
>
> (III.v.80–81)

"Shepherd," in Elizabethan verse, was a conventional term for poet. In the same play is the line:

> When a man's verses cannot be understood, nor a man's good
> wit seconded with the forward child, understanding, it strikes
> a man more dead than a great reckoning in a little room
>
> (III.iii.12–15)

The Author is toying with Marlowe's "Infinite riches in a little room" (*The Jew of Malta*, I.i.37), substituting "great reckoning" for "infinite riches," to create an allusion to the murder. To have one's verses not understood is a greater death than being struck down as Marlowe was.

⁓

Marlowe's candidacy exposes the subjective nature of the Authorship debate. Each heretic makes different assumptions about what the Author knows and has experienced. Advocates for Marlowe see the Author as highly educated and a friend of courtiers, but not a courtier himself. They do not believe the Poet was a soldier or a lawyer. Anti-Stratfordians who think the Author must have studied law or been an aristocrat look elsewhere for a candidate, eventually finding one who satisfies their personal criteria. This is why the twentieth century witnessed an explosion of claimants, from King James (Malcolm X's suspect) to Anne Whateley.

Since 1920, many have turned to Edward de Vere, seventeenth Earl of Oxford. In that year, schoolmaster J. Thomas Looney published his seductive and seminal ideas. It's to those ideas, and the ideas of his followers, that we must now apply our magnifying glass.

CHAPTER 10
The Accused

Edward de Vere, the middle child and only son of John de Vere, sixteenth Earl of Oxford, was born on 12 April 1550. He had a younger sister, Mary, and an elder half-sister, Katherine, who was his father's daughter by his first wife. He had no brothers. This is surprising because fraternal rivalry is such a major theme in the plays that many anti-Stratfordians, especially Baconians, Rutlanders, and Derbyites, think that only a man with a brother could have written *King Lear*, *As You Like It*, *The Tempest*, and the history plays.[1] Oxford does not match their profiles. (Oxfordians scoff at these other camps, but they will not admit that their own profiles, which lead them to de Vere, are just as subjective.)

In November 1558, at the precocious age of eight-and-a-half, Edward enrolled at Cambridge. He was younger than the average "impubes" student; most sons of the nobility turned ten or eleven before they were sent to college. Perhaps he was *too* young. After being in residence for six months, he left to be tutored in the house of Sir Thomas Smith.

In 1562, when Edward was twelve, his father died and he inherited the "proud titles" of Earl of Oxford, Viscount Bulbeck, Baron Scales and Badlesmere, and Lord Great Chamberlain of England. He was sent, like other young earls, to live as a royal ward in the London residence of Sir William Cecil, who would later become Lord Burghley. There, Oxfordians imagine, he was tutored by his mother's brother, Arthur Golding, the man whose translation of *The Metamorphoses* would be widely used in grammar schools. But in fact his tutor was the scholar Lawrence Nowell.[2] Burghley's "orders" for the earl's "exercises" still survive, and they give us a window into what a typical day was like for the young ward:

154

7:00–7:30[a.m.]   Dancing
7:30–8:00   Breakfast
8:00–9:00   French
9:00–10:00   Latin
10:00–10:30   Writing and Drawing
The Common Prayers and so to Dinner
1:00–2:00[p.m.]   Cosmography
2:00–3:00   Latin
3:00–4:00   French
4:00–5:00   Exercises with his pen
The Common Prayers and so to Supper.[3]

Having studied French two hours a day, at thirteen he was able to write a letter in better French than the Author ever demonstrates.[4] In later life, de Vere owned and read books in the language and seems to have been fluent in French conversation. In contrast, the Author's French, as described by the great Edwardian critic Sir Sidney Lee, was "grammatically accurate if not idiomatic."[5] Stiff, in other words. Betraying effort. One need only compare the studied, high-school French of *Henry V* to the assured expression of Oxford's 1563 letter to see that the Author was not as good a linguist as the earl.

Nor was he as good a historian. Arthur Golding praises his nephew's enthusiasm "to read, peruse, and communicate with others as well, the histories of ancient times, and things done long ago"[6] in a dedication to Oxford in 1564. The Author, on the other hand, makes errors in the history plays that no earl would make. Following Holinshed's *Chronicles*, he confuses Sir Edmund Mortimer (who married the daughter of Owen Glendower) with Mortimer's nephew, the fifth Earl of March, who was recognized by Richard II as his heir.

In 1563, de Vere's title was challenged by his half-sister's husband, who questioned the validity of John de Vere's second marriage and, thus, Oxford's legitimacy. Nothing came of this suit, but the threat of bastardy, Oxfordians claim, qualified Edward to create Philip Faulconbridge the Bastard in *King John*.

Less than two years after his father's death, de Vere's mother remarried. According to Oxfordians, this hasty wedding provided the young Oxford with the necessary biographical experience to accurately represent Hamlet's emotions when *his* mother hastily remarries.

In 1564 and 1566, the Queen paid visits to the universities (Cambridge and Oxford), and on both occasions honorary degrees were awarded to distinguished guests, including de Vere.[7] The following year he was admitted to Gray's Inn to study law, although he was never in residence there. He was still living at Cecil House.

In July 1567, he stabbed a drunken undercook named Thomas Bricknell in the leg with a rapier. Bricknell died of the wound a few hours later. "I did my best," Burghley later wrote, "to have the [inquest] jury find the death of the poor man whom he killed in my house to be found *se defendendo*."[8] That is, in self-defense. Burghley must have succeeded well enough because the verdict was *felo-de-se*, death as a result of one's own crime. Bricknell, the jury found, was the aggressor, though Burghley's pity for the "poor man" would seem to indicate he was the victim. Many Oxfordians like to see this episode as the inspiration for Hamlet's stabbing of Polonius behind an arras, but the Author took that event from his source in Belleforest's *Histoires Tragiques* (or a source based on it).

The Bricknell incident, whatever its details, must not have disturbed the Lord Treasurer too greatly. Three years later, Oxford was still living at Cecil House. A ledger entry from 1570 shows he purchased several books at that time: a gilt "Geneva" Bible, Amyot's French translation of Plutarch's *Lives*, and books in Italian and Latin. As we've seen, Amyot's translation was not the version the Author used. The Author did make use of a Genevan Bible, but in the early plays his quotations and references come just as often from the "Bishops" version, a prior English translation.[9]

At the end of March 1570, Oxford joined the Earl of Sussex on his campaign against the Scottish Catholic rebels. He served with Sussex for three or four months, though what his service entailed is unknown.

In May of the following year, he participated in his first tournament and astonished the Queen, as well as the galleries, with his prowess at the tilt against older and more experienced jousters. He was much admired that day, and he was admired at the other tournaments he later entered.

Oxford was suddenly a favorite at court. The Queen, a court observer noted, "delighteth more in his personage, and his dancing and valiantness, than any other."[10] With his star in the ascendant, it was time for Oxford, arguably the most eligible bachelor in England, to take a wife. So just before Christmas 1571, he married Anne Cecil, Burghley's fifteen-year-old daughter, the prototype, Oxfordians say, for Juliet, Ophelia, Desdemona, Anne Page, Coriolanus's wife, and other pure-hearted Shakespearean women.

In 1572, the earl was at the top of Fortune's wheel. He had the ear of the Queen, a powerful father-in-law, and an ally at court in his former commander, the Earl of Sussex. Looking ahead to a magnificent future, he became a generous and sought-after patron of literature and music. The poet Thomas Churchyard and the playwrights John Lyly and Anthony Munday would eventually be in his service.

We now come to the only event in Oxford's life for which there may be a legitimate, though indirect, connection to the Shakespeare plays. In May 1573, two of Oxford's former employees sent a letter to Lord Burghley from Gravesend, where they claimed to be in fear for their lives. They had been riding "peacefully by the highway from Gravesend to Rochester" when three of Oxford's men, who had been hiding in a ditch to waylay them, fired calivers at close range. The bullets whizzed by the startled travelers "within half a foot." Unable to quickly reload (this was the sixteenth century, after all), the attackers fled on horseback toward London. The intended victims, meanwhile, retreated to Gravesend, where they feared other agents of Oxford might murder them. In their letter they politely ("with pardon be it spoken") accuse Oxford of being "the procurer" of their assailants.[11]

Oxfordian B. M. Ward describes this violent encounter as a "hold up . . . on Gad's Hill, near Rochester," even though Gad's Hill is never mentioned in the letter. The reason he does this is to connect the incident to the robbery scene, set at Gad's Hill, in *Henry IV Part One*. The letter, however, details a murder attempt, not a robbery, and it strongly implies the ambush occurred near Gravesend, several miles from Gad's Hill or Rochester. The writers, Fawnt and Wotten, say "we remain here in Gravesend" as if they never really got out of town. Their enemies, they say, "fled towards London"—but if the attack had been at the Gad's Hill/Rochester end of the highway, they logically would have said their assailants fled toward Gravesend (which is in the same direction). For Fawnt and Wotten to return to Gravesend themselves, which they did, they would have had to follow their would-be assassins back up the seven-mile highway where they could be ambushed again! Logically, if the attack had been at Gad's Hill, and their assailants "fled towards London," they should have "remained" in Rochester.

In any case, this episode could not have suggested the Author's scene, because whoever wrote it lifted "Gad's Hill" from a source play, *The Famous Victories of Henry the Fifth*. Ward was well aware of this, and he was reduced to arguing that the Author also wrote *The Famous Victories*, a play about which one commentator said one may search the text "from end to end without finding a decently rhythmical passage."[12] Nonetheless, the robbery in the source play may, in some way, refer to Oxford. Much in

The Famous Victories seems complimentary to de Vere and to his ancestor, the eleventh Earl, who is a prominent character in the play. Whoever wrote the *Famous Victories* (Samuel Rowley has been suggested[13]) was probably seeking Oxford's patronage or at least trying to flatter him. He was not the Author, who follows Holinshed and reduces the role of Oxford's ancestor when he converts the source drama into his *Henry IV* plays and *Henry V*.[14]

In 1575, Oxford set off on a tour of Europe. First, he was in Paris for two months, hobnobbing with politicians and dignitaries. Then he went on to Strasbourg, where he visited the scholar Sturmius. After that, he spent three months in Padua before arriving in Venice in September. While in Venice, he found himself short of funds and borrowed five hundred crowns from a man named Baptista Nigrone. In Padua he had received more money from Pasquino Spinola. Oxfordians believe the Author conflated these two names to forge "Baptista Minola," the father's name in *The Taming of the Shrew*. Suggestive as this reasoning is, when we remember that names—not syllables but full names—from the cast of *Henry V* appear on a Stratford document, we can see that this kind of evidence points more persuasively to Shakespeare than to Oxford.

De Vere's gift for languages no doubt helped him in his travels. Unlike the Author, he spoke Italian well, according to the testimony of Orazio Coquo, a Venetian teenager he met around this time and who lived with de Vere in England for eleven months.[15]

Before he left Venice, word reached the earl that his wife had given birth to a daughter, Elizabeth, the previous July. Pleased, but determined to continue his tour, he journeyed on to Florence, Siena, and, possibly, Sicily. By March 1576 he was in Lyons (France) and the next month back in Paris.

Crossing the English Channel, his ship was seized by Dutch pirates. They stripped Oxford to his undershirt, stole what they desired and then sent the ransacked vessel on its way. Hamlet, of course, is captured by pirates too. But the Dane's vague sketch of the experience, recounted in a letter to his friend Horatio, does not give the impression that something similar once happened to the Author. "Ere we were two days old at sea," Hamlet writes,

> a pirate of very warlike appointment gave us chase. Finding ourselves too slow of sail, we put on a compell'd valor, and in the grapple I boarded them. On the instant they got clear of our ship, so I alone be-

came their prisoner. They have dealt with me like thieves of mercy, but they know what they did: I am to do a good turn for them.

(IV.vi.15–22)

In addition to the obvious differences with Oxford's ordeal, there are no idiosyncratic details here which give the impression of lived life. The pirate vessel is "warlike," there is a "grapple," the thieves expect reward for their mercy. Hamlet's mini-adventure seems to be just a plot convenience, not a memory-based scene.

The pirate encounter was not the earl's only humiliation at the time. While he was in Paris, he had heard a rumor that his daughter wasn't his. Enraged at his wife's disgrace and his own dishonor, he refused to meet his family when he disembarked in London. Despite Anne's pleas of innocence and the apparent untruth of the gossip, he would not allow her to live with him for the next five years. One is reminded that several of the Shakespeare plays—*Othello, Merry Wives of Windsor, Much Ado About Nothing, Cymbeline,* and *The Winter's Tale*—have plots involving virtuous wives whose husbands are misled into thinking they've been unfaithful. It was a common situation in the Author's sources.

Oxford returned from his travels with a taste for Italian fashions and customs. He became one of those dandies Rosalind mocks in *As You Like It*:

Farewell, Monsieur Traveller: look you lisp and wear strange suits; disable all the benefits of your own country; be out of love with your nativity, and almost chide God for making you that countenance you are; or I will scarce think you have swam in a gundello.

(IV.i.33–38)

But his tour had plunged him into debt. By 1577, he owed his creditors six thousand pounds by his own estimate, and he sold four estates to raise funds. ("I fear you have sold your own lands to see other men's," as Rosalind observes.) Selling his inherited lands had become a habit by this time. The earl was always extravagant in his purchases, in his gifts, in outfitting his footmen, in his patronage, and in his risky investments in New World exploration. He was, as Looney imagined the Author, "improvident in money matters."

He was also a poet. The author and scholar Gabriel Harvey commended Oxford in an address in July 1578, remarking that he had "seen many Latin verses of thine, yea, even more English verses are extant."[16]

William Webbe would single Oxford out, in 1586, as "the most excellent" poet among the "Lords and Gentlemen of Her Majesty's Court."[17] The author of *The Arte of English Poesie* (probably George Puttenham) seconded the assessment three years later, and ranked the earl the best "for comedy and interlude." Francis Meres reiterated Puttenham's praise in his *Palladis Tamia* (1598).

In 1579, Oxford and three other lords performed a "device," a short poetic playlet, before the Queen. This performance seems to mark the beginning of the earl's interest in drama. The next year he took over the Earl of Warwick's acting company and, in 1581, he acquired a troupe of boy actors as well. He sponsored the boys for only three years, but the men players seem to have been in his service through the end of Elizabeth's reign. From quarto title pages and the stationers' registry, we know "the Earl of Oxford's Men" performed *The Weakest Goeth to the Wall* (printed 1600) and *The History of George Scanderbarge* (registered 1602). They combined with the Earl of Worcester's Men in 1602 (as a result of Oxford's personal suit to the Queen to tolerate a new men's company), and the merged troupe became Queen Anna's Men in the new reign.[18] For Stratfordians, Oxford's sponsorship of players raises a question: With his own company of actors at his disposal, why would de Vere write plays for the Lord Chamberlain's players? Why deprive his own servants of the Shakespearean masterpieces and leave them with *George Scanderbarge*? (This same reservation, you will recall, was cited for the Earl of Derby.)

Tom Bethell believes Oxford wrote the early Shakespeare plays for court performances and then later revised them for the public theaters.[19] But if that were the case then everyone at court, from Queen Elizabeth to the lowest groom, would have known the Author's true identity. The plays, poems, and Folio, could not have been published without causing someone to blurt the truth somewhere.

Also in 1579, Oxford had a "falling out at tennis" with Philip Sidney, then not yet a knight. The earl, coming "abruptly" into the court, shouted at Sidney to remove himself. But Sidney refused to budge until the earl asked more politely. "This answer," a witness recalled, "like a bellows blowing up sparks of excess already kindled, made my Lord scornfully call Sir Philip by the name of Puppy."[20] Afterward, Sidney challenged Oxford to a duel. But the Queen got wind of it and forbade any violence. She reminded Sidney of the difference between an earl and a gentleman, and she asked him to apologize to his social superior. He refused, bowed sharply, and stormed out of the room.

The tennis court altercation was not the last conflict Oxford had with fellow courtiers. In December 1580, he confessed to the Queen that on his return from the Continent in 1576 he had pledged his allegiance to the Catholic faith along with his friends Lord Henry Howard, Charles Arundel, and Francis Southwell. The Privy Council promptly had all four arrested, though Oxford was soon freed. Under questioning, the others denied all of the earl's charges and countercharged that their accuser was a liar, a blasphemer, an atheist, a drunkard, and a buggerer. Howard even named three boys Oxford sodomized (including Orazio). Having convinced the Queen that Oxford had exaggerated their guilt, the men received only a few months imprisonment, but they were kept under house arrest for much longer. Oxfordians see this episode as the emotional blueprint for the king's uncovering of the treason of Richard Earl of Cambridge, Scroop, and Grey, in *Henry V*.

Meanwhile, Oxford was having an affair with one of the Queen's maids-of-honor, Ann Vavasor. Oxfordians picture her as the original of Beatrice in *Much Ado About Nothing*, Rosalind in *As You Like It*, Rosaline in *Love's Labor's Lost*, and other spirited female characters, though there's no evidence revealing her personality, spirited or otherwise. She is also believed (by some) to be the prototype for the Dark Lady of the Sonnets, even though the latter was clearly married or betrothed ("thy bed-vow broke") and Mistress Vavasor, at the time of the affair, was neither. In March 1581, Ann gave birth to Oxford's illegitimate son, Edward Vere. Elizabeth, who always took personal offense when someone impregnated one of her maids-of-honor out of wedlock, sent father, mother, and newborn to the Tower of London for a few weeks. This imprisonment supposedly gave Oxford the idea for Claudio's incarceration in *Measure for Measure* on the same charge and evidence.

That December the earl finally reconciled with his long-suffering, ever-forgiving wife. They had three more daughters and a son who died in the crib before Countess Anne herself passed away in 1588.

Ann Vavasor's kinsman, the courtier Thomas Knyvet, was not as understanding as Oxford's wife. He attacked the earl and after a brief sword-fight, both men were wounded. For a year afterward, Knyvet's and Oxford's lackeys brawled in the streets like the families in *Romeo and Juliet*. In 1585, Ann's hotheaded brother Thomas sent a formal challenge to the earl, which Oxfordians claim was transformed into Laertes' challenge to Hamlet.

That August, de Vere was given command of the cavalry in Flanders under the field commander Colonel John Norris. Oxford was recalled and replaced in October (like Othello is replaced by Cassio?), but his cousins, Francis and Horace Vere, distinguished themselves against the Spanish in the ensuing months and earned history's appellate "the fighting Veres." Though a "general," Francis's actual military rank was sergeant major general, a rank above captain that, like colonel, never appears in the plays of Shakespeare.

By 1586, Oxford was ruined politically and financially. He had been selling off estates to pay his bills for years, dramatically reducing the value of his earldom. If there was to be an Earl of Oxford in generations to come, Elizabeth would have to provide funds to support him. Which she did. She granted Oxford a pension of a thousand pounds a year. But from then on she never acceded to another petition from the earl; he had exhausted her generosity. In the coming years he sought the governorship of Jersey, the presidency of Wales, and various monopolies; all were denied him.

He continued in his duties as Lord Great Chamberlain, though, attending on the Queen during the victory celebrations after the defeat of the Spanish Armada, serving on the juries that condemned Mary Queen of Scots and, later, the Earl of Essex, and participating in the coronation of James I. But there is no record of him at court after 1588. Ironically, in the 1590s and early 1600s, William Shakespeare the actor was in the monarch's presence more than Oxford, performing at court several times a year.

In 1590, Burghley proposed that Oxford's daughter Elizabeth, then fifteen, should marry one of Burghley's wards, the seventeen-year-old Earl of Southampton. Some Oxfordians believe the first seventeen Sonnets were designed to foster the match, but those poems seem like strange encouragement coming from a potential father-in-law. They never, for example, mention the woman who is his daughter. Elizabeth ended up marrying William Stanley, the sixth Earl of Derby, in 1595. Another daughter, Susan Vere, later wed Philip Herbert, the Earl of Montgomery, one of the "incomparable pair of brethren" to whom the First Folio was dedicated.

In 1591, his wife having died three years earlier, Oxford married Elizabeth Trentham, another of the Queen's maids-of-honor. Two years later she bore him a son, Henry, the future eighteenth Earl.

When the Queen died in 1603, Oxford lamented his benefactor's passing in a moving letter to Robert Cecil:

> I cannot but find a great grief in myself to remember the Mistress which we have lost, under whom both you and myself from our greenest years

have been in a measure brought up; and although it hath pleased God after an earthly kingdom to take her up into a more permanent and heavenly state, wherein I do not doubt but she is crowned with glory; and to give us a prince wise, learned, and enriched with all virtues, yet the long time which we spent in her service, we cannot look for so much left of our days as to bestow upon another, neither the long acquaintance and kind familiarities wherewith she did use us, we are not ever to expect from another prince as denied by the infirmity of age and the common course of reason. In this common shipwreck mine is above all the rest, who least regarded though often comforted of all her followers, she hath left to try my fortune among the alterations of time and chance, either without sail whereby to take advantage of any prosperous gale, or with anchor to ride till the storm be overpast.[21]
[spelling modernized]

Oxford's "great grief," however, is unlike what seems to be the Author's reaction to Elizabeth's death:

> Not mine own fears, nor the prophetic soul
> Of the wide world, dreaming on things to come,
> Can yet the lease of my true love control,
> Suppos'd as forfeit to a confin'd doom.
> The mortal moon hath her eclipse endur'd,
> And the sad augurs mock their own presage,
> Incertainties now crown themselves assur'd,
> And peace proclaims olives of endless age.
> Now with the drops of this most balmy time
> My love looks fresh, and Death to me subscribes,
> Since spite of him I'll live in this poor rhyme,
> While he insults o'er dull and speechless tribes;
> And thou in this shalt find thy monument,
> When tyrants' crests and tombs of brass are spent.
>
> (Sonnet 107)

Since it was a convention of Elizabethan poetry to represent the Queen as the moon, just as they usually meant "poet" by "shepherd," many scholars accept that the line "The mortal moon hath her eclipse endured" refers to the death of Elizabeth. What's interesting is the Sonneteer regards her passing as a "balmy time" when "peace proclaims olives of endless age." And look at the couplet: he seems to be calling the recently dead Elizabeth a tyrant. This attitude is consistent with the Author's Catholic sympathies; as the Queen had stepped up her persecution of Catholics in the 1580s and 1590s, she had become less and less popular with her recusant subjects. (The line "Suppos'd as forfeit to a confined doom" indicates the subject of the sonnet might be the release from prison of the Earl of Southampton in April 1603.)

Oxford's fears about the new King proved to be unfounded. James reconfirmed the earl's thousand-pound annuity and granted his longstanding suit for Waltham Forest and Havering Park. But Oxford's improved fortune was short-lived. In June 1604, he died at Hackney.

～

Handsome and athletic, with a life full of adventure and a personality that was fiery, arrogant, headstrong, profligate, capricious, and lusty, Oxford was indeed like the outsized lords the Author dramatized. And if the Playwright had taken his plots from autobiography instead of sources, perhaps Oxford's life would be an argument for his Authorship. Even so, Oxford may have served as one of the models for various Shakespearean characters. Who knows? The activities of courtiers was the focus of gossip at this time, and the life story of a generous patron would have been common knowledge in literary circles.

Still, Oxford was hardly the Author's only model. If there is a little of Oxford in Hamlet, there's more of the Earl of Essex. Much of what the Author adds to the source story—the poisoning, the love affair with Ophelia against her family's wishes, the play within a play—can be found in Essex's biography. When the Earl of Leicester married Essex's mother, it was rumored he had, like Claudius, poisoned Essex's father in order to woo her. When Essex himself married the daughter of Sir Francis Walsingham, one of Elizabeth's principal advisers, the marriage was opposed by the bride's family, as Ophelia's marriage to Hamlet is opposed by Polonius and Laertes ("he is out of thy star"). Essex was also a poet and patron of players, interested in learning, famously moody and tempermental, known to be abusive to women—even the Queen herself—and liked to wear black. He makes a poignant model for Hamlet given the play's popularity immediately after his execution.

Looney contends that the surly and dislikable character of Bertram in *All's Well That Ends Well* was suggested by Oxford, which is not unbelievable, but it does not make the earl the Author any more than if in some way he served as one of the models for Hamlet. In any case, the Earl of Southampton makes as good a prototype. Like Bertram,

Southampton was an earl, a royal ward, and a General of the Horse, who resisted an arranged marriage and left his country to go to war against his sovereign's wishes.

When it comes to minor characters, Oxfordians, like all heretics, find the originals in people known to their candidate. They claim Malvolio was based on Oxford's rival at court, Sir Christopher Hatton; the faithful steward in *Timon of Athens* was derived from Oxford's faithful steward Robert Christmas; and so forth.[22] What Oxfordians forget is the universality of the Author's characters. In everyone's life is a fat, vivacious uncle who could have inspired Falstaff or a sardonic, fast-talking friend who could have been the original of Mercutio. Finding such archetypes in Oxford's biography proves nothing more than it does when Rutlanders play the game.

The same kind of nonsense can be engaged in by Stratfordians. W. Nicholas Knight suggests the character of Timon of Athens might have been based on Shakespeare's father. Claudio's getting his betrothed with child in *Measure for Measure* is associated with Shakespeare's having done the same. The death of Hamnet Shakespeare in 1596 is alleged to be reflected in Constance's famous speech in *King John*:

> Grief fills the room up of my absent child,
> Lies in his bed, walks up and down with me,
> Puts on his pretty looks, repeats his words,
> Remembers me all his gracious parts,
> Stuffs out his vacant garments with his form.
> Then have I reason to be fond of grief.
>
> (III.iv.94–99)

James Joyce's character Stephen Dedalus speculates in *Ulysses* that Volumnia in *Coriolanus* was patterned after Shakespeare's mother, that the "girls" in *The Tempest*, *Pericles*, and *The Winter's Tale* were based on his daughters, and Cleopatra, Cressida, and Venus were pictures of his wife.[23] Conjecture without proof is a game anyone can play.

What we know for certain about Oxford doesn't fit as well as his advocates would have people believe. The Oxfordians have built a trumped-up case for the earl by ignoring discrepancies and presenting their fantasies as evidence. Their specious arguments are ultimately no more valid than those advanced by other anti-Stratfordians in favor of their own True Authors.

CHAPTER 11
Motive and Means

We're investigating a crime. The crime of fraud. The Earl of Oxford is accused of passing off his writings as the work of the actor William Shakespeare, and the Oxfordians, as detectives, have to establish motive, means, and opportunity. In other words, they have to show (1) that Oxford had a reason—a motive—to disguise his identity and that his heirs had a motive to continue the deception, (2) that there is some connection between Oxford and Shakespeare and thus they had the means to pull off the fraud, and (3) that Oxford's death in 1604 does not preclude him from writing any of the Author's plays—that he had the opportunity.

For a motive, the Oxfordians believe we need look no further than common custom. Drama was not considered respectable, or even literature (much like screenplays today). When Ben Jonson included six plays in his *Works* in 1616, an anonymous wag wrote,

> Pray tell me *Ben*, where doth the mystery lurk,
> What others call a play you call a work.[1]

This prejudice was an extension of the general prejudice against theatre that existed at the time. Players were seen as lowly and disreputable, on the same social level as the prostitutes who cruised the galleries of the playhouses. Theatres like the Rose and the Curtain were offensive to most Londoners, the sites of drunkeness, blasphemy, and crime. The Puritan city council insisted they be built outside the city limits, where they stood beside bawdy houses and bear-baiting arenas. The fact that most dramatic texts were anonymous collaborations plagued their standing as well. Hence the earl's need for a pseudonym.

Poetry was not as scandalous as drama, but it was considered dishonorable for a nobleman, or even a gentleman, to waste his time with such a frivolous hobby. The anonymous author of *The Arte of English Poesie* (1589), probably George Puttenham, complains,

> it is so come to pass that [courtiers] have no courage to write & if they have, yet are they loath to be known of their skill, so as I know very many notable gentlemen in the Court that have written commendably, and suppressed it again, or else suffered it to be published without their own names to it: as if it were a discredit for a gentleman to seem learned, and to show himself amorous of any good art.[2]

[spelling modernized]

Courtiers' verses were usually published without attribution, signed with cryptic initials, or ascribed to "Ignoto," meaning anonymous. If a pseudonym was used, it was something whimsical like "Immerito" (Latin for "unworthy"), which was Spenser's nom de plume on *The Shepheard's Calendar*. Noblemen's poetry was not usually published as their own until after they had died.

For Oxford, though, the cat was out of the bag. The earl's first printed poem appeared in 1573 in a translation by Thomas Bedingfield and bore the title "The Earl of Oxford to the Reader of Bedingfield's *'Cardanus Comfort'.* " Puttenham quotes twelve lines by "Edward Earle of Oxford" in *The Arte of English Poesie*, "which from his excellencie and wit I set down," apparently having copied them from the poet's recitation or manuscript. The anthology *England's Helicon* (1600) sported one poem with the by-line "Earle of Oxenford." In other published works, Gabriel Harvey (1578), William Webbe (1586), Francis Meres (1598), and Henry Peacham (1622) name Oxford as a poet, while Puttenham and Meres commend the earl as one of the best writers of "comedy and enterlude."[3]

It was well known that Oxford was a playwright and poet, so he could not have used a pen name to hide the fact. And since most plays at this time were performed and published without attribution, it would have been easy for Oxford or Derby to write plays anonymously, without a front man, which they probably did.

No, if we're going to come up with a believable motive, we have to assume de Vere felt there was something embarrassing about the Shakespeare works specifically. Perhaps he felt *Venus and Adonis* and *The Rape of Lucrece* were too risqué to ever be associated with him. So he acquired a front man, the actor William Shakespeare, who could pass the poems off as his own. Soon the earl gave him unperformed plays containing vulgar language, bawdy puns, sexual subtext, and uncouth, indelicate poetry. The actor never revealed the secret because he was making money and winning prestige as a writer. As he spent his nights copying the earl's work into his own handwriting, maybe he started to believe he was a poet, a delusion that encouraged him to keep the secret. After his death in 1616, no one—not even Heminges and Condell—knew the truth.

This is the most convincing scenario I can come up with, and it still raises all sorts of questions. Why did Oxford have *Venus* and *Lucrece* published at all? If his embarrassment was so great he could not leave them anonymous but needed to divert suspicions with another man's name, why did he entertain the greater risk of discovery involved in trusting a front man who could betray him at any time? If, as Joseph Sobran suggests, Oxford adopted the actor's name for *Venus and Adonis* in order to deflect suspicion about his homosexual affair with Southampton, why didn't the earl simply dedicate the poem to someone else? And what about Ben Jonson, who "loved the man this side idolatry," knew his face, and saw the race of Shakespeare's mind in his poetry? Where is the evidence that Jonson had something to gain by saying the man he knew was reflected in the plays?

∾

Motive remains unproved. What about means? How did Oxford get the plays to Shakespeare? Oxfordians allege that the Lord Chamberlain's Men were really the Lord *Great* Chamberlain's Men, that Oxford—drumroll please—was actually the actor's patron, not Henry Carey (the Lord Chamberlain) and his son George. The problem is, for a brief time between Henry Carey's death and George's becoming the new Lord Chamberlain, the company seems to have been under the patronage of Lord Hunsdon—George Carey's title. A payment for performances at court was made in 1596 to "John Hemynge and George Bryan servauntes to the late Lorde Chamberlayne and now servauntes to the Lorde Hunsdon."[4] The 1597 quarto of *Romeo and Juliet* states, "it hath been often (with great applause) plaid publiquely, by the right Honourable the L. of Hunsdon his Servants." Clearly, the Careys were the troupe's patrons. In addition, as I noted in the last chapter, Oxford had his own company. There is no evidence Oxford was the patron for a second group of adult actors. In the 1580s his companies are always called the "Earl of Oxford's Men," the "Earl of Oxford's Servants," the "Earl of Oxford's Boys," the "Children of the Earl of Oxford," and so forth. The title of "Lord Great Chamberlain" never appears.[5] Nor is there any indication that the Author's plays were ever performed by Oxford's players, though some of the early works were acted by companies associated with the earls of Derby, Pembroke, and Sussex, according to quarto title pages.[6]

One of Oxford's actors in the 1580s may have been Anthony Munday, whose first stage works were written for the Earl of Oxford's Men. Munday is thought by some to be the link Oxfordians are looking for. *The Book of Sir Thomas More* is a play in manuscript believed to be written partly by Munday and partly by the Author. If the whole of the play could be shown to be the Author's, and if the manuscript could be shown to be all in Munday's handwriting, then there would be a clear connection with Oxford. Unfortunately, the play seems to be the work of five different playwrights and just as many handwritings. Another problem is that Munday left Oxford's service by the 1590s, before the play was written, to become one of the Queen's Messengers of the Chamber. In the ensuing years, he wrote for the rivals of the Lord Chamberlain's company—the Lord Admiral's Men.[7]

Perhaps another link can be made through Shakespeare's fellow, Robert Armin. He remarks in his *Quips Upon Questions*, of 1600, that he would "take my journey (to wait on the right Honourable good Lord my Master whom I serve) to Hackney." Hackney was the town where Oxford was then living, but Armin was never one of the earl's players. He had been with Lord Chandos's Men in Gloucestershire before joining the Chamberlain's. Most likely, the Lord Chamberlain was visiting Oxford or Lord Zouche (who also lived in Hackney) and was bringing along some of his players to attend him or even to perform entertainments in the evening. Rowland Whyte, an observer, described Lord Chamberlain Carey as making such a use of his players when he feasted a visiting dignitary in March 1600.[8]

Oxford and Shakespeare may have been in the same place at the same time at the wedding of the Earl of Derby to Oxford's daughter Elizabeth. As part of the festivities after the ceremony, the Lord Chamberlain's Men performed a play.[9] But there's no evidence the father of the bride attended the performance. So even this connection between Oxford and Shakespeare is dubious. No connection has been found between Oxford and Ben Jonson, the necessary third conspirator, either.

For proof that the earl was hiding behind an actor, Oxfordians point to John Marston's satirical poem "A Toy to Mock an Ape" from *The Scourge of Villanie* (1598). It contains the verses

O what a tricksy learned nicking strain
Is this applauded, senseless, modern vain

When late I heard it from sage *Mutius* lips
How ill me thought such wanton jigging skips
Beseem'd his graver speech. *Far fly thy fame*
Most, most of me belov'd, whose silent name
One letter bounds. Thy true judicial style
I ever honour, and if my love beguile
Not much my hopes, then thy unvalued worth
Shall mount fair place when Apes are turned forth.[10]

[spelling modernized]

Perhaps the "belov'd" writer in the sixth line was indeed Oxford. The letter *E* bounds "Edward de Vere," Oxford's silent name. But Marston does not believe the earl is the Author. (Would anyone call the Author's style "judicial"?) Only wishful thinking makes this passage say what the Oxfordians want it to say—that de Vere will be hailed when the actor/front man Shakespeare is sent packing. In fact, Marston is not referring to writers here at all. "A Toy to Mock an Ape" is a satire on actors. It is acting style not writing style that Marston is talking about. He's criticizing the tricksy (gimmicky), learned, nicking (staccato), senseless, yet applauded, modern style of performing, which makes the actor Mutius's graver speeches appear as wanton jigging skips (a bad dance routine). He's contrasting it with the judicial style of the belov'd actor. This actor's name is silent because it's hidden behind characters, it's bounded by one letter, and its worth will be recognized when the current popular players are hissed from the stage. The actor Marston has in mind is probably Edward Alleyne, whose name was often spelled with a terminal *e*. Richard Archer, Edward Pearce, or even young Edmund Shakespeare, Will's brother, whom Marston could have met through Shakespeare's cousin Thomas Greene, represent other possibilities. Whoever it was, it wasn't Oxford.

In a later part of the poem, Marston jeers at "a youth that hath abus'd his time,/In wronged travel, in that hotter clime" who returns "in clothes Italianate" and "strange fantastic suit shapes."[11] Like the Author, Marston laughed at Italophiles like Oxford, even though he himself studied Italian and wrote plays with Italian themes and sources.

Oxfordians believe another connection is found in Jonson's *Every Man Out of His Humour*. Jonson seems to mock the motto on Shakespeare's grant-of-arms application—*Non Sanz Droict* (old French for "Not Without Justice"). In the play, a fool named Sogliardo describes his new coat of arms as "On a chief argent, a boar's head proper, between two ann'lets sables," and a jester comments, " 'Slud, it's a hog's cheek and puddings, in a pewter field, this." A knight adds, "Let the word be, 'Not without mustard'. Your crest is very rare, sir" (III.iv.81–87). Because the boar was represented on the Vere family arms, it's claimed that Jonson is alluding to Shakespeare's unworthiness and Oxford's true Authorship. But "Not without mustard" is probably an allusion to Nashe's popular book *Pierce Pennilesse His Supplication to the Divell,* in which a vow to give up salt cod is emended "Not without mustard, Good Lord, not without mustard."[12] If Jonson is referring to Shakespeare's motto here, is he really mocking it or is he using it as the template of a proper motto which he warps in order to make the joke? Since Shakespeare's acting company performed the play, it's doubtful they would permit an insult to one of their members.

Still more evidence of a cover-up is gleaned in a 1612 poem written to Jonson by "F. B." (probably Francis Beaumont). It contains the lines:

>   here I would let slip
> (If I had any in me) scholarship,
> And from all Learning keep these lines as [cl]ear
> as Shakespeares best are, which our heirs shall hear
> Preachers apt to their auditors to show
> how far sometimes a mortal man may go
> by the dim light of Nature.[13]

[spelling modernized]

Ogburn and others make a tortuous explication of this fragment.[14] They reason that if "Shakespeares best" lines are clear of learning, his worst are not. And therefore the Author (the man F. B. means by "Shakespeare") was, unlike the actor, a scholar. This may be so, but it doesn't imply that the Author was university educated. F. B. is writing to Ben Jonson after all, a former bricklayer who never attended Oxford or Cambridge. It's just as likely that the "best" are singled out because those are the ones preachers would quote and F. B. wishes to emulate. The last three and a half lines Ogburn sees as ironic: preachers, who, along with their congregations, are not in on the secret of the Poet's true identity, will mistakenly use the Author's poetry to illustrate what an unlearned man can achieve. They unwittingly perpetuate the false idea that the Author was a man of Nature, not a scholar. But even if this reading is correct, it only means posterity will be wrong about Shakespeare's intellectual attainments, not about his identity.

Oxfordians who think "William Shakespeare" was a pseudonym concocted independent of the actor believe their candidate can be tied to the name through the earl's coat of arms as Viscount Bulbeck, which shows a lion brandishing a broken spear. However, an arm shaking a fractured spear is a common heraldic device (my own family's crest has one). Others trace the origin of the name through Gabriel Harvey's 1578 Latin address, in which the orator says of Oxford "vultus tela vibrat"—your countenance shakes spears.[15] But *tela* is more accurately translated as javelins or darts; it has the sense of missiles or weapons that are thrown. "Shakespeare," as Thomas Fuller pointed out in 1662, would be "Hasti-vibrans."[16]

There is simply no existing historical document that connects William Shakespeare to Edward de Vere. Charlton Ogburn understood that this is a huge stumbling block for Oxfordians. He attempted to get around it by proposing a vast conspiracy orchestrated by Burghley's heirs. Unhappy with the humiliating references to their father in the plays, the heirs destroy all evidence of Oxford's Authorship. They weed through the whole country's personal correspondence, burning letters and diaries, and then doctor the records of Shakespeare's life. Out of fear of the Cecils, no one in the know speaks of it ever again—as if a nationwide attempt to destroy private letters and documents would not intensify many people's resolve to pass on the truth.[17]

∽

To prove opportunity, the Oxfordians' first step is to look for evidence that the Author was older than William Shakespeare. So they turn to Edmund Spenser's 1591 cycle of poems *The Teares of the Muses*. In this collection, Spenser writes from the point of view of each of the nine muses as they lament the state of their particular art. Thalia, the muse of Comedy, wails that Sorrow, Barbarism, and Ignorance,

> in the minds of men now tyrannize,
> And the fair Scene with rudeness foul disguise.
>
> All places they with folly have possessed,
> And with vain toys the vulgar entertain;
> But me have banished, with all the rest
> That whilom wont to wait upon my train,
> Fine Counterfe[it]ance and unhurtful Sport,
> Delight and Laughter decked in seemly sort.
>
> All these, and all that else the Comic Stage
> With seasoned wit and goodly pleasance graced;

By which man's life in his likest image
Was limned forth, are wholly now defaced;
And those sweet wits which wont the like to frame,
Are now despised, and made a laughing game.

And he the man, whom Nature self had made
To mock her self, and Truth to imitate,
With kindly counter under Mimic shade,
Our pleasant *Willy*, ah is dead of late:
With whom all joy and jolly merriment
Is also deaded, and in dolour drent.

Instead thereof scoffing Scurrility,
And scornful Folly with Contempt is crept,
Rolling in rhymes of shameless ribaldry
Without regard, or due Decorum kept,
Each idle wit at will presumes to make,
And doth the Learned's task upon him take.

But that same gentle Spirit, from whose pen
Large streams of honey and sweet Nectar flow,
Scorning the boldness of such base-born men,
Which dare their follies forth so rashly throw;
Doth rather choose to sit in idle Cell,
Than so himself to mockery to sell.[18]

[spelling modernized]

Nicholas Rowe, in 1709, was the first to suggest that "Willy" is intended for the Author. He further believed Willy's death is figurative and "that same gentle Spirit" was also "Shakespeare." A few hundred years later, Oxfordians appropriated this reading, substituting their own candidate. Willy, they claim, was a pseudonym for Oxford. And they may have a point. A gentleman-poet, scorning base-born writers, who chooses to stop writing for the stage, sorts well with Oxford. But are the "Spirit" and Willy really the same person? Scholars normally identify Willy as Richard Tarlton or William Knell, the most famous actors (Mimics) of their time who both died in 1588, and the Spirit is usually suspected to be the playwright John Lyly.[19] Oxfordians miss that the Author (or at least his aesthetic) *is* alluded to in the poem but as neither Willy nor the "gentle Spirit." One need only think of the shameless ribaldry, without due decorum of *The Comedy of Errors* ("Dromio: I could find out countries in her. . . . Antipholus: Where Ireland? Dromio: Marry, sir, in her buttocks.

I found it out by the bogs") or *Taming of the Shrew* ("What, my tongue in your tail?"). In later plays the Author will have maids-of-honor make cuckold jokes (*Love's Labor's Lost*) and give a noble youth a line like "The bawdy hand of the dial is upon the prick of noon" (*Romeo and Juliet*). Surely the Author, with his vain toys to entertain the vulgar like *Titus Andronicus*, was the kind of playwright who made Thalia weep.

A similar misappropriation afflicts the Oxfordian view of *Willobie His Avisa* (1594). In this book's introduction to its Canto 13, Henrico Willobego (a thin disguise for the book's author, Henry Willoby) confesses his love for the faithful wife Avisa to "his familiar friend WS who not long before had tried the courtesy of the like passion, and was now newly recovered of the like infection . . ."[20] WS tells HW that he thinks seducing Avisa is

> a matter very easily to be compassed, & no doubt with pain, diligence and some cost in time to be obtained. Thus this miserable comforter comforting his friend with an impossibility, either for that he now would secretly laugh at his friend's folly, that had given occasion not long before unto others to laugh at his own, or because he would see whether another could play his part better than himself, & in viewing afar off the course of this loving Comedy, he determined whether it would sort to a happier end for this new actor, then it did for the old player.[21]

[spelling modernized]

In discussing this passage, Oxfordians assume that WS means William Shakespeare. Since the actor William Shakespeare was only thirty in 1594, and WS is called an "old player," the initials must really refer to the man behind the mask of Shakespeare—de Vere. How the author of this book learned the secret is anybody's guess. Henry Willoby was discovered in the nineteenth century to be a student at St. John's College, Oxford. He had a younger brother Thomas, which confirms the identification because a later edition of *Avisa* contains verses signed "Thomas Willoby, Frater [brother of] Henrici Willoby."[22] Henry was twenty in 1594 and may have regarded the thirty-year-old Shakespeare as old. But if we look at the passage carefully, we can see that WS is no more likely to be an actual player than HW is likely to be an "actor." These labels are part of the extended metaphor of "playing a part" in the "loving Comedy." WS was probably just a fellow student with those initials. By "old player," Willoby was poetically saying "former lover."

It's a stunning coincidence that HW are also the initials of the probable young man in the Sonnets, Henry Writhosley, the Earl of Southampton, and that these initials should be tied to WS in a love triangle. But the situation described in *Avisa* is completely different from the Sonnets, and there are, after all, only twenty-six letters in the alphabet. A different HW (in this case, Henry Willoby) might have a different WS for a friend.

Oxfordians next task is to show that the conventional dating of the Shakespeare plays is wrong. For this, they turn to the documents surrounding the Essex Rebellion. On the eve of the revolt, some of Essex's chief lieutenants decided to foment the passions of their fellow conspirators with a play. A few days before the coup attempt, they bribed the actors at the Globe Theatre to perform the usurpation-themed *Richard II*. (Many scholars assume this performance included a scene, which had been banned, of King Richard's uncrowning. But there is no evidence that it did. And if the scene had indeed been performed, there is a good chance the players would have been arrested.) Chamberlain's man Augustine Phillips was later questioned under oath about the performance. The summary of his "examination" reads as follows:

> He sayeth that on Friday last . . . or Thursday Sir Charles Percy, Sir Joselyne Percy and the Lord Monteagle with some three more spoke to some of the players in the presence of this examinate to have the play of the deposing and killing of Richard the second to be played the Saturday next promising to get them forty shillings more than their ordinary to play it. Where[as] this Examinate and his fellows were determined to have played some other play, holding that play of King Richard to be so old & long out of use as that they should have small or no company at it. But at their request this examinate and his fellows were content to play it the Saturday and had their forty shillings more than their ordinary for it and so played it accordingly.[23]

[spelling modernized]

Oxfordians take gleeful interest in Phillips's contention that the play is "old and long out of use." If Shakespeare wrote it, it could only be, at most, six or seven years old. Scholars, meanwhile, suggest that Phillips might be exaggerating. Two years earlier, John Hayward had dedicated a book to Essex that described Richard II's deposition, and he had been sent to the Tower for life. Phillips may have had Hayward on his mind and was trying to make the play seem more harmless. But it's also possible that, to Phillips, a play which had not been in the repertory for a few years was "old and long out of use." Another possibility is that the players intentionally described the play as old to Sir Charles Percy and his friends in order to haggle a higher fee from them.

Anti-Stratfordians make much of the fact that Phillips was questioned and not Shakespeare. "Why not interrogate the presumed author of the play?" they ask suspiciously. To come up with an answer, let's think about the situation from the Elizabethan authorities' point of view. The play had been approved by the censor (the Master of Revels) several years earlier, so there was no need to talk to its writer; it was the *performance* of the play in connection with Essex that gave offense. But in order to prove the guilt of Essex's followers, it was important to the prosecutors that the actors were innocent of wrongdoing. At the trial, they emphasized the players' reluctance and the forty shilling bribe in order to show the conspirators' treasonous intentions. Francis Bacon later wrote about one of the rebels, "Neither was it casual, but a play bespoken by Merrick. And not so only, but when it was told him by one of the players, that the play was old, and they should have loss in playing it, because few would come to it: there was forty shillings extraordinary given to play it. . . . So earnest he was to satisfy his eyes with the sight of that tragedy, which he thought soon after his lord should bring from the stage to the state, but that God turned it upon their own heads."[24]

By August, Essex and his followers were beheaded or hanged, and the Queen was looking through some records with William Lambarde, the archivist of the Tower of London. He writes,

> her Majestie fell upon the reign of King Richard II, saying, 'I am Richard II. know ye not that?'
>
> W. L. 'Such a wicked imagination was determined and attempted by a most unkind Gent. the most adorned creature that ever your Majestie made.'
>
> Her Majestie. 'He that will forget God, will also forget his benefactors; this tragedy was played forty times in open streets and houses.'[25]

[spelling modernized]

Lambarde seems to have in mind the Earl of Essex as the "unkind Gent," but Oxfordians argue that Elizabeth is thinking of the Author.[26] Since the number of performances has nothing to do with Essex, and since the "most adorned creature" could hardly make Elizabeth think of the actor Shakespeare, she must be alluding to the True Author, the once favored but currently disgraced Earl of Oxford. Stratfordians tend to believe that the Queen's utterances are completely separate thoughts, her first sentence being a response to Lambarde, referring to Essex, and the second representing a return to her initial thought about Richard II. The truth, however, may be that in mentioning the performances of the play she is still speaking of Essex. A year before the rebellion, a document charging Essex with high treason lists among its proofs, "the Earl himself being so often present at the playing [of Richard II's deposing], and with great applause giving countenance and liking to the same."[27] If she has this accusation in mind, the Queen may be implying that Essex personally instigated the forty performances.

Her remark about forgetting God is a euphemism for any breach of the Ten Commandments. It's a phrase that can be found in Burghley's correspondence. "He hath forgotten his duty to God," Burghley wrote of Oxford in 1581, when the earl committed adultery. Oxford had "forgotten God" twenty years earlier, but he was hardly "the most adorned creature" Elizabeth ever made.

The latest attempt to tie Oxford to the Author involves a Genevan Bible that once belonged to Edward de Vere and which today is the property of the Folger Shakespeare Library in Washington D.C. Hundreds of the verses in this volume are marked or underlined and, allegedly, the markings correspond to Biblical allusions in the Author's works. Dave Kathman of the Shakespeare Authorship Website has examined the book and, after making a complete list of the annotations, he found that only about 10 percent of the Author's Biblical allusions were marked. Many of the books the Poet drew heavily from, such as the four gospels, Genesis, Proverbs, and Acts of the Apostles, were hardly touched by the annotator, while some of the annotator's favorite books, like the apocryphal Second Book of Maccabees, Second Book of Esdras, Wisdom, Tobit, and Baruch are all virtually ignored by the Author.[28] Though the Author might have marked more verses than he finally used, the fact that he alluded to more unmarked verses than marked ones means the annotations were most likely not made by the Author.

Let's remember that in Francis Bacon's commonplace book—called Bacon's *Promus of Formularies*—the philosopher recorded 203 English proverbs, three-quarters of which were quoted or alluded to by the Author. These are not marks in a book for which there were thousands of copies; this is much stronger evidence of authorship. Yet, like the Genevan Bible allusions, the general availability of the proverbs renders them insignificant.

We should also remember that the Genevan Bible was not the only English translation the Author knew. In the early plays, he used the Bishops' version just as much. Richmond Noble has shown that in *Henry VI Part One*, *Henry VI Part Two*, *Love's Labor's Lost*, *The Merchant of Venice*, and *Richard II*, the Author's translation of choice was the Bishops'. In *Henry VI Part One*, Talbot's cry "Heavens, can you suffer hell so to prevail?" (I.v.9) echoes the Bishops' rendering of Matthew 16:18, "the gates of hel shall not prevaile against it." The Genevan Bible has "shall not overcome it." The king's assurance that "Our kinsman Gloucester is as innocent/From meaning treason to our royal person/As is the sucking lamb or harmless dove" (III.i.69–71) in *Henry VI Part Two* alludes to a phrase in the Bishops' Matthew 10:16—"harmless as the Doves"; the Genevan says "innocent as the Doves." In *Love's Labor's Lost*, Moth says of Delilah, "she had a green wit" (I.ii.89), which is a pun on Judges 16:8 in the Bishops' translation, "And then the lords of the Philistines brought her [Delilah] seven withs that were green, and never dried, and he bound him therewith." The Genevan has "seven cords," which means that without the Bishops' there would be no joke. Armado's reply, "My love is most immaculate white and red" (I.ii.90) comes from the Bishops' Song of Solomon 5:10, "As for love, he is white and red coloured." The Genevan editors translated this as "My welbeloved is white and ruddie." Later in the play, Berowne's argument that "charity itself fulfills the law" (IV.iii.361) refers to the Bishops' Romans 13:10 "the fulfilling of the law is charitie"; the Genevan has "love." Old Gobbo's epithet for his son, "the boy was the very staff of my age" (II.ii.66–7) in *The Merchant of Venice* is plucked from the Bishops' Tobit 5:23, when Tobias' mother calls him "the staff of our age." In the Genevan, Tobias is "the staff of our hand." When Mowbray swears in *Richard II*, "if ever I were traitor/My name be blotted from the book of life" (I.iii.201–2), he is referring to the Bishops' Revelations 3:5, "and I will not blot out his name out of the booke of life"; the Genevan has "put out." Richard thinks of the same verse later in the play when he says, "Mark'd with a blot, damn'd in the book of heaven" (IV.i.236).[29]

One of the Author's favorite Bible stories comes from the Bishops' version. When the Shunammite woman is asked about her son who has died, the passage reads "Is all well with thee, and with thy husband, and with the ladde? And she answered, All is well." (2 Kings 4:26.) The Genevan text, however, says: "Art thou in health? is thine husband in health? [and] is the childe in health? And she answered, We are in health." The Author made use of this verse, and its paradox that the dead are well because they are beyond cares and in heaven, in *Romeo and Juliet* (IV.v.76), *Henry IV Part Two* (V.ii.3), *Antony and Cleopatra* (II.v.31–3), *The Winter's Tale* (V.i.30), and most memorably in *Macbeth* in the scene in which Macduff is told that his murdered family is "well" (IV.iii. 176–9).

The Author's great affinity for the Bishops' Bible in the early years of his playwriting is strange if he owned a Genevan version in 1570 and read it carefully enough to annotate it. A more likely scenario is that he owned and studied a Bishops' for many years before buying one of the cheap, quarto-sized Genevan Bibles when they flooded the market in the 1580s and 90s, becoming the most popular translation in England. As for de Vere's Bible, the earl (if the markings are his) was clearly attracted to many of the same passages the Author was, and many the Author wasn't. The Poet, on the other hand, was intrigued by many verses that de Vere had no inclination to mark. Oxford's Bible, like the rest of the Oxfordian evidence, proves nothing.

CHAPTER 12
Have the Body

When the actor William Shakespeare died in 1616, the True Author, the man who wrote the Plays and Poems, was already in his grave—or so the Oxfordians insist. For proof, they point to four pre-1616 instances in which "Shakespeare," startlingly, appears to be dead.

The earliest example, Exhibit A, comes at the end of William Barksted's 1607 poem *Myrrha, the Mother of Adonis*. Barksted seems to speak of Shakespeare in the past tense when he writes, "His song was worthy merit." However, look at the whole passage in context:

> But stay my Muse in thine own confines keep,
>   & wage not war with so dear lov'd a neighbor,
> But having sung thy day song, rest and sleep
>   preserve thy small fame and his greater favor:
> His Song was worthy merit (Shakspeare he)
> sung the fair blossom, thou the withered tree
>   *Laurel* is due to him, his art and wit
>   hath purchas'd it, *Cypress* thy brow will fit.[1]
> [spelling modernized except for "Shakspeare"]

It's Barksted's muse—not Shakespeare—who has died and whose brow is fit for cypress. (Sprigs of cypress were symbolic of mourning and used at funerals.) Laurel, the headwear of classical poets, "is due" to Shakespeare, an admission Barksted makes in the present tense. Only the Author's "song," *Venus and Adonis*, is spoken of as belonging to the past, presumably because it was "sung" (composed) fourteen years earlier.

Two years later, in 1609, a quarto edition of *Troilus and Cressida* was published with this unsigned preface:

A NEVER WRITER, TO AN EVER READER. NEWS.

Eternal reader, you have here a new play, never staled with the stage, never clapper-clawed with the palms of the vulgar, and yet passing full of the palm comical; for it is a birth of your brain that never undertook anything comical vainly. And were but the vain names of comedies changed for the titles of commodities, or of plays for pleas, you should see all those grand censors, that now style them such vanities, flock to them for the main grace of their gravities, especially this author's comedies, that are so framed to the life that they serve for the most common commentaries of all the actions of our lives, showing such a dexterity and power of wit that the most displeased with plays are pleased with his comedies. And all such dull and heavy-witted worldlings as were never capable of the wit of a comedy, coming by report of them to his representations, have found that wit there that they never found in themselves and have parted better witted than when they came, feeling an edge of wit set upon them more than they ever dreamed they had brain to grind it on. So much and such savored salt of wit is in his comedies that they seem, for their height of pleasure, to be born in that sea that brought forth Venus. Amongst all there is none more witty than this: and had I time I would comment upon it, though I know it needs not, for so much as will make you think your testern [six-pence] well-bestowed, but for so much worth as even poor I know to be stuffed in it. It deserves such a labor as well as the best comedy in Terence or Plautus. And believe this, that when he is gone and his comedies out of sale, you will scramble for them, and set up a new English Inquisition. Take this for a warning, and at the peril of your pleasure's loss, and judgment's, refuse not, nor like this the less for not being sullied with the smoky breath of the multitude; but thank fortune for the 'scape it hath made amongst you, since by the grand possessors' wills I believe you should have prayed for them rather than been prayed. And so I leave all such to be prayed for, for the state of their wits' healths, that will not praise it. *Vale* [*farewell*]. [2]

Oxfordians smell conspiracy in the line "when he is gone and his comedies out of sale, you will scramble for them, and set up a new English Inquisition. Take this for a warning, and at the peril of your pleasure's loss, and judgment's, refuse not. . . ." The preface-writer knows the Author is dead, they argue, and can't help himself from dropping a hint about it. But look again at what he says: Buy this play now because as soon as this writer dies his plays will no longer be sold, as if the printing presses will stop with his heart like the grandfather's clock in the children's song. It's a fanciful idea to say the least, but the anonymous preface-writer is hawking the play, and he's grasping for any selling point. He must believe the Author is still alive or else, by his own logic, the book would be out of sale.

Spotting the word "ever" in the headline, Oxfordians claim it's intended as an anagram for Vere, that "ever reader" is code for "Vere reader." They also believe that "never clapper-clawed with the palms of the vulgar" points to a nonvulgar Author, and that "grand possessors" refers to Oxford's high-caste literary executors.[3] In fact, the play may have been performed only at the Inns of Court, where its cynicism and satire would have been appreciated. The "grand possessors" probably means the King's Men, who owned the manuscript. Whoever the "never-writer" was, it's almost certain he thought William Shakespeare, very much alive, wrote the play.

That same year (1609), *Shake-speares Sonnets* was published by Thomas Thorpe and printed by George Eld. The book had no dedication from the Author, but it did contain this greeting from Thorpe:

TO.THE.ONLIE.BEGETTER.OF.
THESE.INSUING.SONNETS.
Mr.W.H. ALL.HAPPINESSE.
AND.THAT.ETERNITIE.
PROMISED

BY.

OUR.EVER-LIVING.POET.

WISHETH.

THE.WELL-WISHING.
ADVENTURER.IN.
SETTING.
FORTH.

T.T.

"Ever-living" is an adjective that has never been applied, as far as anyone has discovered, to someone who's still alive.[4] It's been used in the sense of "eternal"—for example, Spenser's "burning starres and everliving fire" (*Faerie Queene*, I.x.50.6)—but never in connection with a living person. Does Thorpe know the Poet's true identity as the deceased Earl of Oxford? Or does he think the actor Shakespeare has passed away—always a good bet in a time when plague ravaged London every few years? Did the mere fact that he acquired such intimate poems lead Thorpe to that conclusion?

To solve the mystery of the "ever-living poet," we must first ponder the Sonnets' most famous secret—the identity of "the onlie begetter": Master WH. Down through the centuries, the word "begetter" in the greeting has been taken to mean either the young man who inspired most of the Sonnets or the middleman who procured the poems for the publisher. Candidates have included William Herbert, third Earl of Pembroke (whose identity Thorpe disguised with the epithet "Mr."); Henry Writhosley, third Earl of Southampton (disguised by the epithet and a reversal of his initials); William Hall, a dealer in literary properties; William Hart, Shakespeare's brother-in-law; William Harvey, Southampton's stepfather; William Hatcliffe, a young gentleman and member of Gray's Inn; Henry Willoby, author of *Willobie His Avisa*; and Will Hughes, a boy whose existence Oscar Wilde surmised from the italicized spelling of *Hews* in Sonnet 20.

"Mr. W.H." was finally unmasked by Professor Donald W. Foster, of Vassar, in 1989. He solved the mystery by doing what any good historian would do: he compared the Sonnets' epigraph to similar greetings from the period. Thumbing through stacks of Renaissance publications, he found the same basic sentence, with varying incidentals, in hundreds of book dedications. Most frequently, it appeared as an epigraph to a longer dedication, such as in another book published by Thorpe, *The Preachers Travels*, by John Cartwright:

> To the Virtuous and Worthy Knight Sir Thomas Hunt, one of his Majesty's Justices of the Peace and Quorum in the County of Surrey, J.C. wisheth all terrestrial and celestial happiness.[5]

In *The Old Man's Lesson*, by Nicholas Breton, Foster discovered,

> To Sir John Linwraye, N.B. wisheth increase of all happiness on earth and the joys of heaven hereafter.[6]

The authorized version of the King James Bible was similarly dedicated to James I, and many authors, including Robert Greene, George Gascoigne, and Thomas Lodge, used the same formulaic greeting, with slight variations, for virtually all their dedications. The only real difference between Thorpe's epigraph and the others' is that Thorpe's initials appear at the bottom rather than before "wisheth," so the verb and the direct object ("all happiness and that eternity promised by our ever-living poet") are necessarily transposed. Instead of the usual formulation (To the addressee the epistler wishes happiness and eternity), Thorpe's greeting has: To the addressee, happiness and eternity wishes the epistler.[7]

Thorpe, then, is the well-wishing adventurer. Such tags as "well-wisher," "well-willer," and "well-wishing friend" were common epithets for the dedication-writer, as in Barnabe Rich's closing to William Corkine: "I shall rest still to wish you well. Your well-willing friend, Barnabe Rych."[8] *To set forth*, in the context of the Jacobean book trade, meant *to publish*, and here Thorpe plays on the term to create the image of a merchant-adventurer setting forth on a voyage.

But who is the "only begetter" and who is the "ever-living poet"? Foster found that the word *begetter* always denoted the person who wrote the work.[9] "If by 'begetter' Thorpe meant anyone other than the author of the *Sonnets*," Foster concluded, "his usage is without parallel."[10] In other words, the addressee of the greeting was William Shakespeare. "Mr. W.H." is really a printer's error for "Mr. W.SH." or "Mr. W.S." One of Eld's compositors overlooked a letter as he was glancing back and forth from Thorpe's handwritten page to his trays of type, or he grabbed the wrong letter, or he reached for an *S* but an *H* had been misfiled, or he misread Thorpe's writing—the *S* and the *H* may have been overlapping and indistinguishable. Whatever happened, "Mr. W. H." was a mistake. And such a mistake was not uncommon. "Without making a careful search," says Foster, "I have come across more than a dozen examples of authors' initials inadvertently misprinted in nearly contemporaneous texts."[11]

This theory fits well with the word "onlie." Common sense dictates that the *only* begetter of the poems would most likely be their author rather than their inspirer, since the Sonnets have *two* inspirers: the young man and the Dark Lady. Foster believes Thorpe wanted to emphasize that Shakespeare was the "only" begetter in order to distinguish the book from collections like *The Passionate Pilgrim*, which had poems by many begetters even though it purported to be "by W. Shakespeare."

The "ever-living poet," then, must be someone other than the Author—someone dead but immortal. In fact, Foster notes, "ever-living" was a conventional epithet for God. Sidney addresses God as "ever-living thee"; Marlowe refers in *Tamburlaine Part One* to "ever-living Jove"; Nicholas Breton calls God "the Ever-Living." Jesus was conventionally "the only and ever-living saviour." In addition, God was sometimes styled an author or poet. For example, the first verse of Psalm 19 was translated, "the firmament proclaims the poetry of His Hands." *The Arte of English Poesie* (1589) stated the comparison bluntly: "A Poet is as much to say as a maker . . . such as (by way of resemblance and reverently) we may say of God."[12] The promised eternity of the fourth line, therefore, is nothing less than heaven. As in other dedications of the time, the publisher is wishing happiness and heaven to the Author of the Poems.

That the Sonneteer wrote no dedication himself has led Oxfordians to assume he was dead. But the Author may not have had anything to do with the Sonnets' publication. And even if he did, poems about homosexual desire and heterosexual adultery are not the kind of gifts one can bestow publicly. To dedicate them to a man would incite speculation that he was the Poet's lover; to dedicate them to a woman would implicate her as an adulteress. Wisely, if he was involved, the Poet knew when to keep his quill in the inkwell.

The fourth alleged reference to the Author's death is in *The Scourge of Folly* (1610), by John Davies of Hereford:

> *To our English Terence Will*: Shake-speare.
>   Epig. 159
>
> Some say (good *Will*) which I, in sport, do sing)
>   Had'st thou not played some Kingly parts in sport,
> Thou hadst been a companion for a *King*;
> And, been a King among the meaner sort.
> Some others rail; but rail as they think fit,
> Thou hast no railing but a reigning Wit:
>   *And* honesty *thou sowest which they do reap*;
>   *So, to increase their* Stock *which they do keep*.[13]

[spelling modernized]

Although this epigram is cryptic, two things are certain: Davies thinks Shakespeare is a poet and player, and thinks he's still alive. Though the second and third lines are in the past tense, they're also in the Elizabethan subjunctive. There's no guarantee Shakespeare will play a "kingly" part in the future so the subjunctive is the proper verb form to use. The sixth line ("Thou hast no railing . . .") is in the present tense, so the man Davies has in mind must be alive.

And it couldn't be Oxford. This poem appears among other theatrical epigrams in Davies' book; it immediately follows verses to the playwrights Samuel Daniel and Ben Jonson, the scene designer Inigo Jones, and Isacke Simonds, who, judging from Davies' lines, was apparently an actor. Davies does not lump Shakespeare with earls or persons of quality. The phrase "in sport" does not, as some Oxfordian commentators believe, imply the Author's acting was not professional. In a later poem in the same volume, Davies uses "in sport" to denote the work of Shakespeare's fellow in the King's Men, Robert Armin:

> *Armin*: what shall I say of thee, but this,
> Thou art a *Fool* and *Knave*? Both? fie, I miss;
> And wrong thee much: sith thou, in *Deed* art neither,
> Although in *Shew*, thou playest both together.
> . . .
> So thou, in sport, the happiest men dost school
> To do as thou dost, *wisely play the fool*.[14]

[spelling modernized]

In addition to the above four documents, Joseph Sobran observes that, "Beginning in 1605, other men's plays were published under his name with apparent impunity."[15] It was in 1605 that Nathaniel Butter issued *The London Prodigal* as "by William Shakespeare." Three years later, Thomas Pavier published *A Yorkshire Tragedy*, "by W. Shakespeare." Neither of these two ever again attributed a non-Shakespearean title to Shakespeare, although both later published bad quartos as well as good.[16] Since these plays were both in the repertory of the King's Men, Butter and Pavier may have made an honest mistake in assuming the works were penned by the company's principal dramatist. Or were they trying to dishonestly capitalize on a popular name? When *Mucedorus* came out in 1610, its title page had the words "Written by William Sh.," a clever way to imply Shakespeare's authorship yet tie the hands of those who might complain—it doesn't say "Shakespeare," after all. The publisher of *Mucedorus*, William Jones, tried the same trick again in 1611 when he put "W. Sh." on the title page of *The Troublesome Reign of King John*. Why curtail the poet's name unless Jones feared retribution for appending it to other men's plays? Which means the Author must have been alive. Other quartos, like *Locrine* (1595), *Thomas Lord Cromwell* (1602), *The Puritan* (1607), and even the first quarto of *The London Prodigal*, claimed to be by "W.S."—perhaps to imply Shakespeare, but perhaps not: There may have been another playwright with those initials. It's also possible that Shakespeare did have a hand in these plays. In the eighteenth century, Richard Farmer noted, "Aulus Gellius informs that some plays are ascribed absolutely to *Plautus* which he only *retouched* and *polished*; and this is undoubtedly the case with our Author [Shakespeare] likewise."[17]

In any case, we can't infer much from the publication of quartos. In Elizabethan England, there was no copyright as we know it today. A printer or publisher could, by an entry in the register of the Stationers Company, "secure the sole right of issuing a work in his possession," as long as it had been approved by government censors. No one else could print a work entered to a particular publisher, regardless of how he had acquired it.[18] So, having no control, the Author may have had little interest in the publication of his plays. He might have felt like John Marston, who writes in the preface to *The Malcontent* (1604), "Only one thing afflicts me, to think that scenes invented, merely to be spoken, should be inforcively [sic] published to be read."[19] But it's possible that Shakespeare the actor was indeed involved in selling some of the plays to printers, especially during times of plague when theatres were closed, and he and his company needed to make up for lost income.[20] After 1603, when they became the King's Men, fewer new plays by the Author came into print—perhaps because they no longer needed the extra money.

≈

All of the alleged allusions to the Author's death assume that the Poet's true identity was an "open secret," that it was generally known that "William Shakespeare" was a smokescreen for Oxford, but no one said anything. Barksted knew the secret and he assumed his readers did too; Thorpe must have known, and must have thought his readers knew, or he wouldn't have called the Author "ever-living"; Davies and *his* readers must have known too.

But a wealth of evidence shows that if there was indeed a secret, it must have been a "closed" one. The inscription under Shakespeare's monument in the chancel of the Stratford church attests he was a writer, and the First Folio bears Shakespeare's name and contains encomiums from his fellow actors, as well as from the stepson of the overseer of his will—

Leonard Digges. Digges's mention of the "Stratford moniment" and his assertion that "Nature only help'd him" prove he believed the actor was the Playwright.

Another believer was Francis Meres. In his *Palladis Tamia*, he assigned twelve plays to Shakespeare before anyone else named their author. He was also the first to speak of Shakespeare writing sonnets when he lauded "his sugar'd sonnets among his private friends." Though Meres calls Shakespeare "the most excellent in [comedy and tragedy] for the stage," he goes on to list the best playwrights in order of social rank:

> These are our best for Tragedie, the Lorde *Buckhurst*, Doctor *Leg* of Cambridge, Doctor *Edes* of Oxforde, maister *Edward Ferris*, the Author of the *Mirrour for Magistrates, Marlow, Peele, Watson, Kid, Shakespeare, Drayton, Chapman, Decker*, and *Benjamin Johnson*. . . . The best for Comedy amongst us bee, *Edward* Earle of Oxforde, Doctor *Gager* of Oxforde, Maister *Rowley* once a rare Scholler of learned Pembrooke Hall in Cambridge, Maister *Edwardes* one of her Majesties Chappell, eloquent and wittie *John Lilly, Lodge, Gascoyne, Greene, Shakespeare, Thomas Nash, Thomas Heywood, Anthony Mundye* our best plotter, *Chapman, Porter, Wilson, Hathway*, and *Henry Chettle*.[21]

If Meres believes Shakespeare and Oxford are the same person, then why does he include Shakespeare among the untitled playwrights? Why does he mention Oxford among the comic but not the tragic writers? Why does he mention both Shakespeare and Oxford in the same list? If he is simply ignorant that Oxford and Shakespeare are the same, then how does he know the Author's private friends and yet not know the secret? How is he so familiar with the Author's Canon yet not know the Poet's identity?

In the face of these questions, the Oxfordians retreat to accusations of conspiracy. Meres, they claim, is trying to create the illusion that Oxford and Shakespeare are different writers. He's working for the hidden cabal that is determined to conceal the truth of the Authorship. But considering that Meres's closest acquaintance in the literary community is the nonuniversity Warwickshireman Michael Drayton, rather than a member of Elizabeth's court, it's more likely he would know people in William Shakespeare's circle than in Oxford's. And since *Palladis Tamia* is almost seven hundred pages long and only sixteen of those pages are devoted to contemporary literary criticism, it would be an idiotic choice for a bullhorn to broadcast a national deception. Like placing the Stratford monument in the chancel of a provincial church, burying subtle propaganda in a book few would read is not a good way to advertise a lie.

The Cambridge students who wrote *The Return from Parnassus Part Two* (performed around 1601) thought Shakespeare was the Author. In the play, the Author is always referred to as "Master Shakspeare" or "Master Shakespeare" to mock the actor's newly acquired title. "O sweet Master Shakespeare!" exclaims one character, a foolish theatre-haunting dandy named Gullio, "I'll have his picture in my study at the court" (lines 1054–55). His picture! Gullio, like Ben Jonson, thinks the Author has a recognizable face.

Sometime between 1598 and 1601, Gabriel Harvey, the Cambridge scholar and son of a rope-maker who had read de Vere's verses in Latin and English, jotted down a note in his copy of Speght's *Chaucer*: "The younger sort take much delight in Shakespeares Venus, & Adonis: but his Lucrece, & his tragedie of Hamlet, Prince of Denmarke, have it in them, to please the wiser sort."[22] But he made no mention that Shakespeare was his old friend Oxford. He went on in the note to praise Sir Edward Dyer's *Amaryllis* and Sir Walter Ralegh's *Cynthia*, recommending them as "Excellent matter of emulation for Spencer, Constable, France, Watson, Daniel, Warner, Chapman, Silvester, Shakespeare, & the rest of owr florishing metricians."[23] If there was a secret, Harvey was out of the loop.

In 1604, the poet Anthony Scoloker in describing the perfect poem suggests, "It should be like the *Never-too-well read Arcadia*, . . . or to come home to the vulgars Element, like *Friendly Shakespeare's Tragedies*."[24] Vulgars' element? No one has told him Shakespeare's plays were written by an earl.

The Revels Account book for 1604–1605, which recorded performances at court, lists "Shaxberd" as the "poet" of "Mesur for Mesur" and "The plaie of Errors" and "the Martchant of Venis," even though for most entries the column for "poet" is blank. The Scotsman who entered Shakespeare's name (look at the spelling) could have discreetly written nothing if he harbored any doubts about the authorship of these plays. And if it was thought that Oxford had written them, one would expect the court to acknowledge the fact as it had acknowledged his compositions in the 1570s and 1580s.

When John Webster's drama *The White Devil* was printed in 1612, Webster provided an introductory author's note, "To the Reader," which singled out some of his colleagues:

For mine own part I have ever truly cherished my good opinion of other men's worthy labors, especially of that full and heightened style of Master *Chapman*: The labor'd and understanding works of Master *Johnson*; the no less worthy composures of the both worthily excellent

Master *Beamont* & Master *Fletcher*: And lastly (without wrong last to be named), the right happy and copious industry of M. *Shake-speare*, M. *Decker*, & M. *Heywood*, wishing what I write may be read by their light.[25]
[spelling modernized except for names]

All of the men Webster extols were alive in 1612. And if the man he meant by "Shake-speare" were dead, Webster would hardly speak of his "right happy and copious industry."

In 1614 Thomas Freeman composed a sonnet, "To Master W. Shake-speare," implying the author he calls "Shakespeare" is alive:

> Shakespeare, that nimble Mercury thy brain,
> Lulls many hundred Argus eyes asleep,
> So fit, for all thou fashionest thy vain,
> At the horse-foot fountain thou hast drunk full deep,
> Virtues or vices the [s]ame to thee all one is:
> Who loves chaste life, there's Lucrece for a teacher:
> Who list read lust there's Venus and Adonis,
> True model of a most lascivious lecher.
> Besides in plays thy wit winds like Meander:
> Whence needy new-composers borrow more
> Then Terence doth from Plautus or Menander.
> But to praise thee aright I want thy store:
> Then let thine own works thine own worth upraise,
> And help t' adorn thee with deserved bays.[26]

The next year, Edmund Howes, an editor of Stow's *Annals*, added to the entry for the year 1614, a list of the "excellent Poets" who flourished during Elizabeth's reign, "according to their priorities as neere as I could."[27] "Sir *Philip Sidney* Knight" and "Sir *Frauncis Bacon* Knight" appear near the top, while "M. *Willi. Shakespeare* gentleman" is in the middle. Even if he thought the Author was no longer among the living, he believed his social rank was no higher than the common gentry.

～

Oxfordians believe the misascription of plays after 1604 implies that the Author was dead. But poems were misascribed to "W. Shakespeare" as early as 1599. In that year, William Jaggard brought out *The Passionate Pilgrim by William Shakespeare*, the collection of miscellaneous poems, some by the Author and never before printed, some available elsewhere, some by other writers, and some of unknown authorship lifted from other dubious compilations. So by the Oxfordians' logic, the Author must have died before 1599!

In 1612, Jaggard brought out a new edition of *The Passionate Pilgrim*, which included two long poems from Thomas Heywood's *Troia Britannica*. Heywood complained about this publication in his *Apologie for Actors* (1612):

> Here likewise, I must necessarily insert a manifest injury done me in that work, by taking the two Epistles of *Paris* to *Helen*, and *Helen* to *Paris*, and printing them in a less volume, under the name of another, which may put the world in the opinion I might steal them from him, and he to do himself right, hath since published them in his own name: but as I must acknowledge my lines not worthy his patronage, under whom he hath published them, so the Author I know much offended with M. Jaggard (that altogether unknown to him) presumed to make so bold with his name.[28]

The result of Heywood's protest was that Jaggard removed Shakespeare's by-line from the cover page—but he kept Heywood's poems in the edition. Since a dead man cannot be "much offended," "William Shakespeare" must have been alive in 1612. Whether he was indeed angry with Jaggard we don't know—Heywood could be exaggerating. But look at the words "altogether unknown to him." How can Heywood state with certainty, and in print no less, what Shakespeare knew or didn't know *unless he was told by Shakespeare?*

In light of this document, it becomes obvious that either Shakespeare really was the Author or he was pretending to be, otherwise he would not be offended that Mr. Jaggard had made "so bold with his name." Regardless of whether he wrote the Plays and Poems, Shakespeare was behaving as if he did.

This complaint also shows that Ben Jonson was not the only literary figure who had personal contact with him. On at least one occasion, Heywood spoke to Shakespeare—the "Author." He showed him a copy of *The Passionate Pilgrim*. Shakespeare denied having seen the book before and cursed Jaggard for abusing his name. Heywood left us a record of their conversation.

CHAPTER 13
The Logjam

One thing Oxfordians and orthodox scholars can (or at least *should*) agree on is the basic order the plays were written. It doesn't take a Ph.D. to see that *Titus Andronicus*, *The Comedy of Errors*, and the *Henry VI* plays come before the great tragedies (they're simply not as good), or that *The Merchant of Venice*, *Henry V*, and *Julius Caesar* fall somewhere in between. Anyone can guess that the poetry of early plays would be plodding and ordinary and rife with unimaginative end-stopped lines—lines that are self-contained and do not spill onto the next—such as these from *The Comedy of Errors*:

> Even now a tailor call'd me in his shop,
> And show'd me silks that he had bought for me,
> And therewithal took measure of my body.
> Sure these are but imaginary wiles,
> And Lapland sorcerers inhabit here.
>
> (IV.iii.7–11)

In the same way, one would guess the verse of late plays would be more complex and have more run-on lines:

> Now I will believe
> That there are unicorns; that in Arabia
> There is one tree, the phoenix' throne, one phoenix
> At this hour reigning there.
>
> (*The Tempest*, III.iii.21–24)

Less obvious is the fact that the Author uses Alexandrines, twelve syllable lines, with increasing frequency throughout most of the Canon.[1] His style develops. In *Antony and Cleopatra, Coriolanus, Cymbeline, The Winter's Tale, The Tempest,* and *Henry VIII,* his verse includes many more lines that end with words like *I, thou, he, she, them, am, is, are, do, have, may, shall,* and so forth. These are called "light endings." The above plays also share a fondness for lines which end with words like *and, or, by, at, from,* and such, which are called "weak endings."[2] In short, these plays had to be written within a few years of each other because their poetry is similar. And their low percentage of end-stopped lines and high percentage of Alexandrines show them to have been composed after the great tragedies.

The exact order of composition—whether *Romeo and Juliet* was written before or after *Richard II*—will probably never be known, but the general sequence has been established. First come the *Henry VI* plays, *Richard III,* the early comedies *The Two Gentlemen of Verona, The Comedy of Error The Taming of the Shrew),* and *Titus Andronicus.* Next are *Love's Labor's Lost, King John, Romeo and Juliet, A Midsummer Night's Dream, Much Ado About Nothing, The Merchant of Venice,* and *Richard II.* Then the *Henry IV* plays, followed by *The Merry Wives of Windsor, Henry V, As You Like It,* and *Julius Caesar.* Next come the great tragedies and problem plays—first *Hamlet, Twelfth Night, Troilus and Cressida, All's Well That Ends Well,* then *Measure for Measure, Othello, King Lear, Macbeth.* After these are the late tragedies— *Antony and Cleopatra, Coriolanus, Timon of Athens,* followed by the romances—*Pericles, Cymbeline, The Winter's Tale, The Tempest.* And finally the collaborations with John Fletcher—*Henry VIII, The Two Noble Kinsmen.*

Dating the plays is a different matter. To determine the upper limit of when a play was written, scholars consult records of publication, licensing documents, records of performances, and references to the play in contemporary works—like Francis Meres's *Palladis Tamia.* The dates of a play's sources and the dates of current events that are alluded to in the play set the lower limit. Since a "bad" quarto of *Romeo and Juliet* was published in 1597, the Author's version had to be written before then, and since it uses John Eliot's *Ortho-epia Gallica* (1593) as a source, *Romeo and Juliet* must postdate 1593. In *Love's Labor's Lost,* the Author alludes to a dancing horse that can count:

> Now here is three studied ere you'll thrice wink; and how easy it is to put years to the word 'three,' and study three years in two words, the dancing horse will tell you.
>
> (I.ii.50–54)

John Banks began showing his performing horse, who counted with hoof-beats, in 1591.[3] There could not have been an earlier counting horse, or else Banks's animal (named "Morocco") would never have become famous. The play, then, must have been written after 1591.

Using these methods, scholars have assigned dates to the late tragedies, the romances, and the collaborations later than 1604. This presents a problem for the Oxfordians, since their man died in that year.

Could the plays have been written earlier? Oxford's partisans say yes, and they point to evidence that shows a *Hamlet* was on the boards by 1589 and a *King Leir* (*sic*) by 1594. This is the passage from Thomas Nashe's introduction to Robert Greene's *Menaphon* (1589), which mentions *Hamlet*:

I'll turn back to my first text, of studies of delight; and talk a little in friendship with a few of our trivial translators. It is a common practice nowadays amongst a sort of shifting companions, that run through every art and thrive by none, to leave the trade of *Noverint* whereto they have been born and busy themselves with the endeavors of Art, that could scarcely latinize their neck verse if they should have need; yet English Seneca read by candlelight yields many good sentences, as *Blood is a beggar*, and so forth: and if you entreat him fair in a frosty morning he will afford you whole *Hamlets* I should say handfuls of tragical speeches. But oh grief! *tempus edax rerum*, what's that will last always? The sea exhaled by drops will in a continuance be dry, and Seneca let blood line by line and page by page at length must needs die to our stage: which makes his famished followers to imitate the Kidde [*sic*] in *Aesop*, who enamored with the Fox's new fangles, forsook all hopes of life to leap into a new occupation, and these men renouncing all possibilities of credit or estimation, to intermeddle with Italian translations: wherein how poorly they have plodded (as those that are neither provincial men, nor are able to distinguish of Articles) let all indifferent Gentlemen that have travailed in that tongue discern by their twopenny pamphlets: & no marvel though their home-born mediocrity be such in the matter; for what can be hoped of those, that thrust *Elysium* into hell and have not learned so long as they have lived in the spheres, the just measure of the Horizon without a hexameter. Sufficeth them to bodge up a blank verse with ifs and ands, & otherwise for recreation after their candle stuff, having starched their beards most curiously, to make a peripatetical path into the inner parts of the City, & spend two or three hours in turning over French *Doudie*, where they attract more infection in one minute, than they can do eloquence all days of their life by conversing with any Authors of like argument. But lest in this declamatory vein, I should condemn all and commend none, I will propound to you learned imitation, those men of import, that have laboured with credit in this laudable kind of Translation; in the forefront of whom, I cannot but place that aged Father *Erasmus*, that invested most of our Greek Writers in the robes of the ancient *Romans*.[4]

[spelling modernized]

Without question, Nashe is speaking here of translators, in particular those who leave the trade of Noverint (i.e., copyist) to become playwrights imitating Seneca—even though they can barely Latinize their neck verse (schoolboy Latin homework, carried around the neck). Despite many good sentences and handfuls of excellent speeches, English Seneca has failed on the stage and forced the imitators to translate Italian pamphlets. In addition, they "starch their beards most curiously" and visit French prostitutes in central London, which would indicate that Nashe has someone specific on his mind—a translator and former copyist with a debauched reputation—not the Earl of Oxford.

Probably he's thinking of Thomas Kyd. Kyd's father was a scrivener ("whereto they have been born"), and his play *The Spanish Tragedy*, from about this time, is an imitation of Seneca. Nashe calls the Goat in Aesop's story a "Kidde," probably to let his readers know whom he's talking about. But Kyd may not be the only writer alluded to. Some scholars have argued that the line "if you entreat him fair in a frosty morning" refers to the ghost in *Hamlet*, a role that, by 1709, tradition claimed was played by William Shakespeare.

Regardless of who wrote the early *Hamlet*, it was not the text we have today. Thomas Lodge, in his *Wits Misery* (1596), invokes "the ghost which cried so miserably at the Theatre like an oyster wife, *Hamlet, revenge*."[5] The one line remembered from the early version does not appear in the editions attributed to the Author.

For *Henry VI Part One*, *Henry VI Part Two*, and *Richard III*, the Author steals passages almost verbatim from the second edition of Holinshed's *Chronicles* (1587), passages which were not in the earlier edition. This means that these three plays could not have been written before that year. But some Oxfordians ask us to believe that in the next two years the Author's poetry and dramatic construction developed at such a rapid pace, he was able to produce *Hamlet* in 1589. This was too much for even Ogburn, and he suggested that the Author continued to rewrite *Hamlet* throughout his life. Many scholars agree with him, though they differ in their identification of the Author.

In 1598, Francis Meres assured his readers that

> As *Plautus* and *Seneca* are accounted the best for Comedy and Tragedy among the Latines: so *Shakespeare* among the English is the most excellent in both kinds for the stage; for Comedy, witnes his *Gentlemen of Verona*, his *Errors*, his *Love labors lost*, his *Love labours wonne*, his *Midsummers night dreame*, & his *Merchant of Venice*: for Tragedy his *Richard the 2. Richard the 3. Henry the 4. King John*, *Titus Andronicus*, and his *Romeo and Juliet*. . . . [6]

He neglects to mention *Hamlet* or *Lear*. He overlooks the three parts of *Henry VI*, *Much Ado About Nothing*, and *The Taming of the Shrew* as well (unless *Love's Labor's Won* is an alternative title for one of those plays), but one would think *Hamlet*, even an embryonic *Hamlet*, would merit a listing. Maybe he thought it was by someone else—as traditional scholarship claims it was.

Meres's list implies a bigger problem for Oxfordians. If the plays were written earlier than scholars suspect, then why does Meres name only relatively juvenile works? Why no great tragedies or problem plays? To answer this, Oxfordians must assume that front man Will Shakespeare is "releasing" the plays on the dates scholars think they were composed. Not only does Shakespeare act as an intermediary, he holds onto each play for a few years in order to make it seem like he's writing them at a reasonable pace. As huge as such an assumption is, it does account for Meres's omissions. It would explain why Samuel Daniel had his *Cleopatra* reprinted in 1607 with alterations suggested by the Author's play, and why Jonson's *Epicoene, or The Silent Woman*, acted in 1610, has critical references to *Coriolanus*. It would justify why *The Winter's Tale* was not licensed for performance until 1610 and why *Henry VIII* is described as a new play in a letter of 1613. Though written earlier, these plays were not performed according to this theory until the dates suggested by the evidence.

To bolster their case, Oxfordians contend that the Author did not use any source published after 1603. As we'll see, this is a false statement. But even if it were true, Oxford still could not have written the late plays. To understand why, remember that sources and topical references set a lower limit for a play's date. Now consider that *Othello* makes use of Richard Knolles's 1603 *History of the Turks* and that *Measure for Measure* contains a reference to a September 1603 proclamation calling for the houses and rooms (i.e., brothels) in London's suburbs to be pulled down:[7]

> POMPEY. You have not heard the proclamation, have you?
> MISTRESS OVERDONE. What proclamation, man?
> POMPEY. All houses in the suburbs of Vienna must be plucked down. . . .
> MISTRESS OVERDONE. But shall all our houses of resort in the suburbs be pulled down?
>
> (*Measure for Measure*, I.ii.94–96, 102)

The Poet borrows from Samuel Harsnet's *Declaration of Egregious Popish Impostures* (1603) in *King Lear*, and from John Florio's 1603 translation of Montaigne's *Essaies* in both *King Lear* and *The Tempest*, so neither of those plays could have been written prior to 1603.

For Oxfordians, this is a logjam. Since their man died on 24 June 1604, in the last year of his life he must have penned all four of the above plays as well as all the plays whose more mature, complex, and subtle poetry shows them to come later—*Macbeth*, the late tragedies, the romances, and the two collaborations. Is such an outpouring possible in a single year? Not bloody likely.

Though Oxfordians would like to simply push the composition of the plays back a few years, this is impossible because many of the dates of earlier plays have been confidently established. *Richard II* could be no earlier than one of its sources, Nashe's *Christ's Tears Over Jerusalem* (1593), nor could *Romeo and Juliet* precede *Ortho-epia Gallica* (1593). *The Merchant of Venice* uses *Have with You to Saffron Walden*, also by Nashe, which was not available even in manuscript before 1595. The reference to Essex's campaign in Ireland in *Henry V* dates that play specifically to 1599.[8] At the start of Act Five, the Chorus exclaims,

> How London doth pour out her citizens!
> The mayor and all his brethren in best sort,
> Like to the senators of th' antique Rome,
> With the plebeians swarming at their heels,
> Go forth and fetch their conqu'ring Caesar in;
> As, by a lower but by loving likelihood,
> Were now the general of our gracious Empress,
> As in good time he may, from Ireland coming,
> Bringing rebellion broached on his sword,

How many would the peaceful city quit,
To welcome him!

(V.cho.24–34)

Essex left for Ireland in March of 1599 and returned, defeated, that September. According to Oxfordians, the Author added these lines for a revival of the play at that time but wrote the bulk of the play earlier. I assume they would say the same thing about the reference in *Henry IV Part Two* to the slaughter in February 1596 by Amurath III of his brothers. The new king, Henry V, addresses his family:

Brothers, you mix your sadness with some fear:
This is the English, not the Turkish court,
Not Amurath an Amurath succeeds,
But Harry Harry.

(*Henry IV Part Two*, V.ii.46–49)

(The Author was apparently untroubled by contemporary references in historical scenes.) In any case, Nashe's *Lenten Stuff* and Crompton's *Mansion of Magnanimitie*, both consulted for *Henry V*, were not accessible before 1598, so that play could be no earlier. In a similar vein, *Julius Caesar* has three sources published in 1599.

Some plays, despite Oxfordian protestations, can only be dated after 1604. The Author of *King Lear* had clearly read a February 1606 pamphlet predicting cataclysms following the previous October's solar and lunar eclipses. "The Earth and Moon's late and horrible obscurations," wrote Edward Gresham,

the frequent eclipsations of the fixed bodies, by the wandering, the fixed stars, I mean the planets, within these few years more than ordinary, shall without doubt have their effects no less admirable, than the positions unusual. Which Peucer with many more too long to rehearse out of continual observation and the consent of all authors noted to be, new leagues, traitorous designments, catching at kingdoms, translation of empire, downfall of men in authority, emulations, ambition, innovations, factious sects, schisms, and much disturbance and troubles in religion and matters of the Church, with many other things infallible in sequent such orbical positions and phenomenes.[9]

In the play, Gloucester recapitulates the idea that planetary positions have "sequent" effects:

These late eclipses in the sun and moon portend no good to us. Though the wisdom of nature can reason it thus and thus, yet nature finds itself scourg'd by the sequent effects. Love cools, friendship falls off, brothers divide: in cities, mutinies; in countries, discord; in palaces, treason; and the bond crack'd 'twixt son and father.

(I.ii.103–9)

Edmund comments on his father's fears:

This is the excellent foppery of the world, that when we are sick in fortune—often the surfeits of our own behavior—we make guilty of our disasters the sun, the moon, and stars, as if we were villains on necessity, fools by heavenly compulsion, knaves, thieves, and treachers by spherical predominance; drunkards, liars, and adulterers by an enforc'd obedience of planetary influence; and all that we are evil in, by a divine thrusting on.

(I.ii.118–26)

And he tells Edgar:

I am thinking, brother, of a prediction I read this other day, what should follow these eclipses.

(I.ii.140–41)

(Apparently, he was reading Gresham.)

I promise you, the effects he writes of succeed unhappily, as of unnaturalness between the child and the parent, death, dearth, dissolutions of ancient amities, divisions in state, menaces and maledictions against king and nobles, needless diffidences, banishment of friends, dissipation of cohorts, nuptial breeches and I know not what.

(I.ii.143–49)

As with all his sources, the Author has brilliantly adapted the pamphlet's predictions to suit his play: Edmund's litany of catastrophes foreshadows the subsequent atrocities in the drama.

For *Macbeth*, many factors indicate a date of 1606. First of all, the play was obviously written to flatter King James, and his reign did not commence until 1603. James was directly descended from five characters in the play, and this fact was referred to in Act Four Scene One when the witches show Macbeth a vision of Banquo's descendants:

> I'll see no more.
> And yet the eighth appears, who bears a glass
> Which shows me many more; and some I see
> That twofold balls and treble septres carry.
>
> (IV.i.118–21)

James was the eighth king descended from Banquo and as the first ruler of England, Scotland, and Ireland, he was the first to carry "treble septres." Secondly, the Author alters his source, Holinshed's *Chronicles*, to make his story inoffensive to the king. In the *Chronicles*, Banquo conspires with Macbeth to kill Duncan, unlike in the play, and the enemy of the Scots in the *Chronicles* are the Danes; the Poet changes them to Norwegians because James's wife was sister to the king of Denmark.

In *The Royal Play of Macbeth*, Henry N. Paul shows how the drama shamelessly celebrates some of James's ideas. James wrote, in his *Counter-Blaste to Tobacco*, published in 1604, "it is the King's part (as the proper Physician of his Politic-body) to purge it of all those diseases by Medicines meet for the same."[10] This idea occurs four times in the play: "Ere human statute purged the gentle weal" (III.iv.75); "Meet we the med'cine of the sickly weal/And with him pour we in our country's purge" (V.ii.27–28); "If thou couldst, doctor, cast/The water of my land, find her disease,/And purge it to a sound and pristine health" (V.iii.50–52); "What rhubarb, cyme or what purgative drug/Would scour these English hence?" (V.iii.55–56). James never knew his mother and was nursed by a Protestant, a fact that inspired his famous response to the Pope when he was asked to change his religion: "I sucked Protestant's milk." In his opening speech to his first English Parliament, on 19 March 1604, he made the statement, "I thank God I sucked the milk of God's truth with the milk of my nurse." In *Macbeth* appears the metaphors, "too full of the milk of human kindness" (I.v.17); "take my milk for gall" (I.v.48); and "the sweet milk of concord" (IV.iii.98). No other play has more than one mother's milk reference, and there are only six others in the Canon. This is probably not coincidental. Nor is it likely to be coincidence that the demonology of the play matches that of James's book *Demonologie*, which appeared in the late 1590s.

In his speech to his first Parliament, the King told them, "I bring you two gifts, one peace with foreign nations, the other union with Scotland."[11] As a result, the phrase "Peace and Unity," which embodied the King's political ideals, became a slogan throughout England.[12] In the year 1606, the phrase was enlarged to become a triplet—Love, Peace, and

Unity. For example, Anthony Nixon wrote in *The Black Year* (published 1606), "Many think well of themselves in making the Doctrine of love, peace and unity, the occasion of strife, contention and heresie."[13] On 31 July of that year, the King and his brother-in-law, King Christian of Denmark, made a ceremonial progress through the city of London and stopped at Cheapside to witness a pageant. For this occasion, John Marston was commissioned to write an address in Latin which glorified Love, Peace, and Unity. Love, as a political virtue, he translated as "Concordia," which Marston represented with an allegorical character. A contemporary observer described the scene like this:

> Divine Concord as sent from Heaven, descended in a cloud from the top unto the middle stage, and with a loud voice, spake an excellent speech in Latin, purporting their hearty welcome, with the heavenly happines[s] of peace and unity amongst Christian Princes, etc. but through the distemperature of the unruly multitude the kings could not well hear it, although they inclined their ears very seriously thereunto.[14]

It was only in this Latin address that the triplet became "Concord, Peace and Unity." And yet in the play we find Malcolm disqualifying himself from kingship with the words,

> Nay, had I pow'r, I should
> Pour the sweet milk of concord into hell,
> Uproar the universal peace, confound
> All unity on earth.
>
> (IV.iii.97–100)

Another account tells us the Grooms of the Chamber were part of the kings' procession that day, and, as we've seen, one of the Grooms of the Chamber was the actor William Shakespeare.

1606 was also the year of the worst hurricane in a generation. Robert Johnston, a Scotsman in London, records,

> Spring was very stormy this year, with violent winds and great tempests. At the end of March a frightful hurricane, which had broken out with fierce wind and much hail, ravaged our ocean, destroyed the shipping and produced great and dreadful shipwrecks, the tops of churches being torn away from the roofs. . . . In Antwerp four towers, the great-

est and highest of all in the city were thrown down. Amongst us there occurred immense destruction of houses, roofs and trees.[15]

A separate account by Edmond Howes relates,

> The twenty nine and thirtieth of March the wind was extreme violent, so as it caused much shipwrack upon the coasts of England, France and the Low countries; it brought in the sea and drowned much cattle; and in Picardy near Dyope, it blew down a steeple which slew four score persons in the fall thereof.[16]

Compare these to lines from Act Four Scene One of *Macbeth*:

> Though you untie the winds, and let them fight
> Against the churches; though the yesty waves
> Confound and swallow navigation up;
> Though bladed corn be lodg'd, and trees blown down;
> Though castles topple on their warders' heads;
> Though palaces and pyramids do slope
> Their heads to their foundations; though the treasure
> Of nature's germains tumble all together,
> Even till destruction sicken.
>
> (IV.i.52–60)

In Elizabethan English, *steeples* and *pyramids* were synonymous. The Author has in mind the same catastrophe at Picardy. The timing of the hurricane, just a week after the beginning of spring, explains this passage:

> As whence the sun 'gins his reflection
> Shipwracking storms and direful thunders break,
> So from that spring whence comfort seem'd to come
> Discomfort swells.
>
> (I.ii.25–28)

Instead of comfort, the return of sunlight brought "shipwracking storms" in 1606.

Equivocation, the use of ambiguous expressions to mislead, is practiced by the apparitions ("none of woman born/Shall harm Macbeth," they say, neglecting to mention that his future assassin would be "from his mother's womb untimely ripp'd"), and the embattled king later begins to "doubt th' equivocation of the fiend." Equivocation is practiced by Ross when he tells Macduff, "No, [your children] were well at peace when I did leave 'em," rather than saying they were dead. The Porter, imagining himself the porter of Hell-gate, jests "here's an equivocator . . . who committed treason enough for God's sake, yet could not equivocate to heaven."

Why is the play drenched in equivocation? In 1606, Father Henry Garnet, the leading Jesuit in England, was accused of conspiring in the Gunpowder Plot, a famous attempt by a group of Catholics to blow up Parliament with kegs of gunpowder. At his trial, Garnet explained the doctrine of equivocation, which permitted Catholics to lie when asked the whereabouts of priests. An account of his long debate with the prosecutor, Lord Edward Coke, was published in May of that year. (The Porter's speech about how drink is an equivocator with lechery seems to be a burlesque of Coke's arguments.) Reporting on the proceedings, the Venetian ambassador wrote that the doctrine had "shocked the ministers and especially the King who is particularly versed in such matters."[17] On the scaffold, Garnet was warned not to equivocate. So it's logical the equivocation in the play would take its inspiration from this episode.

Oxfordians counter that the Author did not have Henry Garnet in mind at all, but rather Robert Southwell.[18] In 1595, Southwell was convicted under a law which said every Jesuit found in England was automatically guilty of treason. At his trial, he admitted to being a Jesuit but argued that the law was unjust since there was no proof he had committed any treasonable act. A good argument, but he was hanged anyway. Equivocation had nothing to do with his case.[19]

In dating *The Tempest*, scholars note parallels between the text and three accounts of a 1609 shipwreck—*A Discovery of the Barmudas*, by Sylvester Jourdain (published October 1610), *A True Declaration of the Estate of the Colonie in Virginia*, which was cobbled together from several documents and appeared in November 1610, and William Strachey's *True Reportory of the Wrack and Redemption of Sir Thomas Gates, Knight* (written in 1610 though not published until 1625; in manuscript, it was shared among members of the Virginia Company who financed the voyage). Many of these parallels involve descriptions of the shipwreck and, as Oxfordians point out, could be coincidental. Every shipwreck, after all, is pretty much the same. But other correspondences are not so easily dismissed.

For example, in his description of the storm, Strachey speaks of a "glut of water,"[20] and Gonzalo, speaking of the boatswain, says,

> He'll be hanged yet,
> Though every drop of water swear against it,
> And gape at wid'st to glut him.
>
> (I.i.58–60)

This is the Author's only use of the word *glut*.[21] Strachey describes "the sharpe windes blowing Northerly"; Prospero mentions "the sharp wind of the north" (I.ii.254). Strachey uses the phrase "bear up" twice—"bearing somewhat up" and "our Governour commanded the Helmeman to beare up"; the phrase also occurs twice in *The Tempest*—"to bear up/Against what should ensue" (I.ii.157–58) and "therefore bear up and board 'em" (III.ii.2–3). The Author's only other use of "bear up" is in *The Winter's Tale*, which, by its poetry, was written at about the same time. Strachey and his fellow mariners were stranded on an island where they found "berries, whereof our men seething, straining, and letting stand some three or four days, made a kind of pleasant drink"; Caliban reminds Prospero, "thou . . . wouldst give me water with berries in't" (I.ii.333–34). *A True Declaration* calls the Bermudas "a place hardly accessible" and "an uninhabited desert," though Jourdain, in *A Discovery*, adds, "yet did we finds there the air so temperate and the Country so abundantly fruitful of all fit necessaries." In the play, Adrian observes, "Though this island seem to be desert . . . uninhabitable and almost inaccessible . . . yet . . . it must needs be of subtle, tender, and delicate temperance" (II.i.35–43). Strachey's account contains a digression that mentions Aeneas, followed by another digression that mentions Dido; *The Tempest* contains a digression on Aeneas and Dido too:

> GONZALO. Not since widow Dido's time.
> ANTONIO. Widow? a pox o' that! How came that widow in? Widow Dido!
> SEBASTIAN. What if he had said "widower Aeneas" too? Good Lord, how you take it!
>
> (II.i.77–81)

Strachey describes "great strokes of thunder, lightning, and rain in the extremity of violence"; in the play, the Author uses the word "thunderstroke" twice (II.i.204; II.ii.108)—his only uses of the word in the Canon. Strachey describes "boske [small bushes] running along the ground"; Ceres, in Prospero's "pageant," mentions "my bosky acres" (IV.i.81)—

likewise the Author's only use of this word. There are many, many more correspondences from the flora and fauna of the island to unusual words like *hoodwink*, not to mention basic plot elements including the storm, the separation of the flagship from its fleet, its apparant loss, the survival of everyone aboard, conspiracies, drunken sailors and dangerous natives.[22]

Without a doubt, the Author read Strachey. So, without a doubt, de Vere cannot be the Author.

Had Strachey's account been written in 1602, there is no question Oxfordians would argue its use is obvious and that their man, as an earl and an investor in exploration from as early as 1577, would have had the best access to it—even though he was not himself an investor in the Virginia Company. As it happens, William Shakespeare was not an investor in the Virginia Company either. But Dudley Digges, stepson of Shakespeare's executor Thomas Russell, was. As was Sir Henry Rainsford of Clifford Chambers, two miles south of Stratford. Both Rainsford and Shakespeare were left bequests in John Combe's will, Shakespeare's son-in-law was Rainsford's physician, and Shakespeare's houseguest Thomas Greene was Rainsford's friend, so it's likely Shakespeare knew him. William Leveson, who was in charge of attracting investors for the Virginia Company, had acted as a trustee in the 1599 purchase of shares in the Globe; Shakespeare would have known him too.

Another post-1604 play is *Henry VIII*. Because it celebrates the birth of Queen Elizabeth, Oxfordians like to think it must have been written during her reign. But the play is sympathetic to Katherine of Aragon, Henry's first wife, and could never have passed the censors during Elizabeth's lifetime. In fact, the play belongs to a cultural revival of interest in Elizabeth in the second decade of the seventeenth century. John Speed wrote her biography in 1611, and William Leigh published a collection of sermons in 1612 entitled *Queen Elizabeth Paralleled in the Princely Virtues with Daniel, Joshua, Hezekia*. In the mid-1600s, Bishop Godfrey Goodman summarized this phenomenon:

[A]fter a few years, when we had experience of the Scottish Government . . . the Queen did seem to revive, then was her memory much magnified—such ringing of bells, such public joy and sermons in commemoration of her, the picture of her tomb painted in many churches.[23]

When their honeymoon with James was over, the English looked back nostalgically to their previous monarch. *Henry VIII* fits like a puzzle piece into this time.

≈

Now we come to the collaborations. The Oxfordians cannot explain how their man could coauthor plays with John Fletcher, a playwright whose earliest known piece is from 1606. So they offer the seemingly sensible theory that the Author, being dead, left several unfinished manuscripts which were completed by other hands.[24] These would include *Timon of Athens*, *Pericles*, *Henry VIII*, and *The Two Noble Kinsmen*. But this idea ignores the division of labor in these plays, which is inconsistent with one writer completing the other's work. In *Henry VIII*, the two distinct styles (one very similar to the Author's late style and one very similar to Fletcher's[25]) exist in parts of the play that are dependent on scenes supplied by the other man. The Author's scene between an old lady and Anne Bullen requires Anne's previous introduction, which was written by Fletcher. Fletcher introduces the Cranmer story, which the Author then picks up. Both men seem to be working from the same plan, each writing individual scenes, in a typical Elizabethan collaboration—two or more poets could, in this way, write separate sections simultaneously and compose a play twice as fast. In *The Two Noble Kinsman*, the Author's three brief scenes involving the Jailer's Daughter are not connected with each other nor are they important by themselves; they depend upon Fletcher's more substantial contribution to the subplot. Therefore, like the *Henry VIII* sections, these scenes must have been written in collaboration. The Oxfordian response to this argument has been to deny the Author had anything to do with *The Two Noble Kinsmen*, despite the evidence of verse tests, comparisons of style, and the title page of the 1634 quarto, which reads "written by the memorable worthies of their time, Mr. John Fletcher, and Mr. William Shakspeare, Gent."

In the past twenty years, Middleton has been thought to have collaborated with the Author on *Timon of Athens*.[26] As with Fletcher, the parts assigned to Middleton are so large and necessary (the second scene of Act One, the whole of Act Three, the second halves of two long scenes in Act Four), it's unlikely the play was left unfinished and then completed by the collaborator.

≈

Let's say that the plays were written earlier than the dates assigned to them. This means the Author could not have learned from many of the writers who are generally believed to have influenced him. Lyly, Marlowe, Spenser, Chapman, Daniel, Jonson, Beaumont, and Fletcher, must all have read his work, but he could not have read theirs. Influences flow in only one direction, and he becomes the originator of almost every trend in contemporary drama—Senecan tragedies, history plays, Elizabethan satires, Jacobean comedy, antimasques, and more. *Cymbeline* and *The Winter's Tale* must be models for the plays of Beaumont and Fletcher, not conscious imitations of the duo's manner, because the pair did not begin writing until Oxford was dead. The whimsical and elaborate Stuart court masques must have been inspired by the similar masque scene in *The Tempest*, because the first such masque was in 1605.

In this way, the Oxfordian's Author is even more of a superman than the Stratfordian's. And he was not only a visionary artist but a prophet. In *Lear*, in 1603, he writes of "these late eclipses of the sun and moon" and then two years later, there are lunar and solar eclipses two weeks apart.[27] He writes a play, *Macbeth*, which is pervaded with the idea of equivocation, and then three years later the word takes on treasonous significance. He imagines a shipwreck in 1604 and five years afterwards it is enacted in life, right down to the bosky acres and berry wine.

Of course, coincidences happen all the time, and it's possible they could account for some of the apparent fortunetelling on the part of the Author. But when coincidences pile up, as they do in this case, it's time to look to a logical explanation. Logically, the events came first. The plays were influenced by the events. And the Earl of Oxford was silent in his grave.

CHAPTER 14
Grief and Strife

To find holes in the Oxfordian case is easy enough, and, in theory, it shouldn't be difficult to out and out disprove it. All one has to do is compare the Works to the writings and poems of Oxford—the earl left seventy-six letters and memoranda (all but two in his own hand) as well as sixteen (possibly twenty) poems and the introduction to Thomas Bedingfield's translation of *Cardanus Comfort*.[1] But the nature of the two bodies of work (one largely plays, the other largely letters) and their sizes (Oxford's surviving output comes to only a few thousand words while the Author's Canon has millions) makes comparing them problematic.

Let's take vocabulary. Several words in Oxford's letters don't appear in the Works. Because the earl's sample size is small, this is significant. But an author's vocabulary for letter writing is different from his artistic vocabulary. It's perfectly normal to use words in a letter that one would not use in a play or poem. So vocabulary differences prove nothing. It's suspicious that eighteen of Oxford's letters (written between 1594 and 1599) discuss his desire to be granted control of Her Majesty's tin mines, and yet the word *tin* never appears in the Author's Canon—but perhaps Oxford made a conscious effort to avoid the word in his plays, fearing it might give away his identity. It's equally suspicious that an evocative word like *brandel*, meaning shake or unsettle (as one might unsettle sediment), would be used in an image in personal correspondence—"brandel the clearness of your guiltless conscience"[2]—but not in a work of art by the same writer. Still, it proves nothing. Similar words like *immerse* and *recede* never appear in the Canon either, yet we would not be surprised to find them in letters by the Author.

The same two pitfalls, sample size and kind of writing, complicate comparisons of style. We can say Oxford and the Author share a penchant for interchanging parts of speech, for paradoxes, antitheses, and gerunds, while the Author's imagery, personifications, and metaphors are missing from the letters—but again the discrepancy proves nothing. Letters are not works of art. The same two weaknesses exist in computer analyses of word-use patterns. Even when only poetry is compared, the sample of the earl's verse (476 lines) is too small to establish word patterns that can be convincingly contrasted with the Author's.

So what *can* we look at?

Well, there's spelling. The First Folio substitutes "dg" for "g" in many words, which is characteristic of the Midlands. In Stratford documents, *digging* is spelled "dydgen" and *nutmegs* is "nutmedggs."[3] In the same way, the first edition of the Sonnets renders *privilege* as "priviledge." The Folio *Merchant of Venice* spells *hugged* "hudg'd" in the line "Hudg'd and embraced by the strumpet wind" (II.vi.16), and *acknowledge* appears in the Folio, all six times, as it's rendered today—we have adopted the Midlands spelling. The Earl of Oxford, however, spells *acknowledge* eight times as "acknowlege" and once as "acknowne." He spells the past tense "acknowlegged" and "acknowlegd," the gerund "acknowleginge," and the subjunctive "acknowlegethe"—he never adds the "d" before the "g."

By examining Oxford's manuscripts, Alan H. Nelson, de Vere's most recent biographer, has found the earl's spelling was full of idiosyncracies.[4] De Vere tended to write "cowld" for *could*, "showld" for *should*, and "wowld" for *would*. Almost always he wrote "lek" for *like*, even when *like* was a root word such as in *mislike*, which he spelled "misleke." He often put a "t" at the end of *although*, *enough*, *though*, and *through* and spelled *slip* as "slypte" and *highness* as "hightnes." Some of his characteristic spellings include "accept" for *except*, "agers" for *agents*, "churge" for *church*, "impodent" for *impudent*, "lenghe" for *length*, "mythinks" for *methinks*, "oft" for *ought*, "obsurdite" for *absurdity*, "reame" for *realm*, "subiest" for *suggest*, "Wesmester" for *Westminster* and "yowse" for *use*. In some cases, he adds syllables such as when he writes "importunate" for *importune*. Likewise, he always writes his own name as "Oxenford" or "Oxenforde." If the earl wrote the plays, would not the characters called "Oxford" be addressed as "Oxenford"? And wouldn't Baptista Minola's first line in *The Taming of the Shrew* be "Gentlemen, importunate no further," rather than "importune me no further"?

Oxford's most characteristic spellings, Nelson observes, never occur in the Author's Works. And what are believed to be idiosyncratic spellings by the Author, such as "scilens" for *silence*, never occur in Oxford's manuscripts. Oxfordians argue that the printers changed the spelling, and they could be right. Compositors, setting the letters of type, routinely changed authors' spellings according to their own individual preferences.[5] But even with the alterations by professional scribes, editors, and printers, it seems unlikely that no trace of the Author's signature spellings would remain in his published works (at least those published under the name William Shakespeare). To account for this, Oxfordians must once again resort to an assumption. They must assume that Will Shakespeare copied the plays and poems into his own hand, with his own spelling. This theory would explain why his fellows found hardly a blot in his papers and why Warwickshire renderings of words are found in the plays. To persuade Oxfordians otherwise, we'll have to look elsewhere.

According to Nelson, Oxford's spelling of *likelihoods* as "leklywhodes" and *falsehood* as "falswhood" reveal *e*-for-*i* and *wh*-for-*h* substitutions that are characteristic of an East Anglian dialect.[6] Growing up in Essex and Cambridge, he acquired the local pronunciations of words. This gave me an idea. It occurred to me that if Oxford's provincial accent was evident in his spelling, it would also show itself in his rhymes. My wife, who is from the Midwest, pronounces *Mary*, *merry*, and *marry* all in the same way and would rhyme them all with *hairy*, while I, being from New York, would rhyme *hairy* only with *Mary*, because I pronounce the other words differently. For me, *Mary*, *merry*, and *marry* have three distinct vowel sounds. Perhaps, like midwesterners and New Yorkers, Oxford and the Author rhymed words in different ways. We can see this is true for the Author and Milton. Milton, in "On the Morning of Christ's Nativity" (1629), rhymes "God" with "abode,"[7] implying that he pronounced the word *God* with a long "o"; meanwhile, the Author, in *Cymbeline* and *Timon of Athens*, rhymes "gods" with "odds," implying a short, open, "ah"-sounding "o."

So I began to study Oxford's verse. To be honest, I had little hope of success. Most of the rhymes in de Vere's extant poetry are commonplace, so there was little chance they would not be found in the Author's immense and varied Canon. In addition, pronunciation-expert Helge Kökeritz tells us that "already in the sixteenth century, and probably earlier, there had apparently developed a rhyming tradition that was to some extent independent of the contemporary pronunciation. Each new generation of poets preferred to use more or less the same rhymes as the preceding one and continued to do so long after some of the syllables they coupled in rhyme had ceased to be pronounced alike. . . . This is the genesis of the eye rhyme, e.g. love:prove, good: blood, still a characteristic of English prosody."[8] In other words, rhyming patterns were conventional and not dependent on pronunciation. To make matters worse, Londoners at this time pronounced the same word in different ways. For example, *sea* was spoken as *see* (with a long "e") but also as *say* (i.e., with a long "a" sound). The influx of people from other parts of England encouraged these double and even triple pronunciations, which poets took advantage of to facilitate their rhyming.[9]

On the bright side, the small quantity of Oxford's verse would be an ally. Because I'm comparing something small (fewer than 250 rhyme pairs) to something large (all of the Author's rhymes), finding just one discrepancy would be significant. It would mean that Oxford saw a rhyme where the Author did not and was therefore, most likely, a different person.

The first doubtful rhyme that caught my eye was from Oxford's poem that begins "I am not as I seem to be":

> And Caesar that presented was,
> With noble Pompeye's princely hedd,
> As 'twere some judge, to rule the case,
> A floud of teares, he semde to shedd.[10]

"Was" and "case"? In another poem possibly by Oxford, one that begins "Sitting alone upon my thought in melancholy mood," he rhymes "face" with "glasse." This was not unusual at the time. In the sixteenth century, *ace* and *ass* were homonyms for many speakers.[11] Yet in all the Author's plays and poems, there is only one instance of a word that is rhymed with *face* rhyming with a word that is rhymed with *glass*, and it's a dubious example.[12] *The Comedy of Errors* contains this speech:

> O villain, thou hast stol'n both mine office and my name:
> The one ne'er got me credit, the other mickle blame.
> If thou hadst been Dromio to-day in my place,
> Thou wouldst have chang'd thy face for a name, or thy name
>   for an ass.

> (III.i.44–46)

This passage comes at the end of a long section, all in rhymed couplets, which contains the rhyme "pass:ass." The odd meter of the last line may indicate the writer is aware he is only rhyming the consonant "s"—a poetic technique called *consonance*—and he's doing it for emphasis. It's really "face" he's rhyming with "place."

Oxford's poem "Love Compared to a Tennis Play" contains the rhyme "shows:lose":

> Whereas the heart at Tennis plays and men to gaming fall,
> Love is the Court, Hope is the House, and Favour serves the
>   Ball.
> The Ball itself is True Desert, the Line which Measure shows
> Is Reason, whereon Judgment looks how players win or lose.

A similar rhyme occurs only once in the Works. In the play-within-a-play in *Hamlet*, the Player King declaims,

> What to ourselves in passion we propose,
> The passion ending, doth the purpose lose.
>
> (III.ii.194–95)

Everywhere else the Author rhymes "lose" with "choose" and "abuse." Since he also puns on "lose-loose," he probably pronounced the word as we do in America today. "Lose" with a long "o" was an older pronunciation.[13] Perhaps the Author was using it here to call attention to this important couplet—important because it expresses the ultimate theme of the play. Other writers, however, preferred the long "o." Spenser commonly rhymed "lose" with "expose," "dispose," "rose," and so forth, and Oxford seems to have done the same.

In another poem possibly by Oxford, a poem entirely in rhyming couplets, the earl makes a rhyme of "head" and "had":

> I went to gather Strawberries tho' when woods and groves were
>   fair
>   And parch'd my face with Phoebus lo, by walking in the air.
> I lay me down all by a stream and banks all over head,
>   And there I found the strangest dream, that ever young man
>   had.

[spelling modernized]

Nothing similar exists in the Canon, even though *head* seems to have been pronounced in two different ways—with a short "e" vowel sound like in *bed* and with a long "a," rhyming with *made*. But maybe this poem is not by Oxford, and that's why it contains a non-"Shakespearean" rhyme.

Here are some lines that Steven W. May has determined are "definitely" by de Vere:

> I live abrod but styll in secreat greef,
> Then least alone when most I seeme to lurke;
> I speak of peace, and lyve in endless stryfe,
> And when I playe than are my thoughts at worke.

The Author never rhymes *strife* with anything but *life* and *wife* (and, by extension, *knife*—which he rhymes with the other two). *Grief* he rhymes with *brief, chief, relief,* and *thief.* For the Poet, *grief:strife* was not a possible pair. But for Oxford, it was. That he rhymes these words shows nothing about pronunciation—based on the spelling and other rhymes, Oxford may have pronounced these words in more than one way, with different vowel sounds—but it does show he thought *grief:strife* an acceptable rhyme, while in a much bigger sample, it seems never to have occurred to the Author.

One thing that definitely never occurred to the Author was to rhyme a word that ended with an "s" with a word that did not. Yet Oxford, in 368 lines (not counting the possible lines), does this twice. Once in "Love Compared to a Tennis Playe" he rhymes "proves" and "Love":

> And lo, the Racket is Free will, which makes the Ball rebound,
> And noble Beauty is the chase, of every game the ground.
> But Rashness strikes the Ball awry, and where is Oversight?
> 'A Bandy ho!' the people cry, and so the Ball takes flight.
> Now in the end Goodliking proves
>   Content the game and gain.
> Thus is a tennis knit I Love,
>   A Pleasure mix'd with Pain.

He rhymes "flames" with "dame" in the poem that begins "A crown of bays shall that man wear":

> Drown me with trickling tears,
>   you wailful wights of woe;
> Come help these hands to rend my hairs,
>   my rueful haps to show.

On whom the scorching flames
  of love doth feed you see;
Ah a lalalantida, my dear dame,
  hath thus tormented me.

Sometimes the Author rhymed a terminal "s" with a terminal "s" *sound*, as in "enemies:cowardice" and "fleet'st:sweets" but he always rhymes the "s," even in the assonant rhyme "designs:times" in *Richard III*.

    Singulars:plurals, *was:case*, *grief:strife*—Oxford and the Author rhymed words differently. And probably they pronounced words differently, too. Without question, and with a certainty Oxfordians would find good enough when applied to any other candidate, we can conclude: These are two different poets. Unless he altered the way he rhymed words, the Earl of Oxford did not write the poetry of William Shakespeare.

CHAPTER 15
All Conspiracy Theories Are Alike

The medieval nominalist William of Ockham created the philosophical tool called Ockham's Razor. Usually stated as "The simplest explanation is most likely to be right," it's in fact a warning against sloppy reasoning. What Ockham actually said was, "Assumptions must not be multiplied beyond necessity." Don't assume what you don't *have* to assume. Applying this rule to the Oxford theory we can see it's riddled with wild, improbable assumptions. Here are just a few:

1. For some reason yet to be determined, writing plays and narrative poems anonymously was unsatisfactory for the earl, so he enlisted William Shakespeare as his front man.

2. All evidence of any connection between the two has been either lost or destroyed.

3. People acquainted with the semi-literate actor never realized he couldn't write the witty and elegant plays, or if they did, they kept their mouths shut. Shakespeare was able to convince all those around him of his authorship or to enlist them in the plot.

4. And what a plot it must have been! Beginning in 1593, when the name "William Shakespeare" was first attached to a production of the Author's quill (the narrative poem *Venus and Adonis*), the hoax continued for decades, after the Author's death, after the death of the front man, after the publication of the First Folio—as long as anyone who knew the truth survived. The scheme was so successful that no public doubts about Shakespeare's authorship arose for 232 years and the actual Author was not identified for 72 more.

5. As a poet, the earl made huge leaps, including changing his characteristic rhyming pattern. The extant poems by de Vere, all of which are plainly inferior to the Author's, must have been composed when the earl was a young man.

6. In his forties, he wrote dedications to the Earl of Southampton, a man whom he was trying to marry to his daughter, first pretending to be a solicitous poet and then pretending their relationship had grown closer.

7. He wrote plays for one company of actors while patronizing another, denying his own players popular works like *Hamlet*.

8. As a writer, he was not influenced by Beaumont, or Fletcher, or Jonson, or Middleton, or Stuart court masques.

9. Topical references that date some plays to the late 1590s were added at the time of performance, not when the plays were written.

10. The order of composition of the plays, as determined by the development of their poetry, is wrong. *Othello, King Lear, Macbeth, Measure for Measure*, and *The Tempest* must have been his last plays, all written in the final year of his life, while plays conventionally dated between 1604 and 1611, like *Antony and Cleopatra, Coriolanus, Cymbeline*, and *The Winter's Tale*, were really composed earlier.

11. Plays like *Timon of Athens, Pericles, Henry VIII*, and *The Two Noble Kinsmen* were not collaborations, but were left unfinished at the time of his death and completed by other hands.

12. The evidences that the Strachey letter of 1609 was a principal source for *The Tempest* are just astounding coincidences.

13. Shakespeare released the plays at a rate of about two a year even after Oxford's death, thus *The Winter's Tale* was not licenced until 1610 and *Henry VIII* was called a "new" play in 1613.

14. Shakespeare or someone else changed Oxford's characteristic spelling for every published work.

Etc., etc., etc.—the list is endless.

When applied to history, Ockham's Razor militates against conspiracy theories. And anti-Stratfordianism, regardless of candidate, is a conspiracy theory. Denial of Shakespeare follows exactly the same flawed reasoning as Holocaust denial, though obviously it lacks the same moral dimension. First, the theorists reject the most obvious explanation of an event because it conflicts with a deeply held subjective opinion: the plays must have been written by a scholar-lawyer-nobleman; the Germans could never have attempted systematic genocide. Then, the theorists reinterpret evidence to fit their fixed idea. Rather than letting the facts speak for themselves, they assume their conclusion and regard every piece of evidence in its light: the authors of the Parnassus plays believed Shakespeare was illiterate; the ovens at Auschwitz baked bread. Meanwhile, facts that contradict the theory are explained by conspiracy: Ben Jonson is lying; death camp survivors are lying. Any absences of evidence, like mention of books in Shakespeare's will or missing birth records for Holocaust victims, are regarded as proof of a hoax.

The same dynamic is at work in the Kennedy assassination theories and in doubts about the *Apollo 11* lunar landing. A subjective opinion is held to be sacrosanct—Lee Harvey Oswald did not shoot John F. Kennedy; the United States could not have landed a man on the moon. Evidence is reinterpreted—smoke near the grassy knoll came from a second gunman's rifle; NASA's mock-up lunar surface was where the moonwalks were staged. Inconvenient facts are explained by conspiracy— doctors who performed the autopsy on Kennedy are lying; astronauts are lying. The arguments of the Flat Earth Society follow the same pattern.

Because all contrary evidence is explained away, conspiracy theories are really not theories at all. They are faiths. A good theory can be proven false—it's falsifiable—but Authorship theories are not. If Anne Shakespeare's grave were exhumed and a sonnet signed by Shakespeare were found to be clutched in her skeletal fingers, it would not convince the Oxfordians. They would claim he had copied the poem from Oxford's papers and was taking advantage of his position as front man to pretend to be a poet for his wife. This is what is meant by unfalsifiable. Belief overwhelms rational perception. A subjective opinion is valued over objective evidence.

For this reason, despite my subtitle, there can never be an end to the Authorship Question. No appeal to evidence can ever convince true believers, because nothing can disprove their fixed idea.

Many anti-Stratfordians will not even acknowledge they are conspiracy theorists. They don't believe in a cover-up or that Shakespeare acted as a front man; they think the plays were somehow simply misascribed. But every heretic believes in at least one conspiracy, a conspiracy in academia. They think that for the past century and a half university professors have blinded themselves to the truth because they have a vested interest in maintaining the "fiction" of William Shakespeare, that the academics prefer an Author we know little about so they can project their own biases onto the Works. The anti-Stratfordians refuse to accept that many scholars *have* looked into their arguments but have found them unsound. They refuse to accept that there is a fundamental difference between speculation based on evidence and speculation based on subjective opinion.

Their case against Shakespeare is a con game. And like all con games, it's based on misdirection. By separating the business documents from the literary ones, the Stratford records from the London records, the plays from the life, they create two constructs: Master Shakspere and the Author—one an actor-businessman and the other an educated, aristocratic man of letters. Part of the blame for the creation of these constructs must lie with the man himself. If he had severed his ties with Stratford and moved to London permanently, if he had acquired more enemies willing to gossip about him, if he had gotten himself arrested or sued, we would probably know more about his life and personality. Had he not tried to create two lives for himself, one in the city and one in the country, it would be less easy for others to do it for him. But Shakespeare's two lives are united—by the monument, the Folio, Ben Jonson's testimony, later testimony of actors, and circumstantial evidence, all of which must be condemned as part of a cover-up in order for the anti-Stratfordians to prevail.

Though believing themselves to be amateur historians, the Oxfordians approach evidence in a way that is, in fact, anti-historical. Rather than putting documents like *Groats-worth of Wit* and *Henry VI Part Three* together, they keep them apart lest "Shakescene" be a reference to Shakespeare. They look at portions of documents, such as Nashe's introduction to *Menaphon*, instead of wholes. They call opinions (like Twain's) evidence and omissions (like Shakespeare's lack of personal correspondence) proof. They dismiss "the Stratford man" as a candidate because their idea of him does not conform with their idea of the Author. In reality, the Oxfordians are not looking for the Author at all—they are looking for Oxford, and like Baconians and Derbyites before them, they inevitably find their man.

To be sure, we must make a few assumptions if we are to believe William Shakespeare wrote the Works. But I submit that each of the assumptions is reasonable.

1. His handwriting was better than his signatures.

This is true for most people, and other factors—like unsharpened quills, arthritis, ill health, or writer's cramp—may have contributed to the imperfect state of his autograph. It must also be considered that none of the extant signatures was penned before 1612; they may all postdate his writing career.

2. He attended grammar school.

Given his father's position as an alderman and former Bailiff, it would have been very unusual if Shakespeare hadn't gone to the King's Free School in Stratford. The fact that he became an actor means he had to learn to read somewhere, and grammar school would have been the likely place. There, he would have studied Latin. Even though there's no record of his education, there's no record of Ben Jonson's or George Chapman's either, and yet both of them demonstrate a command of Latin.

3. He knew some French.

There were plenty of French tutors, teach-yourself-French books, and French expatriates in London at the time, and it's logical that some French must have been comprehensible by the popular audience or the scenes in French would never have been written. We know he lived with a bilingual family in 1604 and that his ne'er-do-well son-in-law Thomas Quiney knew some French. Because the plays don't indicate an author with a profound knowledge of the language, he wouldn't have had to have been fluent, in any case. Where he learned his French is unknown, but then no one knows where John Marston learned Dutch for *The Dutch Courtesan*, where Ben Jonson learned Spanish for *The Alchemist*, or where George Chapman learned German for *Alphonsus Emporer of Germany*, either.

4. He knew some law.

Other playwrights use similar legal phrases; law language was the idiom of the time. Much of his legal vocabulary came from his sources, but he also might have learned it from the work of other writers—or from the street. Court procedures and legal contracts were familar to many people. Self-educated Ben Jonson parodies the language of a formal legal agreement in the Induction to *Bartholomew Fair*. It's probably not a coincidence that the real estate and property cases he would have observed at the Stratford Court of Record and the law cases he was named in, such as *Shakespeare v. Lambert*, involve precisely the aspects of law that the Author is most familiar with.

    5. He was intimate with falconry.

Hawking would have been a natural pastime for would-be gentlemen like Shakespeare and his father, John. The sport's popularity among the rising middle class was satirized by Jonson.

    6. He had access to translations now lost, or he learned their content indirectly.

Others who had read the Italian originals may have supplied him with some plots; Robert Armin could have done so. Armin probably didn't join the Lord Chamberlain's Men until 1598 or 1599, but there were many Italian speakers in London, and an entire expatriate community. The advertisement in *Painter's Palace of Pleasure* implies that manuscript translations did exist for several allegedly untranslated authors.

    7. He was younger than the references to old age in the Sonnets suggest.

Sonnet 138—which contains the line "And wherefore say not I that I am old?"—was written when he was at most thirty-four, but it may not be autobiographical. Alternatively, his feeling old may be in relation to the young friend and the dark mistress. Or he may be speaking of feeling old spiritually, as when Macbeth laments his "way of life is fallen into the sear, the yellow leaf." Or, perhaps, Shakespeare indeed thought of himself as old even in his early thirties. Life expectancy was shorter then.

    At its root, the Authorship Question is about Shakespeare's education. The heretics assume the false premise that the Author could not have rhetorical sophistication without an aristocratic upbringing or two magical years in a university. If Shakespeare had gone to Cambridge, his vocabulary and knowledge of the classics would seem to be explicable, and it's safe to say there would be no doubts about his authorship.

    The controversy is also about our discomfort with greatness. Emerson writes in his Journals, "Is it not strange that the transcendent men, Homer, Plato, Shakespeare confessedly unrivalled, should have questions of identity and of genuineness raised respecting their writings?"[1] In the same vein, J. M. Robertson observed, "It is very doubtful whether the Baconian theory would ever have been framed had not the idolatrous Shakespeareans set up a visionary figure of the Master."[2] It's not coincidental the doubts about Shakespeare began in the nineteenth century as the cult of Shakespeare arose. In this century, some have taken to believe that

Einstein's wife was the real genius and the physicist unfairly took the credit. It's always the most important historical events or figures whose reality is doubted. As no less an expert than Adolf Hitler observed, "The great masses of people . . . will more easily fall victim to a big lie than to a small one."[3] Which is why there has never been a Jonson Authorship Question. We don't wonder how a bricklayer's apprentice who probably left school before age thirteen could write genuinely learned plays like *Sejanus* because Jonson doesn't mean that much to us. We don't revere him as mysteriously superhuman, so there's no need to make him more like us.

Shakespeare, of course, wasn't superhuman either. He was an upper–middle-class actor-playwright who never learned to empathize completely with the servant classes beneath him. He had small French, less Italian, good Latin, and little if any Greek. His plots he took from sources, and his dialogue he often contrived by rewriting others' passages. As an actor, he would have traveled from town to town throughout his nation, sometimes by ship, and he would have visited the palaces and great manor houses of the monarch and the ruling class, but he probably never went abroad. He was a man of superior imagination and observation, not extraordinary experience. We do not have a list of the books he read or the people he knew, but there is enough evidence to satisfy any open-minded historian that Shakespeare indeed wrote the matchless poetry attributed to him.

Anti-Stratfordianism is not valueless, though. It exposes how little we really know about the Elizabethan period. By and large, of course, Oxfordians know even less, which its why it should not surprise us when even highly intelligent people like Sigmund Freud or actors like Orson Welles and John Gielgud doubt Shakespeare's authorship. They lack knowledge, not intelligence. The same is true for professors. Oxfordian Louis Benezet was a professor of philosophy and education, not history. Derbyite A. W. Titherley's specialty was organic chemistry. The few anti-Stratfordian literature professors, like Daniel Wright of Concordia University in Oregon, have not examined their own false assumptions. Their folly is like that of their nonliterary colleagues—amusing but not dangerous.

I find it much more disturbing when three Supreme Court Justices ignore hard documentary evidence in favor of suppositional circular reasoning and declare themselves Oxfordians. In 1987 a moot-court debate between Oxfordians and orthodox partisans was held at The American University, presided over by Supreme Court Justices Harry Blackmun,

William Brennan, and John Paul Stevens. The judges found in favor of the Stratford man, but Justice Blackmun was unconvinced. "If I had to rule on the evidence presented," he declared, "it would be in favor of the Oxfordians."[4] Later, nagging doubts swayed Stevens, and Justice Lewis Powell confessed that he had "never thought the man of Stratford-upon-Avon wrote the plays of Shakespeare."[5] This brings me to the real dangers of the Authorship Question.

What happens when the intelligentsia embrace a conspiracy theory? Doesn't a kind of thinking become legitimized? Reasoning like that of the Authorship theorists has led juries to believe in police conspiracies and thus to dismiss valid evidence and acquit murderers. Similar reasoning has led many Americans to believe that a government cover-up prevents anyone from learning the truth about UFOs or the assassination of John F. Kennedy[6]; their distrust has fueled the militia movement and made the 1995 Oklahoma City bombing seem almost inevitable. Today, Holocaust denial is ridiculous, but what about three hundred years from now, when the survivors are all dead and the original films of them are carefully preserved in vaults, the province only of scholars, as is the case with Shakespeare today? Will easily doctored computer images be trusted? Will the century's greatest atrocity be widely considered a hoax? I don't mean to be alarmist. Conspiracy thinking has been around a long time. In medieval France, lonely old women with pet cats and skin blemishes were routinely burned as witches. Assume a conspiracy and anything—or anyone—can be called into question. With the advent of the Internet, imaginary conspiracies can spread as never before, threatening our perception of the world in which we live. But we needn't resign ourselves to living with paranoia. We can start by disbelieving ideas—like the Authorship Question—that rest upon, are based on and require acceptance of unproven conspiracies.

For most people, though, it really doesn't matter who wrote Shakespeare's plays. They don't care. For most people it doesn't matter whether the Earth revolves around the sun, either. The sun will "rise" tomorrow morning and we will still have the plays. But for those of us who would like to deepen our appreciation of Shakespeare and unlock some of his secrets, it does matter. What we think is true affects the way we look at the world. It colors our understanding, for better and worse. "If you get [the Author] wrong," Oxford partisan Charles Vere has warned, "you get the Elizabethan Age wrong."[7] I would go further and say we get ourselves wrong. The idea that one must be born an earl to empathize with earls is a misunderstanding of the power of human imagination. It's a child's view of reality, in which one can gain knowledge only through experience. How we look at history and reality matters. We can try to make sense of the world and make decisions based on reason, or we can cling to our prejudices. We can defend our wrong ideas to the death or be open to the possibility of changing our minds. The time has come for Oxfordians to make that choice. They need to realize they're looking through the wrong end of the telescope, and they should stop inviting the unwitting to take a peek. "I know who really wrote Shakespeare" is nothing more than "I know where ya got those shoes," except the Oxfordians have also conned themselves. It's time to strike the tent. The show's over. *La commedia e finita*. It's time for every conspiracy theorist to step off the intellectual carousel and become, in the words of an alderman's son from Stratford, "as one new-risen from a dream."

Notes

PROLOGUE: SLEIGHT OF HAND

1. Tom Bethell, "The Case for Oxford," *The Atlantic Monthly* 268, no. 4 (October 1991): 48.

2. Diana Price uses this tactic as her basic methodology in *Shakespeare's Unorthodox Biography* (Westport, CT: Greenwood Press, 2001).

3. In *Shakespeare, in Fact* (New York: Continuum, 1994), Irvin Matus refutes several Oxfordian contentions, often with original and valuable scholarship, but he doesn't address what the doubters think they see in the plays nor does he show the flaws in the skeptics' reasoning.

4. In Cervantes' novel, the character Carrasco disguises himself as the Knight of the White Moon, but for the purpose of my metaphor I prefer the version in Dale Wasserman's musical, *Man of La Mancha*.

CHAPTER 1: TWO SHAKESPEARES

1. *First Folio* (London: Isaac Jaggard and Edward Blount, 1623), opposite title page.

2. Ibid., sig. A2.

3. Ibid., sig. A7.

4. Ibid., sig. A4.

5. See Henrietta Bartlett and Alfred W. Pollard, eds., *A Census of Shakespeare's Plays in Quarto 1594–1709* (New Haven: Yale University Press, 1939).

6. *The Return from Parnassus Part Two*, lines 1766–73 in J. B. Leishman, ed., *Pilgrimage to Parnassus: The Three Parnassus Plays (1598–1601)* (London: Nicolson and Watson, 1949), 337. Jonson gave the poets a pill in his play *Poetaster*. Scholars are uncertain in what way Shakespeare gave Jonson a "purge."

7. Edmund K. Chambers, *William Shakespeare: A Study in Facts and Problems*, vol. 2 (Oxford: Clarendon Press, 1930), 243.

8. Ibid., 226. Heretics (e.g., Joseph Sobran) see something unusual in the scarcity of literary tributes at the actor's death. Similarly, there's no documentary evidence for a shower of praise on the death of the playwright Francis Beaumont, who also died in 1616. The earliest notice of Beaumont's death (that we have) is in the same two poems that contain the earliest mention of Shakespeare's. The first printed eulogy specifically for Beaumont was in the 1629 edition of his brother Sir John Beaumont's poems. See Bernard Newdigate, *Michael Drayton and His Circle* (Oxford: Basil Blackwell, 1941), 219.

9. *A Banquet of Jeasts or Change of Cheare* (1630), in C. M. Ingleby et al., eds., *The Shakspere Allusion Book: A Collection of Allusions to Shakspere from 1591 to 1700*, vol. 1 (London: Oxford University Press, 1932), 347.

10. Chambers, *William Shakespeare*, vol. 2, 245.

11. Ibid., 249–50.

12. Ibid.

13. Ingleby et al., 455.

14. Ibid.

15. Chambers, *William Shakespeare*, vol. 2, 245.

16. Ibid., 249–50.

17. Ibid., 264.

18. S. Schoenbaum, *Shakespeare's Lives* (Oxford: Clarendon Press, 1970), 129.

19. Chambers, *William Shakespeare*, vol. 2, 271.

20. Schoenbaum, *Shakespeare's Lives*, 548.

21. Ibid., 534.

22. Ibid., 539.

CHAPTER 2: THE THIRD MAN

1. Ben Jonson, *Discoveries 1641 and Conversations With William Drummond of Hawthornden 1619*, ed. G. B. Harrison (New York: Barnes and Noble, 1966), *Conversations*, 4.

2. *First Folio* (London: Isaac Jaggard and Edward Blount, 1623), sig. A4.

3. Jonson, *Conversations*, 4.

4. Jonson, *Discoveries*, 70.

5. Jonson, *Conversations*, 3.

6. Jonson, *Discoveries*, 37.

7. Epigram XXIII, "To John Donne," in C. H. Herford, Percy Simpson, and Evelyn Simpson, eds., *Ben Jonson*, vol. 8 (Oxford: Oxford University Press, 1925–1952), 34.

8. Jonson, *Conversations*, 4–7.

9. Ibid., 4, 8.

10. Edmund K. Chambers, *William Shakespeare: A Study in Facts and Problems*, vol. 2 (Oxford: Clarendon Press, 1930), 205.

11. He says the same thing in his epigram "To William Camden," which begins: "Camden, to whome I owe all that I am in arts." Herford, et al., *Ben Jonson*, vol. 8, 31.

12. The cited episode is from *The Winter's Tale*, but the geographical error is not the Author's. He lifted the Bohemian shipwreck from the novel on which the play was based. Robert Greene, See Geoffrey Bullough, Narrative and Dramatic Sources of Shakespeare (New York: Columbia University Press, 1957–1975), vol. 8, 156–99.

13. Jonson, *Discoveries*, 28–29. The example Jonson gives does not appear in the Folio; it has been replaced with: "Know Caesar doth not wrong nor without cause/Will he be satisfied" (*Julius Caesar*, lines 1254–55). Since it's doubtful Jonson would remember a single line from many years earlier, it's possible Jonson himself, as one of the editors of the Folio, altered the line.

14. *First Folio* (London: Isaac Jaggard and Edward Blount, 1623), sig. A3.

15. A Jonson coinage that, from the context of the poem, seems to mean "purchased material."

16. Herford, et al., *Ben Jonson*, vol. 8, 44–45.

17. H. N. Gibson, *The Shakespeare Claimants* (New York: Barnes and Noble, 1962), 45. The *Oxford English Dictionary* lists the earliest use as 1581 in Sidney's *Apologie for Poesie*: "The cause why [Poesie] is not esteemed in England, is the fault of Poet-apes, not Poets."

18. Chambers, *William Shakespeare*, vol. 2, 260.

19. Francis Meres, *Palladis Tamia: Wit's Treasury* (1598; repr., New York: Garland Publishing, 1973), 282.

20. Ibid., 283.

21. Thomas Legge, LL.D., the author of *Richardus Tertius* (1579), was the vice chancellor of Cambridge University at the same time Meres was studying there for his M.A. (1587–1591). If he did not actually meet Legge, he saw him at convocations and probably learned at Cambridge the names of the plays Legge had written.

22. Meres, *Palladis Tamia*, 281.

CHAPTER 3: THE VACUUM

1. Mark Twain, *Is Shakespeare Dead?: From My Autobiography* (New York: Harper and Row, 1909), 49.

2. Edgar Innis Fripp, *Shakespeare: Man and Artist*, vol. 1 (London: Oxford University Press, 1938), 43.

3. Park Honan, *Shakespeare: A Life* (Oxford: Oxford University Press, 1998), 311.

4. The "book" in this case may be a legal document listing properties owned rather than a book in the ordinary sense, but John would still, logically, have to be able to read it.

5. Charles Nicholl, *The Reckoning: The Murder of Christopher Marlowe* (New York: Harcourt Brace and Co., 1992), 95.

6. Fripp, *Shakespeare: Man and Artist*, vol. 1, 83–84.

7. Honan, *Shakespeare: A Life*, 48.

8. Richard Jr. writes in part: "gratias tibi ago quia a teneris, quod aiunt, unguiculis, educasti me in sacrae doctrinae studiis usque ad hunc diem" [I thank you that from tender—which they say—fingernails, you have educated me in the studies of sacred doctrines to this day.] The phrase "a teneris, ut Graeci dicunt, unguiculis" is from Cicero's *Epistolae ad Familiares*. See Marcus Tullius Cicero, *Letters to Friends*, vol. 1, D. R. Shackleton Bailey, ed. (Cambridge, MA: Harvard University Press, 2001), 98. Richard has changed "as the Greeks say" to "which they say."

9. Edmund K. Chambers, *William Shakespeare: A Study in Facts and Problems*, vol. 2 (Oxford: Clarendon Press, 1930), 101–2. Sturley advises in part: "Hoc movere et quantum in te est permovere ne negigas" [Don't neglect to move in this and, as much as is in you, move deeply.]

10. *The Return from Parnassus Part Two*, lines 1766–1773, in J. B. Leishman, ed., *Pilgrimage to Parnassus: The Three Parnassus Plays (1598–1601)* (London: Nicolson and Watson, 1949), 337.

11. See Honan, *Shakespeare: A Life*, 36–39.

12. Facsimiles of this and most of the following records can be found in S. Schoenbaum, *William Shakespeare: A Documentary Life* (New York: Oxford University Press, 1975).

13. Robert Greene, *Greene's Groats-Worth of Wit* (Menston: Scolar Press, 1969), sig. E4–F2.

14. All quotations from the Works are from G. Blakemore Evans et al., eds., *The Riverside Shakespeare*, 2nd ed. (Boston: Houghton Mifflin, 1997).

15. A. D. Wraight and Virginia F. Stern, *In Search of Christopher Marlowe* (New York: Vanguard Press, 1965), 197. Writer Jay Hoster, advocating the same theory, is cited in Joseph Sobran, *Alias Shakespeare* (New York: The Free Press, 1997), 34.

16. See, for example, Diana Price, *Shakespeare's Unorthodox Biography* (Westport, CT: Greenwood Press, 2001), 49.

17. Edmund K. Chambers, *The Elizabethan Stage*, vol. 2 (Oxford: Clarendon Press, 1923), 301–38.

18. Henry Chettle, *Kind-Harts Dreame* (London: William Wright, 1592), sig. A3–4. "Facetious" in the passage is from the Latin *facetus*, meaning fine or elegant.

19. Lukas Erne has argued that Chettle is actually apologizing to George Peele ("Biography and Mythography: Rereading Chettle's Alleged Apology to Shakespeare," *English Studies* 79 [1998]: 430–40), a view that Brian Vickers endorses in his *Shakespeare, Co-Author* (Oxford: Oxford University Press, 2002), 141. But the condescension in the phrases "his demeanor no less civil" and "di-

verse of worship have reported his uprightness of dealing which argues his honesty" do not fit well on "George Peele, M.A. Oxford," as he styled himself. And it seems to be the usury charge that Chettle is referring to.

20. Frederick S. Boas, *Marlowe and His Circle* (Oxford: Clarendon Press, 1929), 13.

21. Irvin Leigh Matus, *Shakespeare, in Fact* (New York: Continuum, 1994), 28–30. Diana Price would have us believe a hyphen indicates a pseudonym. (Price, *Shakespeare's Unorthodox Biography*, 60.) But the fact that it was used in the names of other nonfictional people, living and dead, shows this was not necessarily the case. It's also possible that the four publishers who hyphenated the Author's name indeed thought "Shakespeare" was a pseudonym, but they were wrong.

22. *Merchant of Venice*, V.i.59; *Taming of the Shrew*, II.i.349; II.i.353.

23. Honan, *Shakespeare: A Life*, 259–60.

24. Chambers, *William Shakespeare*, vol. 2, 20.

25. Leishman, *Pilgrimage to Parnassus*, 350.

26. Chambers, *William Shakespeare*, vol. 2, 20.

27. Ibid., 72.

28. Gerald Eades Bentley, "Shakespeare and the Blackfriars Theatre," *Shakespeare Survey* 1 (1948): 40. Between 1603 and 1613, the King's Men gave "at least 138 royal performances." (Honan, *Shakespeare: A Life*, 302.)

29. Charlton Ogburn, *The Mysterious William Shakespeare* (McLean, VA: EPM Publications, 1992), 30–31.

30. Vickers, *Shakespeare, Co-Author*, 291–332.

31. Chambers, *William Shakespeare*, vol. 2, 66.

32. See Vickers, *Shakespeare, Co-Author*, 333–432, and John Freehafer, "*Cardenio*, by Shakespeare and Fletcher," *Publications of the Modern Language Association of America* 84 (1969): 501–13.

33. Chambers, *William Shakespeare*, vol. 2, 249.

34. David Riggs, *Ben Jonson: A Life* (Cambridge, MA: Harvard University Press, 1989), 160.

35. Schoenbaum, *Documentary Life*, 220.

36. Ian Wilson, *Shakespeare: The Evidence* (New York: St. Martin's Press, 1993), 371.

37. See Chambers, *William Shakespeare*, vol. 2, 52–57, 67. In *Witter v. Heminges and Condell* (1619), the defendants recount the shifting history of who owned what shares in the Globe Theatre. If Shakespeare had parted with his share and not passed it on to his heirs, Heminges and Condell probably would have mentioned its sale or testified to its dissolution, as they do with every other share. They affirm at the end of their statement that they have not "made or contrived to themselves or to any other person or persons any estate or estates . . . other than is above mentioned," except for one to Nathan Field. So Shakespeare likely retained his share and bequeathed it to John and Susanna Hall.

38. Greene reports that he wrote a letter to Shakespeare on 23 December 1614, implying Shakespeare was not in Stratford. See Chambers, *William Shakespeare*, vol. 2, 142–43.

39. Greene notes that in September "W Shakspeare" spoke to Greene's brother John, a Stratford burgess. The conversation may have taken place in London, but since no location is specified scholars assume the two men were in Stratford. Shakespeare's absences contradict Nicholas Rowe's 1709 statement that the poet is said to have spent some years before his death "at his native Stratford" and that the "latter part of his life was spent . . . in ease, retirement and the conversation of his friends." (Chambers, *William Shakespeare*, vol. 2, 268.)

40. Michael Wood, *Shakespeare* (New York: Basic Books, 2003), 339.

41. Honan, *Shakespeare: A Life*, 397.

42. Heywood in his dedication to *The English Traveller* (1633); see *The Dramatic Works of Thomas Heywood*, vol. 4 (New York: Russell and Russell, 1964), 5. Middleton in his dedication to *The Witch* (1624); see *The Works of Thomas Middleton*, vol. 5, A. H. Bullen, ed. (New York: AMS Press, 1964), 355.

43. See Matus, *Shakespeare, in Fact*, 73.

44. Ibid., 25.

45. James G. McManaway, *The Authorship of Shakespeare* (Ithaca, NY: Cornell University Press, 1962), 29.

CHAPTER 4: REASONABLE DOUBTS

1. J. Thomas Looney, *"Shakespeare" Identified in Edward de Vere the Seventeenth Earl of Oxford* (New York: Duell, Sloan, and Pearce, 1920), 92–103.

2. C. L. Barber and Richard Wheeler, "Shakespeare in the Rising Middle Class," in Norman N. Holland, Sidney Homan, Bernard J. Paris, eds., *Shakespeare's Personality* (Berkeley: University of California Press, 1989), 18.

3. Peter Brook, *The Shifting Point* (New York: Harper and Row, 1987), 75–76.

4. T. S. Eliot, *Selected Essays 1917–1932* (New York: Harcourt Brace, 1932), 108.

5. John Rigby Hale, "Shakespeare and Warfare," in John F. Adams, ed., *William Shakespeare: His World, His Work, His Influence* (New York: Charles Scribner's Sons, 1985), 94.

6. Caroline F. E. Spurgeon, *Shakespeare's Imagery and What It Tells Us* (1935; repr., Boston: Beacon Press, 1958), 36.

7. Ibid., 39.

8. Ibid., 76.

9. Paul A. Jorgensen, *Shakespeare's Military World* (Berkeley: University of California Press, 1956), 8.

10. See, for example, Peele's *The Battle of Alcazar* and Kyd's *The Spanish Tragedy* in, respectively, *The Life and Works of George Peele*, vol. 2, Charles Tayler Prouty, general editor (New Haven: Yale University Press, 1961), 296–347 and

The Works of Thomas Kyd, Frederick S. Boas, ed. (Oxford: Clarendon Press, 1955), 4–99.

11. W. G. Boswell-Stone, *Shakespeare's Holinshed* (1896; repr., New York: Benjamin Blom, 1966), 207.

12. Hale, "Shakespeare and Warfare," 95.

13. Thomas Heywood, *The Dramatic Works of Thomas Heywood*, vol. 1 (New York: Russell and Russell, 1964), 20.

14. All Marlowe quotations are from Fredson Bowers, ed., *The Complete Works of Christopher Marlowe* (London: Cambridge University Press, 1973).

15. Duff Cooper, *Sergeant Shakespeare* (London: Rupert Hart-Davis, 1949), 9. In his book, Cooper attributes all of the Author's knowledge to experience without once comparing the plays to their sources or to other Elizabethan dramas.

16. Hale, "Shakespeare and Warfare," 95.

17. Ibid.

18. One exception is Thomas Kyd, who gives his character Hieronomo the rank of "Knight Marshal" (I.i.96) and writes of "Don Pedro, their chief horsemen's corlonell" (I.i.40) in *The Spanish Tragedy*. Another is Jonson, who refers to "Sergeant-Major" and "Lieutenant Corlonell" in *Every Man in His Humour* (III.v.26–27).

19. Edmund K. Chambers, *The Elizabethan Stage*, vol. 2 (Oxford: Clarendon Press, 1923), 90. All three were in service to the Earl of Leicester. Probably they were musicians, since it is in this capacity the latter two were sent by Leicester from the Low Countries to the court of Denmark at Helsingor (Elsinore).

20. Jorgensen, *Shakespeare's Military World*, 130.

21. Ibid.; 2,800 men were levied in 1594; 1,806 in 1595; 8,840 in 1596; 4,835 in 1597; 9,164 in 1598 and 7,300 in 1599.

22. Leslie Hotson makes a convincing case that it was Thomas Digges's *Stratioticos* (1579), reprinted by Richard Field in 1590, that the Author uses in *Henry V*. See Leslie Hotson, *I, William Shakespeare Do Appoint Thomas Russell Esquire* (New York: Oxford University Press, 1938), 118–22.

23. Sister Miriam Joseph, *Shakespeare's Use of the Arts of Language* (New York: Hafner Publishing Company, 1966), 4.

24. H. N. Gibson, *The Shakespeare Claimants* (New York: Barnes and Noble, 1962), 188.

25. The medical doctor in *The Merry Wives of Windsor* may have been named after John Caius (1510–1573), a prominent physician who was also founder and master of Caius College at Cambridge from 1559 until his death. But the French character bears no other resemblance to his English namesake, and the real Dr. Caius was sufficiently famous (and notorious for his Catholicism) that the Author did not need to know him personally in order to refer to him.

26. Only in *Hamlet* does the word "school" denote university, and there only twice. Claudius tells Hamlet, "For your intent/In going back to school in Wittenberg,/It is most retrograde to our desire" (I.ii.112–14), but the king may be

using the word to belittle the place. To Horatio, Hamlet describes Rosencrantz and Guildenstern as his "school-fellows," but he may mean that he knew them in grammar school, since presumably Horatio would have been acquainted with them at Wittenberg. This idea is supported by Claudius, who refers to Rosencrantz and Guildenstern as "being of so young days brought up with" Hamlet (II.ii.11). And the prince himself refers to the "consonancy of our youth" (II.ii.284), not to recent college days.

27. The character designated "Pedant" in *Taming of the Shrew* is an academic in name and costume only. He is really a businessman of some sort who has "bills for money by exchange/From Florence" (IV.iii.89–90).

28. Holofernes replies to Sir Nathaniel, "Novi hominem tanquam te" [I know the man as I know you], which is Lily's illustration for the syntax of adverbs. Sir Toby reminds Sir Andrew, "diluculo surgere," an abbreviation of "diluculo surgere saluberrimum est" [Rising early in the morning is healthy] (II.iii.1–3), which is a maxim from Lily. And Benedick refers to the book's classification of interjections by emotion: "interjections? Why then some be of laughing, as, ah, ha, he!" (IV.i.21–22). Lily has "Laughing: as Ha ha he."

29. T. W. Baldwin, *William Shakspere's Small Latine & Lesse Greeke*, vol. 1 (Urbana: University of Illinois Press, 1944), 562.

30. His knowledge of other writers, as far as has been discovered, seems to come solely from English translations, not the original Latin versions.

31. Rosalind Miles, *Ben Jonson: His Craft and Art* (Savage, MD: Barnes and Noble, 1990), 5.

32. Baldwin, *Small Latine & Lesse Greeke*, vol. 2, 72–76. Oxfordians must assume Edward de Vere was reading a grammar-school rhetoric textbook at the age of twenty-three or older.

33. Baldwin, *Small Latine & Lesse Greeke*, vol. 2, 671.

34. V.H.H. Green, *A History of Oxford University* (London: B. T. Batsford, 1974), 53.

35. See A. L. Rowse, *Christopher Marlowe: His Life and Work* (New York: Harper and Row, 1964), 21–23.

36. John Lawson and Harold Silver, *A Social History of Education in England* (London: Methuen and Co., 1973), 92, 95, 99.

37. J. M. Robertson, *The Baconian Heresy: A Confutation* (New York: E. P. Dutton, 1913), 194–95.

38. Stanley W. Wells and Gary Taylor, eds., *William Shakespeare: A Textual Companion* (Oxford: Clarendon Press, 1987), 114–15. Brian Vickers has recently shown that these lines were likely written by George Peele. See Brian Vickers, *Shakespeare, Co-Author* (Oxford: Oxford University Press, 2002), 148–243.

39. John Churton Collins, *Studies in Shakespeare* (Westminster: Archibald Constable and Company, 1904), 68–69.

40. Plutarch, *Plutarch's Lives of the Noble Grecians and Romans Englished by Sir Thomas North, Anno 1579*, vol. 6, ed. George Wyndham (New York: AMS Press, 1967), 25–26.

41. Jacques Amyot, *Plutarch: Les vies des hommes illustres* . . . , vol. 2 (Paris: Pierre Cheuillot, 1579), 1211.

42. Thomas North, *Plutarke of Choeronea: The lives of the Noble Grecians and Romans* . . . , vol. 4 (1579; London: The Nonesuch Press, 1930), 450.

43. Ibid., 335.

44. Gibson, *Shakespeare Claimants*, 174.

45. Quiney wrote, "Bien heureux est celui qui pour devenise sage/Qui pour le mal d'autrui fait son appranti/cage," substituting "devenise" for "devenir" and "appranticage" for "apprentissage." In English, the lines mean "Happy is he who, to become wise, serves his apprenticeship from the misfortune of others." See Charles Hamilton, *In Search of Shakespeare* (San Diego: Harcourt Brace Jovanovich, 1985), 93.

46. John Florio, *Florio His First Fruites* (London: Thomas Woodcock, 1578), 34; *Florios Second Frutes* (London: Thomas Woodcock, 1591), 106. Florio writes, "*Venetia, chi non ti vede non ti pretia.* . . ." The spelling changes may indicate a different source, or that Holofernes, the foolish pedant character who quotes it, is a poor scholar. He misquotes Latin texts also.

47. For example, Jonson uses the same fencing terms as the Author in *Every Man in His Humour* (1598): "your punto, your reverso, your stoccata, your imbroccato, your passada, your montanto" (IV.vii.76–79). *Cornuto* appears in Day's *The Travailes of Three English Brothers* (1607). Dekker uses *bona-roba* in *The Honest Whore Part Two* (printed 1630). *Cielo* and *terra*, in *Love's Labor's Lost*, are copied out of Florio's 1598 Italian dictionary, *World of Words*, along with their definitions: "*cielo*, heaven, the skie, the firmament or welkin. . . ." (*World of Words*, 72); "*terra*, the element called earth, anie ground, earth, countrie, province, region, land, soile. . . ." (*World of Words*, 417). Compare to *LLL*, IV.ii.5–7: "*caelo*, the sky, the welkin, the heaven, and anon falleth like a crab on the face of *terra*, the soil, the land the earth."

48. I'm counting Pistol's "Si fortuna me contento, sperato me contento," which he repeats twice in *Henry IV Part Two* in differing versions, as mangled Spanish rather than mangled Italian, though it is a hash of both; and neither.

49. Florio, *First Fruites* (1578), sig. ***iii.

50. Ben Jonson, *Discoveries 1641 and Conversations with William Drummond of Hawthornden 1619*, ed. G. B. Harrison (New York: Barnes and Noble, 1966), *Conversations*, 5.

51. Geoffrey Bullough, *Narrative and Dramatic Sources of Shakespeare*, vol. 2 (New York: Columbia University Press, 1957–1975), 274.

52. Based on its title, the play *The History of Felix and Feliomena*, which is now lost, was probably a dramatization of the story in Montemayor's *Diana* that was the basis for *Two Gentlemen of Verona* and *Twelfth Night*. If so, this could have been the Author's source.

53. Richard Farmer, *An Essay on the Learning of Shakspeare Addressed to Joseph Craddock, Esq.* (1767; repr., New York: AMS Press, 1966), 69.

54. Ibid., 70.

55. Kathleen M. Lea, *Italian Popular Comedy*, vol. 2 (1931; repr., New York: Russell and Russell, 1962), 374.

56. See Frances A. Yates, *John Florio: The Life of an Italian in Shakespeare's England* (Cambridge: Cambridge University Press, 1934).

57. Lea, *Italian Popular Comedy*, 353.

58. Ibid., 381.

59. David Riggs, *Ben Jonson: A Life* (Cambridge, MA: Harvard University Press, 1989), 47.

60. Thomas Heywood, *An Apology for Actors* (1612; repr., New York: Garland Publishing, 1973), sig. E2.

61. Andrew Grewar, "Shakespeare and the Actors of the Commedia Dell'Arte," in David J. George and Christopher J. Gossip, eds., *Studies in the Commedia Dell'Arte* (Cardiff: University of Wales Press, 1993), 27.

62. Harley Granville Barker, *Prefaces to Shakespeare*, vol. 4 (Princeton: Princeton University Press, 1946), 98.

63. Murray J. Levith, *Shakespeare's Italian Settings and Plays* (New York: St. Martin's Press, 1989), 16.

64. Ibid., 44.

65. Ibid., 70–71.

66. Ibid., 31.

67. It has been alleged that the Sagittary, mentioned in *Othello*, was the official residence of the commanders of the Venetian galleys. If this was so, the Author didn't know it. In the play, the Sagittary is an inn where Cassio finds Othello when the general can not be found "at his lodging." In other words, the one thing the Sagittary is not is Othello's official residence. See Horatio F. Brown, *Studies in the History of Venice*, vol. 2 (London: J. Murray, 1907), 177. Possibly, like the Elephant in *Twelfth Night*, the Sagittary was an inn in London.

68. Edmund K. Chambers, *William Shakespeare: A Study in Facts and Problems*, vol. 1 (Oxford: Clarendon Press, 1930), 61; Joseph Sobran, *Alias Shakespeare* (New York: The Free Press, 1997), 67; Tom Bethell, "The Case for Oxford," *The Atlantic Monthly* 268, no. 4 (October 1991): 58.

69. Quoted in Charlton Ogburn, *The Mysterious William Shakespeare* (McLean, VA: EPM Publications, 1992), 303.

70. Geoffrey Bullough, *Narrative and Dramatic Sources of Shakespeare*, vol. 1 (New York: Columbia University Press, 1957–1975), 445.

71. In 1925, "Gobbo" was discovered in the parish registers of Titchfield, the Earl of Southampton's home, as a family name, but this has since been discovered to be a misreading of "Hobbes." See G.P.V. Akrigg, *Shakespeare and the Earl of Southampton* (Cambridge, MA: Harvard University Press, 1968), 223.

72. Two such maps are in Sebastian Münster's *Cosmographia Universale* (Cologne: Arnold Birckmann, 1575). The one reproduced is from page 157.

73. Levith, *Shakespeare's Italian Settings*, 18.

74. Ibid., 26.

75. Ibid., 21.

76. G. H. McWilliam, *Shakespeare's Italy Revisited* (Leicester: Leicester University Press, 1974), 15.

77. Levith, *Shakespeare's Italian Settings*, 18.

78. Ogburn, *Mysterious William Shakespeare*, 305.

79. Ernesto Grillo, *Shakespeare and Italy* (1949; repr., New York: Haskell House Publishers, 1973), 132.

80. Levith, *Shakespeare's Italian Settings*, 90.

81. In *Twelfth Night*, however, the Author does not use "the Lady of Strachy" as an idiom for a haughty woman. Malvolio says, "the Lady of Strachy married the yeoman of the wardrobe" as if she were a real person. In fact, as Muriel St. Clare Byrne points out, Katherine Willoughby, dowager duchess of Suffolk, married a servant. Her story was told in Foxe's *Book of Martyrs*, a volume which at the time was second-only to the Bible in popularity. Her stepdaughter, Frances, Duchess of Suffolk, married her groom of the chamber. See M. St. Clare Byrne, "The Social Background," in Harley Granville Barker and G. B. Harrison, eds., *A Companion to Shakespeare Studies* (1934; repr., Cambridge: Cambridge University Press, 1977), 211. So it seems several Elizabethan noblewomen married servants, and the "Lady of Strachy" is probably a fictitious exemplar. The referenced line in *Othello* reads, "Why, masters, ha' your instruments been in Naples, that they speak i'th' nose thus?" Naples was associated with venereal disease perhaps because its inhabitants speak nasally, a symptom of syphillis. How Neapolitans speak was probably common knowledge or the audience would never have gotten the joke! The only other alleged Italian expression is "by the ears" in *All's Well That Ends Well*. "The florentines and senoys are by th' ears," meaning at war. It also appears in *Coriolanus*— "Were half to half the world by th' ears...." C. T. Onions, in *A Shakespeare Glossary*, ed. Robert D. Eagleson, (Oxford: Oxford University Press, 1986) notes that the expression was originally said of animals, which makes sense since animals tend to fight by biting each other's ears. Chambers observes it was used in a legal deposition to describe a fistfight involving James Burbage, Richard's father (Chambers, *Elizabethan Stage*, vol. 2, 384–92). It's an English phrase as much as an Italian one. Grillo finds the expression "sano come un pesce" [sound as a fish] in *Two Gentlemen of Verona*. The Author, however, never writes "sound as a fish"; this is the dialogue in the play:

> SPEED. But shall she marry him?
> LANCE. No.
> SPEED. How then? Shall he marry her?
> LANCE. No, neither.
> SPEED. What, are they broken?
> LANCE. No; they are both as whole as a fish.
>
> (II.v.14–19)

Clearly the Author has the anatomy of a fish in mind, its head and body all of a piece, not its health.

CHAPTER 5: LAWYER'S FINGERS

1. Paul S. Clarkson and Clyde T. Warren, *The Law of Property in Shakespeare and Elizabethan Drama* (1942; repr., New York: Gordian Press, 1968), xvii.

2. Quoted in Clarkson and Warren, *Law of Property*, xix.

3. W. Nicholas Knight, *Shakespeare's Hidden Life: Shakespeare at the Law 1585–1595* (New York: Mason and Lipscomb, 1973), 80.

4. Mark Twain, *Is Shakespeare Dead?: From My Autobiography* (New York: Harper and Row, 1909), 15–16.

5. This contrivance, however, seems to have been part of the traditional story. See O. Hood Phillips, *Shakespeare and the Lawyers* (London: Methuen, 1972), 100.

6. Pointed out by R. F. Fuller. Quoted in Phillips, *Shakespeare and the Lawyers*, 92.

7. Phillips, *Shakespeare and the Lawyers*, 127.

8. Clarkson and Warren, *Law of Property*, 59.

9. Ibid., 285.

10. Phillips, *Shakespeare and the Lawyers*, 189.

11. Clarkson and Warren, *Law of Property*, 112–13.

12. See J. M. Robertson, *The Baconian Heresy: A Confutation* (New York: E. P. Dutton, 1913), 90–92.

13. Phillips, *Shakespeare and the Lawyers*, 191.

14. Clarkson and Warren, *Law of Property*, 286.

15. Phillips, *Shakespeare and the Lawyers*, 186.

16. Ibid., 35.

17. Thomas Nashe, *The Works of Thomas Nashe*, vol. 1, ed. Robert B. McKerrow (Oxford: Basil Blackwell, 1966), 189.

18. Quoted in Robertson, *Baconian Heresy*, 141.

19. Knight, *Shakespeare's Hidden Life*, 162.

20. S. Schoenbaum, *Shakespeare's Lives* (Oxford: Clarendon Press, 1970), 21.

21. Knight, *Shakespeare's Hidden Life*, 56–57.

22. On the other hand, the sonnet's imagery is related to *The Merchant of Venice*—the Poet casts himself as Bassanio, his friend as Antonio, and his lover as Shylock. The poem's legalese may derive from the same source as the play.

CHAPTER 6: THE COURTIER'S TONGUE

1. Joseph Sobran, *Alias Shakespeare* (New York: The Free Press, 1997), 166.

2. Oscar G. Brockett, *History of the Theatre*, 7th ed. (Boston: Allyn and Bacon, 1995), 159. In "An Essay of Dramatick Poesie" (1668), John Dryden said, "Beaumont and Fletcher understood and imitated the conversation of gentlemen much better [than the Author]."

3. George Puttenham, *The Arte of English Poesie* (1589; repr., Cambridge: Cambridge University Press, 1936), 145.

4. C. L. Barber and Richard Wheeler, "Shakespeare in the Rising Middle Class," in Norman N. Holland, Sidney Homan, Bernard J. Paris, eds., *Shakespeare's Personality* (Berkeley: University of California Press, 1989), 35.

5. Dennis Kay, *William Shakespeare: Sonnets and Poems* (New York: Twayne Publishers, 1998), 130.

6. Muriel St. Clare Byrne, "The Social Background," in Harley Granville Barker and G. B. Harrison, eds., *A Companion to Shakespeare Studies* (1934; repr., Cambridge: Cambridge University Press, 1977), 190.

7. Ibid., 208.

8. Ibid., 209.

9. Ibid., 199.

10. Ibid., 200.

11. Ibid.

12. Ibid., 200–201.

13. Ibid., 202.

14. Ibid.

15. Rev. T. F. Thiselton Dyer, *Folk-Lore of Shakespeare* (1883; repr., New York: Dover Publications, 1966), 394.

16. Colonel H. Walrond, "Archery," in Sir Walter Alexander Raleigh et al., eds., *Shakespeare's England*, vol. 2 (1916; repr., Oxford: Clarendon Press, 1950), 376–79.

17. Quoted in Raleigh et al., eds., *Shakespeare's England*, vol. 2, 389.

18. A. Forbes Sieveking, "Fencing and Duelling," in Raleigh et al., eds., *Shakespeare's England*, vol. 2, 390.

19. J. W. Fortescue, "Hunting," in Raleigh et al., eds., *Shakespeare's England*, vol. 2, 342.

20. Ibid., 344.

21. John Dover Wilson, ed., *Life in Shakespeare's England* (1913; repr., Cambridge: Cambridge University Press, 1978), 16.

22. John Manningham, *The Diary of John Manningham of the Middle Temple*, ed. Robert Parker Sorlien (Hanover, NH: University Press of New England, 1976), 123.

23. Quoted in A. Forbes Sieveking, "Games," in Raleigh et al., *Shakespeare's England*, vol. 2, 465.

24. Caroline F. E. Spurgeon, *Shakespeare's Imagery and What It Tells Us* (1935; repr., Boston: Beacon Press, 1958), 33.

25. Henry Thew Stephenson, *The Elizabethan People* (New York: Henry Holt and Company, 1910), 110–11.

26. Ben Jonson, *Ben Jonson*, vol. 3, eds. C. H. Herford, Percy Simpson, and Evelyn Simpson (Oxford: Oxford University Press, 1925–1952), 305.

27. Edgar Innis Fripp and Richard Savage, eds., *Minutes and Accounts of the Corporation of Stratford-upon-Avon and Other Records, 1553–1620*, vol. 4 (London: Oxford University Press, 1924–1929), 5.

28. Gerald Lascelles, "Falconry," in Raleigh et al., *Shakespeare's England*, vol. 2, 351.

29. Stephenson, *Elizabethan People*, 115.

30. Alan H. Nelson, *Monstrous Adversary* (Liverpool: Liverpool University Press, 2003), 68–70, 261–65, 277–78.

31. Sir Philip Sidney, *Astrophel and Stella* (1591; repr., Menston: Scolar Press, 1970), 17 (Sonnet 41), 22 (Sonnet 53).

32. H. N. Gibson, *The Shakespeare Claimants* (New York: Barnes and Noble, 1962), 238.

33. Abel Lefranc, *Sous le masque de William Shakespeare*, trans. Cecil Cragg (1918; Braunton, England: Merlin, 1988), 260–68.

34. Sir Thomas Coningby, *Journal of the Siege of Rouen* (1591), vol. 1, quoted in G. B. Harrison, ed., *The Elizabethan Journals* (Garden City, NY: Anchor Books, 1965), 40–42.

35. Geoffrey Bullough, *Narrative and Dramatic Sources of Shakespeare*, vol. 1 (New York: Columbia University Press, 1957–1975), 429.

36. John Chamberlain, *The Letters of John Chamberlain*, vol. 1, ed. Norman Egbert McClure (Philadelphia: The American Philosophical Society, 1939), 183–84.

37. Francis Meres, *Palladis Tamia: Wit's Treasury* (1598; repr., New York: Garland Publishing, 1973), 178.

38. Some scholars prefer as the model for Polonius the prolix author of *The Counselor*, a book of advice on affairs of state, published in English translation in 1598. The author, known as Goslicius, was a Polish bishop and statesman—hence the character's name: Polonius. See Bullough, *Narrative and Dramatic Sources*, vol. 7, 44–45.

39. John Chamberlain, *The Chamberlain Letters*, ed. Elizabeth McClure Thomson (New York: G. P. Putnam's Sons, 1965), 7.

40. Quoted in Kay, *Sonnets and Poems*, 19.

41. Edmund K. Chambers, *Elizabethan Stage*, vol. 2 (Oxford: Clarendon Press, 1923), 308.

42. Ibid., 323.

43. W. G. Boswell-Stone, *Shakespeare's Holinshed* (1896; New York: Benjamin Blom, 1966), 258.

CHAPTER 7: THE SONNETEER

1. Whether the discrepancies between Jaggard's versions and the 1609 versions are the result of a thief's faulty memory or the Author's revision is unknown.

2. I omit mention of Sonnet 108 because in that poem it is personified Love that has suffered the "dust and injury of age" and the "necessary wrinkles," and ultimately appears "dead"; not the speaker.

3. Byron, *The Poetical Works of Byron*, ed. Robert F. Gleckner (Boston: Houghton Mifflin Company, 1975), 206.

4. A. H. Bullen, ed., *Some Longer Elizabethan Poems* (New York: Cooper Square, 1964), 169.

5. The composition of sonnet cycles was a European vogue that flourished in England after the publication of Sidney's *Astrophel and Stella* in 1591. Henry Constable's *Diana* (1592), Samuel Daniel's *Delia* (1592), Barnabe Barnes's *Parthenophil and Parthenophe* (1593), Giles Fletcher's *Licia* (1593), Thomas Lodge's *Phillis* (1593), Michael Drayton's *Idea's Mirrour* (1594), William Percy's *Coelia* (1594), Richard Barnfield's *Cynthia* (1595), Bartholomew Griffin's *Fidessa* (1596), and William Smith's *Chloris* (1596) were all sonnet cycles with a thread of a story that preceded the Author's. Twelve hundred sonnets have survived in print from the 1590s.

6. See Helen Vendler, *The Art of Shakespeare's Sonnets* (Cambridge, MA: Harvard University Press, 1997).

7. See Park Honan, *Shakespeare: A Life* (Oxford: Oxford University Press, 1998), 292.

8. It's actually dated "March 1601," but for the Elizabethans the new calendar year began on 25 March.

9. John Manningham, *The Diary of John Manningham of the Middle Temple*, ed. Robert Parker Sorlien (Hanover, NH: University Press of New England, 1976), 75. Mr. Towse (or "Towes") was an anecdotalist of the Inner Temple (Honan, *Shakespeare: A Life*, 263). The story re-emerged in the eighteenth century even before Manningham's diary was discovered; it was gossip that had spread beyond the Inns of Court.

10. Joseph Sobran quotes the "public honor" part of the line, but turns a blind eye to the "proud titles" in making his case for Oxford.

11. Michael Wood, *Shakespeare* (New York: Basic Books, 2003), 184.

12. Sir Philip Sidney, *The Poems of Sir Philip Sidney*, ed. William A. Ringler (Oxford: Clarendon Press, 1962), 179–80.

13. Ibid., 224.

14. By the 1590s, "thou"—once upon a time the singular of "you"—had become archaic and was reserved for literature. It expressed social difference: Poets conventionally employed "thou" as a sign of humility when addressing a paramour, a god, a muse, or their lord, whereas a lord might use it in addressing his vassal. And anyone might use it to express contempt or superiority. See Andrew Gurr, "You and Thou in Shakespeare's Sonnets," *Essays in Criticism* 32 (January 1982): 13.

15. Lisa Jardine and Alan Stewart, *Hostage to Fortune: The Troubled Life of Francis Bacon* (New York: Hill and Wang, 1999), 169.

16. It has been suggested that one of his inspirers was an apprentice actor in an acting company who played women's roles convincingly.

17. Vendler, *Art of Shakespeare's Sonnets*, 15.

18. For commentary on the Sonnets thgat assumes a homosexual relationship, see Bruce R. Smith's *Homosexual Desire in Shakespeare's England* (Chicago: Chicago University Press, 1991).

19. See Sir Philip Sidney's *Astrophel and Stella* (1591), Henry Constable's *Diana* (1592), Samuel Daniel's *Delia* (1592), Barnabe Barnes's *Parthenophil and Parthenophe* (1593), Thomas Lodge's *Phillis* (1593), Richard Barnfield's *Cynthia* (1595), and so forth.

20. For example, Sir Christopher Hatton writes to Elizabeth, "No death, no, not hell, shall ever win of me my consent so far to wrong myself again as to be absent from you one day. . . . I lack that I live by . . . Love me, for I love you."

CHAPTER 8: FOOTPRINTS IN THE GARDEN

1. Park Honan, *Shakespeare: A Life* (Oxford: Oxford University Press, 1998), 305.

2. G.P.V. Akrigg, *Shakespeare and the Earl of Southampton* (Cambridge, MA: Harvard University Press, 1968), 223.

3. S. Schoenbaum, *William Shakespeare: A Documentary Life* (New York: Oxford University Press, 1975), 39.

4. Edmund K. Chambers, *William Shakespeare: A Study in Facts and Problems*, vol. 1 (Oxford: Clarendon Press, 1930), 396.

5. I omit from this paragraph Katherine Hamlett of Tiddington, who drowned in the Avon in 1580. It has been suggested that her death was the inspiration for the similar demise of Ophelia in *Hamlet*, a theory based largely on Katherine's surname. It seems to me this supposed connection is too tenuous, proves nothing, and may very well be a genuine coincidence.

6. Honan, *Shakespeare: A Life*, 72.

7. Hilda M. Hulme, *Explorations in Shakespeare's Language* (New York: Barnes and Noble, 1962), 334.

8. Edgar Innis Fripp, *Shakespeare: Man and Artist*, vol. 1 (London: Oxford University Press, 1938), 79–80.

9. See Honan, *Shakespeare: A Life*, 37n.

10. Caroline F. E. Spurgeon, *Shakespeare's Imagery and What It Tells Us* (1935; repr., Boston: Beacon Press, 1958), 110.

11. The Earl of Oxford was also connected to bear-baiting, as a sponsor. In 1597 the city of Coventry paid five shillings to the Earl of Oxford's "beareward." See Alan H. Nelson, *Monstrous Adversary* (Liverpool: Liverpool University Press, 2003), 391.

12. Spurgeon, *Shakespeare's Imagery*, 125.

13. Robert McCrum, William Cran, and Robert McNeil, *The Story of English* (New York: Penguin Books, 1986), 101.

14. Ivor Brown in Reginald Charles Churchill, *Shakespeare and His Betters* (London: M. Reinhardt, 1958), xiii.

15. Hulme, *Explorations*, 331.

16. George Wilkes and J. W. Tavener, *Shakespeare from an American Point of View* (London: Low, Marston, Seale and Rivington, 1877), 463.

17. Arthur Conan Doyle, *The Sign of Four* (1889; repr., New York: Ballantine Books, 1975), 43.

CHAPTER 9: SUSPECTS

1. G.P.V. Akrigg, *Shakespeare and the Earl of Southampton* (Cambridge, MA: Harvard University Press, 1968), 96. In a letter of the time, Rowland Whyte reported that Southampton and Rutland "pass away the time merely in going to plays every day."

2. John Michell, *Who Wrote Shakespeare?* (London: Thames and Hudson, 1996), 212.

3. Lisa Jardine and Alan Stewart, *Hostage to Fortune: The Troubled Life of Francis Bacon* (New York: Hill and Wang, 1999), 261.

4. Ibid., 160.

5. For a fuller account, see Akrigg, *Shakespeare and the Earl of Southampton*, 109–19.

6. Individual theorists differ in what character they associate with which personage; these are merely representative. Even so, many deniers, including Marlovian William Honey and Anthony Bacon partisan Olive Driver, agree with them. See Olive W. Driver, *The Bacon-Shakespearean Mystery* (Northampton, MA: Kraushar Press, 1960), 209–11, and William Honey, *The Life, Loves, and Achievements of Christopher Marlowe Alias Shakespeare* (London: Pisces Press, 1982), 478–85.

7. In 1594, he collaborated with Christopher Yelverton in producing *The Misfortunes of Arthur*. He was the principal organizer of the Gray's Inn Christmas Revels that same year. In 1613, he was responsible for the masque given jointly by Gray's Inn and the Inner Temple to celebrate the marriage of the King's daughter to the Elector Palatine, and in 1615, he spent £2000 in organizing *The Masque of Flowers*.

8. Francis Bacon, *Francis Bacon: A Critical Edition of the Major Works*, ed. Brian Vickers (Oxford: Oxford University Press, 1996), 386.

9. Ibid., 420.

10. Francis Bacon, *Sylva Sylvarum: A Natural History in Ten Centuries* (1627; repr., Whitefish, MT: Kessinger Publishing, 2004), 68.

11. Edward D. Johnson, *Bacon-Shakespeare Coincidences* (London: The Bacon Society, 1948), 5.

12. J. M. Robertson, *The Baconian Heresy: A Confutation* (New York: E. P. Dutton, 1913), 518–19.

13. Edmund K. Chambers, *William Shakespeare: A Study in Facts and Problems*, vol. 2 (Oxford: Clarendon Press, 1930), 323.

14. Michell, *Who Wrote Shakespeare?*, 218.

15. Chambers, *William Shakespeare*, vol. 2, 327.

16. Stanley W. Wells and Gary Taylor, eds., *William Shakespeare: A Textual Companion* (Oxford: Clarendon Press, 1987), 76.

17. H. N. Gibson in *The Shakespeare Claimants* (1962) and John Michell in *Who Wrote Shakespeare?* (1996), to give two examples.

18. Joseph Hall, *Satires*, ed. Samuel Weller Singer (London: R. Triphook, 1824), 27.

19. John Marston, *The Poems of John Marston*, ed. Arnold Davenport (Liverpool: Liverpool University Press, 1961), 65–66.

20. Ibid., 83.

21. Joseph Hall, *The Poems of Joseph Hall*, ed. Arnold Davenport (Liverpool: Liverpool University Press, 1969), 94.

22. See Arnold Davenport's introduction to Hall, *Poems*, xlix–lviii.

23. Steven W. May, "The Poems of Edward de Vere, Seventeenth Earl of Oxford and of Robert Devereux, Second Earl of Essex," *Studies in Philology* 77, no. 5 (1980): 11–12.

24. Joseph Sobran, *Alias Shakespeare* (New York: The Free Press, 1997), 232.

25. The same goes for Oxford who writes, "While the grass grows the silly horse starves" in a 1576 letter. Even though Hamlet quotes the same adage, " 'While the grass grows'—the proverb is something musty" (III.ii.343–44), and quotes it in a similar context, it proves nothing. Joseph Sobran calls their mutual citing of this quotation: "evidence" (Sobran, *Alias Shakespeare*, 192).

26. William F. Friedman and Elizabeth S. Friedman, *The Shakespearean Ciphers Examined* (Cambridge: Cambridge University Press, 1957), 194. In fairness to Elizabeth Wells Gallup, whose findings I am citing, Montaigne and Cervantes were not revealed by her inconsistent and faulty application of the so-called "bilateral cipher." Other cipher systems named the French essayist and the Spanish novelist as front men for Bacon.

27. Caroline F. E. Spurgeon, *Shakespeare's Imagery and What It Tells Us* (Boston: Beacon Press, 1958), 192–93.

28. See Spurgeon, *Shakespeare's Imagery*, 195–99.

29. Alfred Harbage, *William Shakespeare: A Reader's Guide* (New York: Farrar, Straus and Giroux, 1963), 33.

30. A. W. Titherley, *Shakespeare's Identity: William Stanley, Sixth Earl of Derby* (Winchester: Warren and Son, 1952), 30.

31. Chambers, *William Shakespeare*, vol. 1, 358–61. Scholars who believe this theory assume the play was written to be presented at a wedding because of its marital theme and final speeches which bless "this hallowed house" and the "bride-bed." They note that the Derby wedding took place in January 1595, about the time the play is thought to have been composed. But it's just as likely the play was written as a commercial comedy and *chosen* to be presented at the marriage of the Lord Chamberlain's granddaughter in February 1596. It was at that time that the final speeches were probably inserted between the end of the last scene and Puck's epilogue.

32. A letter from Derby to the Mayor of Chester survives in which the earl

supports the Earl of Hertford's Players in their petition to use the town hall. See Edmund K. Chambers, *The Elizabethan Stage*, vol. 2 (Oxford: Clarendon Press, 1923), 117.

33. Edmund Spenser, *The Works of Edmund Spenser*, vol. 7, eds. Charles Grosvenor Osgood and Henry Gibbons Lotspeich (Baltimore: The Johns Hopkins Press, 1947), 160.

34. Chambers, *Elizabethan Stage*, vol. 2, 127.

35. A. L. Rowse, *Christopher Marlowe: His Life and Work* (New York: Harper and Row, 1964), 27.

36. Ibid., 30.

37. Charles Nicholl, *The Reckoning: The Murder of Christopher Marlowe* (New York: Harcourt Brace and Co., 1992), 179.

38. Calvin Hoffman, *The Murder of the Man Who Was "Shakespeare"* (New York: J. Messner, 1955), 49.

39. Nicholl, *The Reckoning*, 87.

40. Ibid.

41. All details from the inquest report are from Leslie Hotson's English translation of the original Latin in Della Hilton, *Who Was Kit Marlowe?* (New York: Taplinger Publishing, 1977), 140–41.

42. Nicholl does not conclude that all four were secretly working for the Cecils, but it's a logical inference since they were all meeting in a Cecil safe house.

43. Nicholl, *The Reckoning*, 267.

44. See A. D. Wraight, *The Story That the Sonnets Tell* (1994).

45. H. N. Gibson, *The Shakespeare Claimants* (New York: Barnes and Noble, 1962), 131.

46. Nicholl, *The Reckoning*, 19.

47. In 1901, Dr. T. C. Mendenhall compared word-length frequencies of selected Elizabethan writers and discovered that Shakespeare and Marlowe used words of the same length at the same rate per thousand words. Word-length frequencies did not produce a unique fingerprint, however, as he himself disclosed. A friend of his, Prof. Shaler of Harvard, had written a play "in the spirit and style of the Elizabethan Age" and produced the same frequencies as Marlowe and Shakespeare. His method was more like a blood type; it could be used to eliminate suspects, but not prove anything. Even so, the effect of spelling changes made by Elizabethan copyists and printers renders Mendenhall's frequencies worthless. See George McMichael and Edgar M. Glenn, *Shakespeare and His Rivals* (New York: The Odyssey Press, 1962), 108–9.

48. Spurgeon, *Shakespeare's Imagery*, 13.

CHAPTER 10: THE ACCUSED

1. Of course, whether the Author had a brother is impossible to deduce from the Works, and one's opinion is entirely subjective.

2. Alan H. Nelson, *Monstrous Adversary: The Life of Edward de Vere, 17th Earl of Oxford* (Liverpool: Liverpool University Press, 2003), 37.

3. Ibid.

4. Reproduced in Charlton Ogburn, *The Mysterious William Shakespeare* (McLean, VA: EPM Publications, 1992), 441. It begins: "Monsieur, j'ai receu vos lettres, plaines d'humanite et courtoysie, et fort resemblantes a vostre grand'amour et singuliere affection envers moy, comme vrais enfans devement procreez d'une telle mere, pour la quelle je me trouve de jour en jour plus tenu a v[otre] h[onneur] vos bons admonestments pour l'observation du bon ordre selon vos appointemens, je me delibere (dieu aidant) de garder en toute diligence, comme chose que je cognois et considere tendre especialement a mon propre bien et profit."

5. Quoted in Tom Bethell, "The Case For Oxford," *The Atlantic Monthly* 268, no. 4 (October 1991): 50.

6. B. M. Ward, *The Seventeenth Earl of Oxford, 1550–1604, from Contemporary Documents* (London: John Murray, 1928), 23–24.

7. Nelson, *Monstrous Adversary*, 42, 45.

8. Ibid., 48.

9. Richmond Noble, *Shakespeare's Biblical Knowledge and Use of the Book of Common Prayer* (New York: Macmillan, 1935), 43, 47, 75–76.

10. Sobran, *Alias Shakespeare*, 117.

11. Ward, *Seventeenth Earl of Oxford*, 91.

12. H. Dugdale Sykes, *Sidelights on Elizabethan Drama* (1924; New York: Barnes and Noble, 1966), 53.

13. By H. Dugdale Sykes (1924).

14. Charlton Ogburn points out that the robbery in *The Famous Victories* takes place in May of the fourteenth year of Henry IV's reign, but the king died that March. Since Oxford's "robbery" took place in May of the fourteenth year of Elizabeth's reign, he argues, the author of *The Famous Victories* must have stretched Henry's reign by two months in order to associate the two events. (Ogburn, *Mysterious William Shakespeare*, 529.) But May 1573 was the fifteenth year of Elizabeth's reign, not the fourteenth.

15. Nelson, *Monstrous Adversary*, 157.

16. Ward, *Seventeenth Earl of Oxford*, 157–58.

17. Nelson, *Monstrous Adversary*, 385–86.

18. Edmund K. Chambers, *The Elizabethan Stage*, vol. 2 (Oxford: Clarendon Press, 1923), 101–2; vol. 4, 334–35.

19. Bethell, "The Case for Oxford," 47.

20. Fulke Greville, quoted in Nelson, *Monstrous Adversary*, 196.

21. Ogburn, *Mysterious William Shakespeare*, 759. Original in Nelson, *Monstrous Adversary*, 419.

22. Sobran, *Alias Shakespeare*, 189.

23. James Joyce, *Ulysses* (1918; repr., New York: Random House, 1946), 206.

CHAPTER 11: MOTIVE AND MEANS

1. Ben Jonson, *Ben Jonson*, vol. 9, eds. C. H. Herford, Percy Simpson, and Evelyn Simpson (Oxford: Oxford University Press, 1925–1952), 13.

2. George Puttenham, *The Arte of English Poesie* (1589; repr., Cambridge: Cambridge University Press, 1936), 61.

3. Puttenham, *Arte of English Poesie*, 63; Meres, *Palladis Tamia*: *Wits Treasury* (1598; repr., New York: Garland Publishing, 1973), 283b.

4. Edmund K. Chambers, *William Shakespeare*: *A Study in Facts and Problems*, vol. 2 (Oxford: Clarendon Press, 1930), 321.

5. See Edmund K. Chambers, *The Elizabethan Stage*, vol. 2 (Oxford: Clarendon Press, 1923), 100–102. See also Irvin Leigh Matus, *Shakespeare, in Fact* (New York: Continuum, 1994), 225–28.

6. See Bartlett and Pollard, *A Census of Shakespeare's Plays in Quarto 1594–1709* (New Haven: Yale University Press, 1939).

7. Chambers, *Elizabethan Stage*, vol. 3, 444–45.

8. S. Schoenbaum, *William Shakespeare*: *A Compact Documentary Life* (New York: Oxford University Press, 1977), 213.

9. See Chambers, *William Shakespeare*, vol. 1, 358–61.

10. John Marston, *The Scourge of Villanie* (1599; repr., New York: Barnes and Noble, 1966), 94–95.

11. Ibid., 97.

12. Thomas Nashe, *Pierce Pennilesse His Supplication to the Divell*, ed. G. B. Harrison (1592; repr., New York: Barnes and Noble, 1966), 26.

13. Chambers, *William Shakespeare*, vol. 2, 224.

14. Charlton Ogburn, *The Mysterious William Shakespeare* (McLean, VA: EPM Publications, 1992), 109.

15. For a translation of part of Harvey's address, see Ogburn, *Mysterious Shakespeare*, 597.

16. Chambers, *William Shakespeare*, vol. 2, 245.

17. Ogburn, *Mysterious William Shakespeare*, 198–99, 203–4.

18. Edmund Spenser, *The Works of Edmund Spenser*, vol. 8, eds. Charles Grosvenor Osgood and Henry Gibbons Lotspeich (Baltimore: The Johns Hopkins Press, 1947), 68–69.

19. Chambers, *William Shakespeare*, vol. 2, 186.

20. Henry Willoby, *Willobie His Avisa* (1594; repr., New York: Barnes and Noble, 1966), 116.

21. Ibid.

22. Leslie Hotson, *I, William Shakespeare Do Appoint Thomas Russell Esquire* (New York: Oxford University Press, 1938), 57–58.

23. Chambers, *William Shakespeare*, vol. 2, 325.

24. Ibid., 326.

25. Ibid., 326–27.

26. Ogburn, *Mysterious William Shakespeare*, 10.

27. Chambers, *William Shakespeare*, vol. 2, 323.

28. Dave Kathman, *The Shakespeare Authorship Page*, http://www.clark.net/pub/tross/ws/will.html.

29. See also Naseeb Shaheen, *Biblical References in Shakespeare's Plays* (Newark, DE: University of Delaware Press, 1999), 41–44.

CHAPTER 12: HAVE THE BODY

1. Edmund K. Chambers, *William Shakespeare: A Study in Facts and Problems*, vol. 2 (Oxford: Clarendon Press, 1930), 216.

2. Ibid., 216–17.

3. See Charlton Ogburn, *The Mysterious William Shakespeare* (McLean, VA: EPM Publications, 1992), 205–6.

4. Donald W. Foster, "Master W. H., R.I.P.," *Publications of the Modern Language Association of America* 102 (January 1987): 46.

5. Ibid., 44.

6. Ibid.

7. Ibid., 42–45.

8. Ibid., 44.

9. The only exception is in Samuel Daniel's *Delia* (1592). In the prefatory sonnet to the Countess of Pembroke, Daniel says his verse has been "begotten by thy hand and my desire." Yet, Foster observes, "since Daniel presents his conceit as a conscious reversal of the customarily assigned roles, taking care to explain his variation, the 'exception' is unexceptional" (Foster, "Master W. H.," 45). The word *father* in Dekker's dedication of *News from Hell* may refer to a patron, but Dekker still figures as the "begetter."

10. Foster, "Master W. H.," 45.

11. Ibid., 49.

12. George Puttenham, *The Arte of English Poesie* (1589; repr., Cambridge: Cambridge University Press, 1936), 3.

13. John Davies, *The Scourge of Folly* (London: Richard Redmer, 1610), 76–77.

14. Ibid., 228–29.

15. Joseph Sobran, *Alias Shakespeare* (New York: The Free Press, 1997), 140.

16. *A Yorkshire Tragedy* had the same by-line in 1619 because its title page was reprinted.

17. Richard Farmer, *An Essay on the Learning of Shakspeare Addressed to Joseph Craddock, Esq.* (1767; repr., New York: AMS Press, 1966), 33.

18. Peter Alexander, *Shakespeare's Life and Art* (New York: New York University Press, 1967), 32. Not every published work, though, was entered in the Stationers Register, including some "good" Shakespeare quartos.

19. John Marston, *The Malcontent* (1604; Menston: Scolar Press, 1970), sig. A2.

20. Brian Vickers, *Shakespeare, Co-Author* (Oxford: Oxford University Press, 2002), 6.

21. Francis Meres, *Palladis Tamia*: *Wits Treasury* (1598; repr., New York: Garland Publishing, 1973), 283–83b.

22. Chambers, *William Shakespeare*, vol. 2, 196–98.

23. Ibid.

24. Ibid., 214–15.

25. Ibid., 218.

26. Ibid., 220.

27. Ibid., 221.

28. Thomas Heywood, *An Apology for Actors* (1612; repr., New York: Garland Publishing, 1973), sig. G4.

CHAPTER 13: THE LOGJAM

1. Frank Ernest Halliday, *A Shakespeare Companion 1550–1950* (London: Gerald Duckworth and Co., 1952), 681.

2. Peter Alexander, *Shakespeare's Life and Art* (New York: New York University Press, 1967), 46–47.

3. Ibid., 87.

4. Thomas Nashe, *Preface to Robert Greene's Menaphon* (1589; repr., New York: Garland Publishing, 1973), sig. **3.

5. Edmund K. Chambers, *William Shakespeare*: *A Study in Facts and Problems*, vol. 1 (Oxford: Clarendon Press, 1930), 411.

6. Francis Meres, *Palladis Tamia*: *Wit's Treasury* (1598; New York: Garland Publishing, 1973), 282.

7. Ian Wilson, *Shakespeare*: *The Evidence* (New York: St. Martin's Press, 1993), 301.

8. Some scholars, like W. D. Smith, believe the reference is to Essex's successor in Ireland, Lord Mountjoy, which would date the play even later.

9. Edward Gresham, ed., *Strange fearful & true newes, which happened at Carlstadt in the kingdome of Croatia . . . which prophisied many strange and fearfull things* (London: G. Vincent and W. Blackwall, 1606.) It's also quoted by Nigel Davies in "The Place 2 Be: Why Oxford Wasn't Shakespeare," (http://geocities.com/Athens/Troy/4081/Oxford.html).

10. Quoted in Henry N. Paul, *The Royal Play of Macbeth* (New York: Macmillan, 1950), 391.

11. Ibid., 361.

12. Ibid.

13. Ibid.

14. Ibid., 362–63.

15. Ibid., 250.

16. Edmond Howes, quoted in Paul, *Royal Play*, 251.

17. Ibid., 239.

18. For example, see Joseph Sobran, *Alias Shakespeare* (New York: The Free Press, 1997), 150.

19. See Paul, *Royal Play*, 244.

20. All Strachey references can be found in Geoffrey Bullough, *Narrative and Dramatic Sources of Shakespeare*, vol. 8 (New York: Columbia University Press, 1957–1975), 275–94. The comparisons with *The Tempest* can be found in Dave Kathman's *"Dating The Tempest," The Shakespeare Authorship Page* (http://www.shakespeareauthorship.com.html).

21. The word *glutted*, meaning overfed, appears in *Henry IV Part One* (III.ii.84). But only in *The Tempest*, where "glut" means to drown, is the word associated with too much water.

22. See Dave Kathman's *"Dating The Tempest," The Shakespeare Authorship Page* (http://www.shakespeareauthorship.com.html).

23. Quoted in Anne Barton, *Ben Jonson, Dramatist* (Cambridge: Cambridge University Press, 1984), 309.

24. For example, Tom Bethell, "The Case for Oxford," *The Atlantic Monthly* 268, no. 4 (October 1991): 61.

25. The nineteenth-century critic Charles Lamb captured the difference in styles: "[Fletcher's] ideas are more slow; his versification, though sweet, is tedious: it stops every moment, he lays line upon line, making up one after the other, adding image to image so deliberately that we see where they join: [the Author] mingles everything, he runs line into line, embarrasses sentences and metaphors; before one idea has burst its shell, another is hatched out and clamorous for disclosure." See Frank Kermode, *Shakespeare's Language* (New York: Farrar Straus Giroux, 2000), 308.

26. See Brian Vickers, *Shakespeare, Co-Author* (Oxford: Oxford University Press, 2002), 244–90.

27. Irvin Leigh Matus, *Shakespeare, in Fact* (New York: Continuum, 1994), 155.

CHAPTER 14: GRIEF AND STRIFE

1. The number of poems is based on Steven W. May's assessment of sixteen poems as "definitely" by Oxford and four poems "possibly" by him.

2. Alan H. Nelson, *Monstrous Adversary* (Liverpool: Liverpool University Press, 2003), 401.

3. Hilda M. Hulme, *Explorations in Shakespeare's Language* (New York: Barnes and Noble, 1962), 316.

4. Nelson, *Monstrous Adversary*, 64–66.

5. The variant spellings in the 1609 edition of the Sonnets, for example, have led scholars to conclude that the type was set by two compositors—one who favors "shall be," "rich," "flower," and "doost," and one who has a fondness for italics and prefers "shalbe," "ritch," "flowre," and "dost."

6. Nelson, *Monstrous Adversary*, 65.

7. John Milton, *Complete Poems and Major Prose*, ed. Merritt Y. Hughes (Indianapolis: Bobbs-Merrill Publishing, 1957), 43–50.

8. Helge Kökeritz, *Shakespeare's Pronunciation* (New Haven: Yale University Press, 1953), 31.

9. Ibid., 10.

10. Steven W. May, "The Poems of Edward de Vere, Seventeenth Earl of Oxford and of Robert Devereux, Second Earl of Essex," *Studies in Philology* 77, no. 5 (1980): 28. All Oxford poem quotations are from May, "Poems of Edward de Vere," 25–42.

11. Kökeritz, *Shakespeare's Pronunciation*, 89.

12. The epilogue of *The Two Noble Kinsmen* rhymes "face" and "has," but this is widely believed to have been written by Fletcher, and Oxfordians contend the whole play is Fletcher's.

13. Kökeritz, *Shakespeare's Pronunciation*, 231.

CHAPTER 15: ALL CONSPIRACY THEORIES
ARE ALIKE

1. Quoted in Marjorie Garber, *Shakespeare's Ghost Writers* (New York: Methuen, 1987), 10.

2. J. M. Robertson, *The Baconian Heresy: A Confutation* (New York: E. P. Dutton, 1913), 4.

3. Adolf Hitler, *Mein Kampf*, trans. Ralph Mannheim (Boston: Houghton Mifflin Company, 1971), 231.

4. Quoted in Charlton Ogburn, *The Mysterious William Shakespeare* (McLean, VA: EPM Publications, 1992), vi.

5. Ibid.

6. The endless conspiracy theories surrounding the Kennedy assassination have possibly clouded the search for facts that might lead to a *real* conspiracy. Oswald was definitely the shooter, but it has not been determined if anyone else was involved.

7. Quoted in Irvin Leigh Matus, *Shakespeare, in Fact* (New York: Continuum, 1994), 15.

Bibliography

All quotations from the Works of Shakespeare are from *The Riverside Shakespeare*, 2nd edition, ed. G. Blakemore Evans et al. (Boston: Houghton Mifflin Company, 1997).

Adams, John F., ed. *William Shakespeare: His World, His Work, His Influence*. New York: Charles Scribner's Sons, 1985.

Akrigg, G.P.V. *Shakespeare and the Earl of Southampton*. Cambridge, MA: Harvard University Press, 1968.

Alexander, Peter. *Shakespeare's Life and Art*. New York: New York University Press, 1967.

Amyot, Jacques. *Plutarch: Les vies des hommes illustres.* . . . 2 vols. Paris: Pierre Cheuillot, 1579.

Bacon, Delia. *The Philosophy of the Plays of Shakespeare Unfolded*. Boston: Ticknor and Fields, 1857.

Bacon, Francis. *Francis Bacon: A Critical Edition of the Major Works*. Edited by Brian Vickers. Oxford: Oxford University Press, 1996.

———. *Sylva Sylvarum: Or a Natural History in Ten Centuries*. Whitefish, MT: Kessinger Publishing, 2004.

———. *Works*. 14 vols. Edited by James Spedding, Robert Leslie, and Douglas Denon Heath. London: Longman, Green, Longman and Roberts, 1858–1874.

Baldwin, T. W. *William Shakspere's Small Latine & Lesse Greeke*. 2 vols. Urbana: University of Illinois Press, 1944.

Bakeless, John. *The Tragicall History of Christopher Marlowe*. 2 vols. Hamden, CT: Archon Books, 1964.

Barker, Harley Granville. *Prefaces to Shakespeare*. 5 vols. Princeton: Princeton University Press, 1946.

Barker, Harley Granville, and G. B. Harrison, eds. *A Companion to Shakespeare Studies*. 1934. Cambridge: Cambridge University Press, 1977.

Bartlett, Henrietta, and Alfred W. Pollard, eds. *A Census of Shakespeare's Plays in Quarto 1594–1709*. New Haven: Yale University Press, 1939.

Barton, Anne. *Ben Jonson, Dramatist*. Cambridge: Cambridge University Press, 1984.

Barton, Sir Dunbar P. *Links Between Shakespeare and the Law*. 1929. New York: Benjamin Blom, 1971.

Bate, Jonathan. *The Genius of Shakespeare*. Oxford: Oxford University Press, 1998.

Beaumont, Francis, and John Fletcher. *The Dramatic Works in the Beaumont and Fletcher Canon*. 10 vols. Edited by Fredson Bowers. Cambridge: Cambridge University Press, 1996.

Bentley, Gerald Eades. *The Profession of Dramatist in Shakespeare's Time, 1590–1642*. Princeton: Princeton University Press, 1971.

———. *The Profession of Player in Shakespeare's Time, 1590–1642*. Princeton: Princeton University Press, 1984.

———. "Shakespeare and the Blackfriars Theatre." *Shakespeare Survey* 1 (1948): 38–50.

Bethell, Tom. "The Case for Oxford." *The Atlantic Monthly* 268, no. 4 (October 1991): 45–61.

Blayney, Peter W. M. *The First Folio of Shakespeare*. Washington, DC: Folger Library Publications, 1991.

Boas, Frederick S. *Marlowe and His Circle*. Oxford: Clarendon Press, 1929.

Boswell-Stone, W. G. *Shakespeare's Holinshed*. 1896. New York: Benjamin Blom, 1966.

Bradbrook, M. C. *The Rise of the Common Player*. Cambridge, MA: Harvard University Press, 1962.

———. *Shakespeare the Craftsman*. London: Chatto and Windus, 1969.

Brockett, Oscar G. *History of the Theatre*. 7th ed. Boston: Allyn and Bacon, 1995.

Brook, Peter. *The Shifting Point*. New York: Harper and Row, 1987.

Brooks, Alden. *Will Shakspere and the Dyer's Hand*. New York: Charles Scribner's Sons, 1943.

Brown, Horatio F. *Studies in the History of Venice*. 2 vols. London: J. Murray, 1907.

Brownlee, A. *William Shakespeare and Robert Burton*. Reading: Bradley and Son, 1960.

Bullen, A. H., ed. *Some Longer Elizabethan Poems*. New York: Cooper Square, 1964.

Bullough, Geoffrey. *Narrative and Dramatic Sources of Shakespeare*. 8 vols. New York: Columbia University Press, 1957–1975.

Burgess, Anthony. *Nothing Like the Sun*. New York: W. W. Norton and Co., 1964.

Byron, George Gordon, Baron. *The Poetical Works of Byron*. Edited by Robert F. Gleckner. Boston: Houghton Mifflin Company, 1975.

Camden, William. *Remaines, Concerning Britaine*. London: S. Waterson, 1623.

Carson, Neil. *A Companion to Henslowe's Diary*. Cambridge: Cambridge University Press, 1988.

Chamberlain, John. *The Chamberlain Letters*. Edited by Elizabeth McClure Thomson. New York: G. P. Putnam's Sons, 1965.

——. *The Letters of John Chamberlain*. 2 vols. Edited by Norman Egbert McClure. Philadelphia: The American Philosophical Society, 1939.

Chambers, Edmund K. *The Elizabethan Stage*. 4 vols. Oxford: Clarendon Press, 1923.

——. *William Shakespeare: A Study in Facts and Problems*. 2 vols. Oxford: Clarendon Press, 1930.

Chandler, David. "A Further Reconsideration of Heywood's Allusion." *Elizabethan Review* 3 (Fall 1995): 15–24.

Chapman, George. *The Plays of George Chapman*. 2 vols. Edited by Thomas M. Parrott. New York: Russell and Russell, 1961.

Chettle, Henry. *Kind-Harts Dreame*. London: William Wright, 1592. Quarto.

Churchill, Reginald Charles. *Shakespeare and His Betters*. London: M. Reinhardt, 1958.

Cicero, Marcus Tullius. *Letters to Friends*. 3 vols. Edited by D. R. Shackleton Bailey. Cambridge, MA: Harvard University Press, 2001.

Clarkson, Paul S., and Clyde T. Warren. *The Law of Property in Shakespeare and Elizabethan Drama*. 1942. New York: Gordian Press, 1968.

Collins, John Churton. *Studies in Shakespeare*. Westminster: Archibald Constable and Company, 1904.

Cooper, Duff. *Sergeant Shakespeare*. London: Rupert Hart-Davis, 1949.

Coryate, Thomas. *Coryats Crudities*. 1611. London: Scolar Press, 1978. Facsimile.

Daniel, Samuel. *Complete Works in Verse and Prose*. 5 vols. Edited by Alexander B. Grosart. New York: Russell and Russell, 1963.

Davies, John. *The Scourge of Folly*. London: Richard Redmer, 1610. Octavo.

Dekker, Thomas. *The Dramatic Works of Thomas Dekker*. 4 vols. Edited by Fredson Bowers. Cambridge: Cambridge University Press, 1964.

Dictionary of National Biography. 20 vols. Edited by Leslie Stephen and Sidney Lee. Oxford: Oxford University Press, 1921–1922.

Drayton, Michael. *The Works of Michael Drayton*. 5 vols. Edited by J. William Hebel. Oxford: Shakespeare Head Press, 1961.

Driver, Olive W. *The Bacon-Shakespearean Mystery*. Northampton, MA: Kraushar Press, 1960.

Durning-Lawrence, Edwin. *Bacon Is Shake-Speare*. New York: The John McBride Company, 1910.

Dyer, Rev. T. F. Thiselton. *Folk-Lore of Shakespeare*. 1883. New York: Dover Publications, 1966.

Eccles, Mark. *Shakespeare in Warwickshire*. Madison: University of Wisconsin Press, 1961.

Eliot, T. S. *Selected Essays 1917–1932*. New York: Harcourt Brace, 1932.

England's Helicon. 1600. London: Scolar Press, 1973. Facsimile.

Erne, Lukas. "Biography and Mythography: Rereading Chettle's Alleged Apology to Shakespeare." *English Studies* 79 (1998): 430–40.

Evans, Alfred J. *Shakespeare's Magic Circle*. Freeport, N.Y.: Books for Libraries Press, 1970.

Farmer, Richard. *An Essay on the Learning of Shakspeare Addressed to Joseph Craddock, Esq.* 1767. New York: AMS Press, 1966. Facsimile.

Finkelpearl, Philip J. *John Marston of the Middle Temple*. Cambridge, MA: Harvard University Press, 1969.

Florio, John. *Florio His First Fruites*. London: Thomas Woodcock, 1578.

———. *Florios Second Frutes*. London: Thomas Woodcock, 1591.

———. *A Worlde of Wordes*. London: Edward Blount, 1598.

Foakes, R. A., and R. T. Rickert, eds. *Henslowe's Diary*. Cambridge: Cambridge University Press, 1961.

Foster, Donald W. "Master W. H., R.I.P." *Publications of the Modern Language Association of America* 102 (January 1987): 42–54.

Fox, Levi. "An Early Copy of Shakespeare's Will." *Shakespeare Survey 4* (1951): 69–77.

Freehafer, John. "*Cardenio*, by Shakespeare and Fletcher." *Publications of the Modern Language Association of America* 84 (1969): 501–13.

———. "Leonard Digges, Ben Jonson and the Beginning of Shakespeare Idolatry." *Shakespeare Quarterly* 21 (Winter 1970): 63–75.

Freeman, Arthur. *Thomas Kyd: Facts and Problems*. Oxford: Clarendon Press, 1967.

Friedman, William F., and Elizabeth S. Friedman. *The Shakespearean Ciphers Examined*. Cambridge: Cambridge University Press, 1957.

Fripp, Edgar Innis. *Shakespeare: Man and Artist*. 2 vols. London: Oxford University Press, 1938.

Fripp, Edgar Innis, and Richard Savage, eds. *Minutes and Accounts of the Corporation of Stratford-upon-Avon and Other Records, 1553–1620*. 5 vols. London: Oxford University Press, 1924–1929.

Garber, Marjorie. *Shakespeare's Ghost Writers*. New York: Methuen, 1987.

Gaskell, Philip. *A New Introduction to Bibliography*. Oxford: Oxford University Press, 1972.

George, David J., and Christopher J. Gossip, eds. *Studies in the Commedia Dell'Arte*. Cardiff: University of Wales Press, 1993.

Gibson, H. N. *The Shakespeare Claimants*. New York: Barnes and Noble, 1962.

Green, V.H.H. *A History of Oxford University*. London: B. T. Batsford, 1974.

Greene, Robert. *Greene's Groats-Worth of Wit*. 1592. Menston: Scolar Press, 1969. Facsimile.

Greenwood, George. *The Shakespeare Problem Restated*. 1908. Westport, CT: Greenwood Press, 1970.

Greg, W. W. *Some Aspects and Problems of London Publishing Between 1550 and 1650*. Oxford: Clarendon Press, 1956.

————., ed. *English Literary Autographs, 1550-1650*. Oxford: Oxford University Press, 1925–1932.

Gresham, Edward, ed. *Strange, fearful & true newes, which happened at Carlstadt in the kingdome of Croatia . . . which prophisied many strange and fearfull things*. London: G. Vincent and W. Blackwall, 1606. Octavo.

Grillo, Ernesto. *Shakespeare and Italy*. 1949. New York: Haskell House Publishers Ltd., 1973.

Grosart, Alexander B., ed. *The Life and Complete Works in Prose and Verse of Robert Greene*. 15 vols. 1881–1886. New York: Russell and Russell, 1964.

Guicciardini, Francesco. *The History of Italy*. 1540. Edited by Sidney Alexander. Princeton: Princeton University Press, 1969.

Gurr, Andrew. "You and Thou in Shakespeare's Sonnets." *Essays in Criticism* 32 (January 1982): 9–25.

Hall, Joseph. *The Poems of Joseph Hall*. Edited by Arnold Davenport Liverpool: Liverpool University Press, 1969.

————. *Satires*. Edited by Samuel Weller Singer. London: R. Triphook, 1824.

Halliday, Frank Ernest. *The Life of Shakespeare*. London: Gerald Duckworth and Co., 1961.

————. *A Shakespeare Companion 1550–1950*. London: Gerald Duckworth and Co., 1952.

Hamilton, Charles. *In Search of Shakespeare*. San Diego: Harcourt Brace Jovanovich, 1985.

Hammer, Paul E. J. *The Polarisation of Elizabethan Politics: The Political Career of Robert Devereux, 2nd Earl of Essex, 1585–1597*. Cambridge: Cambridge University Press, 1999.

Harbage, Alfred. *William Shakespeare: A Reader's Guide*. New York: Farrar, Straus and Giroux, 1963.

Harrison, G. B., ed. *The Elizabethan Journals*. 2 vols. Garden City, NY: Anchor Books, 1965.

Hart, Joseph C. *The Romance of Yachting: Voyage the First*. New York: Harper and Brothers, 1848.

Heywood, Thomas. *An Apology for Actors*. 1612. New York: Garland Publishing, 1973. Facsimile.

————. *The Dramatic Works of Thomas Heywood*. 6 vols. New York: Russell and Russell, 1964.

————. *The English Traveller*. London: R. Raworth, 1633. Quarto.

Hilton, Della. *Who Was Kit Marlowe?* New York: Taplinger Publishing, 1977.

Hoffman, Calvin. *The Murder of the Man Who Was "Shakespeare."* New York: J. Messner, 1955.

Holland, Norman, Sidney Homan, and B. J. Paris, eds. *Shakespeare's Personality*. Berkeley: University of California Press, 1989.

Honan, Park. *Shakespeare: A Life*. Oxford: Oxford University Press, 1998.

Honey, William. *The Life, Loves and Achievements of Christopher Marlowe Alias Shakespeare*. London: Pisces Press, 1982.

Honigmann, E.A.J. *Shakespeare's Impact on His Contemporaries*. London: Macmillan, 1982.

Hotson, Leslie. *I, William Shakespeare Do Appoint Thomas Russell Esquire*. New York: Oxford University Press, 1938.

Hulme, Hilda M. *Explorations in Shakespeare's Language*. New York: Barnes and Noble, 1962.

Ingleby, C. M., L. Toulmin Smith, F. J. Furnivall, eds. *The Shakspere Allusion Book*: *A Collection of Allusions to Shakspere From 1591 to 1700*. 2 vols. London: Oxford University Press, 1932.

Jardine, Lisa, and Alan Stewart. *Hostage to Fortune*: *The Troubled Life of Francis Bacon*. New York: Hill and Wang, 1999.

Johnson, Edward D. *Bacon-Shakespeare Coincidences*. London: The Bacon Society, 1948.

Jonson, Ben. *Ben Jonson*. 11 vols. Edited by C. H. Herford, Percy Simpson, and Evelyn Simpson. Oxford: Oxford University Press, 1925–1952.

———. *Discoveries 1641 and Conversations With William Drummond of Hawthornden 1619*. Edited by G. B. Harrison. New York: Barnes and Noble, 1966.

Jorgensen, Paul A. *Shakespeare's Military World*. Berkeley: University of California Press, 1956.

Joseph, Sister Miriam. *Shakespeare's Use of the Arts of Language*. New York: Hafner Publishing Company, 1966.

Jowett, John. "Johannes Factotum: Henry Chettle and *Greene's Groatworth of Wit*." *Papers of the Bibliographical Society of America* 87 (December 1993): 453–86.

Joyce, James. *Ulysses*. 1918. New York: Random House, 1946.

Kathman, Dave, and Terry Ross. *The Shakespeare Authorship Page*. http://www.shakespeareauthorship.com.html.

Kay, Dennis. *William Shakespeare*: *Sonnets and Poems*. New York: Twayne Publishers, 1998.

Kermode, Frank. *Shakespeare's Language*. New York: Farrar Straus Giroux, 2000.

Knight, W. Nicholas. *Shakespeare's Hidden Life*: *Shakespeare at the Law 1585–1595*. New York: Mason and Lipscomb, 1973.

Kökeritz, Helge. *Shakespeare's Pronunciation*. New Haven: Yale University Press, 1953.

Kotsiopoulos, George. *The Art and Sport of Falconry*. Chicago: Argonaut Publishers, 1969.

Kyd, Thomas. *The Works of Thomas Kyd*. Edited by Frederick S. Boas. Oxford: Clarendon Press, 1955.

Lawson, John, and Harold Silver. *A Social History of Education in England*. London: Methuen and Co., 1973.

Lea, Kathleen M. *Italian Popular Comedy*. 2 vols. 1931. New York: Russell and Russell, 1962.

Lefranc, Abel. *Under the Mask of William Shakespeare*. 1918. Translated by Cecil Cragg. Braunton: Merlin, 1988.

Leishman, J. B., ed. *Pilgrimage to Parnassus: The Three Parnassus Plays (1598–1601)*. London: Nicolson and Watson, 1949.

Lever, J. W. *The Elizabethan Love Sonnet*. London: Methuen, 1956.

Levith, Murray J. *Shakespeare's Italian Settings and Plays*. New York: St. Martin's Press, 1989.

Looney, J. Thomas. *"Shakespeare" Identified in Edward de Vere the Seventeenth Earl of Oxford*. New York: Duell, Sloan and Pearce, 1920.

Maguire, Laurie E. *Shakespearean Suspect Texts: The "Bad" Quartos and Their Contexts*. Cambridge: Cambridge University Press, 1996.

Manningham, John. *The Diary of John Manningham of the Middle Temple*. Edited by Robert Parker Sorlien. Hanover, NH: University Press of New England, 1976.

Marlowe, Christopher. *The Complete Works of Christopher Marlowe*. 2 vols. Edited by Fredson Bowers. London: Cambridge University Press, 1973.

Marston, John. *The Malcontent*. 1604. Menston: Scolar Press, 1970. Facsimile.

———. *The Poems of John Marston*. Edited by Arnold Davenport. Liverpool: Liverpool University Press, 1961.

———. *The Scourge of Villanie*. 2nd ed. 1599. New York: Barnes and Noble, 1966. Facsimile.

Matus, Irvin. "The Case for Shakespeare." *The Atlantic Monthly* 268, no. 4 (October 1991): 64–72.

———. *Shakespeare, in Fact*. New York: Continuum, 1994.

May, Steven W. *The Elizabethan Courtier Poets*. Columbia: University of Missouri Press, 1991.

———. "The Poems of Edward de Vere, Seventeenth Earl of Oxford and of Robert Devereux, Second Earl of Essex." *Studies in Philology* 77, no. 5 (1980).

McCrum, Robert, William Cran, and Robert McNeil. *The Story of English*. New York: Penguin Books, 1986.

McManaway, James G. *The Authorship of Shakespeare*. Ithaca, NY: Cornell University Press, 1962.

McMichael, George, and Edgar M. Glenn. *Shakespeare and His Rivals*. New York: The Odyssey Press, 1962.

McWilliam, G. H. *Shakespeare's Italy Revisited*. Leicester: Leicester University Press, 1974.

Mendenhall, T. C. "A Mechanical Solution of a Literary Problem." *The Popular Science Monthly* 60 (December 1901): 97–105.

Meres, Francis. *Palladis Tamia: Wit's Treasury*. 1598. New York: Garland Publishing, 1973. Facsimile.

Michell, John. *Who Wrote Shakespeare?* London: Thames and Hudson, 1996.

Middleton, Thomas. *The Witch.* c. 1626. Edited by W. W. Greg. Oxford: Oxford University Press, 1950.

———. *The Works of Thomas Middleton.* 8 vols. Edited by A. H. Bullen. New York: AMS Press, 1964.

Miles, Rosalind. *Ben Jonson: His Craft and Art.* Savage, MD: Barnes and Noble, 1990.

Milton, John. *Complete Poems and Major Prose.* Edited by Merritt Y. Hughes. Indianapolis: Bobbs-Merrill Publishing, 1957.

Milward, Peter. *Shakespeare's Religious Background.* Bloomington: Indiana University Press, 1973.

Morgan, J. Appleton. *A Study in the Warwickshire Dialect.* New York: The Shakespeare Press, 1899.

Münster, Sebastian. *Cosmographia Universale.* . . . Cologne: Arnold Birckman, 1575.

Nashe, Thomas. *Pierce Pennilesse His Supplication to the Divell.* 1592. Edited by G. B. Harrison. New York: Barnes and Noble, 1966.

———. *Preface to Robert Greene's Menaphon.* 1589. New York: Garland Publishing, 1973. Facsimile.

———. *The Works of Thomas Nashe.* 5 vols. Edited by Robert B. McKerrow. Oxford: Basil Blackwell, 1966.

Nelson, Alan H. *Alan H. Nelson Home Page.* http://ist-socrates.berkeley.edu/~ahnelson.html.

———. *Monstrous Adversary: The Life of Edward de Vere, 17th Earl of Oxford.* Liverpool: Liverpool University Press, 2003.

Newdigate, Bernard. *Michael Drayton and His Circle.* Oxford: Basil Blackwell, 1941.

Nicholl, Charles. *The Reckoning: The Murder of Christopher Marlowe.* New York: Harcourt Brace and Co., 1992.

Noble, Richmond. *Shakespeare's Biblical Knowledge and Use of the Book of Common Prayer.* New York: Macmillan, 1935.

North, Thomas. *Plutarke of Choeronea: The lives of the Noble Grecians and Romans.* . . . 5 vols. 1579. London: The Nonesuch Press, 1930.

Ogburn, Charlton. *The Mysterious William Shakespeare.* 1984. McLean, VA: EPM Publications, 1992.

Onions, C. T. *A Shakespeare Glossary.* Edited by Robert D. Eagleson. Oxford: Oxford University Press, 1986.

The Oxford English Dictionary. 20 vols. 2nd edition. Oxford: Clarendon Press, 1989.

Paul, Henry N. *The Royal Play of Macbeth.* New York: Macmillan, 1950.

Peele, George. *The Life and Works of George Peele.* 3 vols. Charles Taylor Prouty, general editor. New Haven: Yale University Press, 1952–1970.

Phillips, O. Hood. *Shakespeare and the Lawyers*. London: Methuen, 1972.

Plutarch. *Plutarch's Lives of the Noble Grecians and Romans Englished by Sir Thomas North, Anno 1579*. 6 vols. Edited by George Wyndham. New York: AMS Press, 1967.

Price, Diana. *Shakespeare's Unorthodox Biography*. Westport, CT: Greenwood Press, 2001.

Puttenham, George. *The Arte of English Poesie*. 1589. Edited by Gladys Doidge Willcock and Alice Walker. Cambridge: Cambridge University Press, 1936.

Raleigh, Sir Walter Alexander, Sir Sidney Lee, and C. T. Onions, eds. *Shakespeare's England*. 2 vols. 1916. Oxford: Clarendon Press, 1950.

Riggs, David. *Ben Jonson: A Life*. Cambridge, MA: Harvard University Press, 1989.

Robertson, J. M. *The Baconian Heresy: A Confutation*. New York: E. P. Dutton, 1913.

Rowse, A. L. *Christopher Marlowe: His Life and Work*. New York: Harper and Row, 1964.

———. *Eminent Elizabethans*. Athens, GA: University of Georgia Press, 1983.

Schoenbaum, S. *Shakespeare's Lives*. Oxford: Clarendon Press, 1970.

———. *William Shakespeare: A Compact Documentary Life*. New York: Oxford University Press, 1977.

———. *William Shakespeare: A Documentary Life*. New York: Oxford University Press, 1975.

Shaheen, Naseeb. *Biblical References in Shakespeare's Plays*. Newark, DE: University of Delaware Press, 1999.

———. "Shakespeare's Knowledge of Italian." *Shakespeare Survey* 47 (1994): 161–69.

Shakespeare Oxford Society Home Page. http://www.shakespeare-oxford.com.html.

Shakespeare, William. *Mr. William Shakespeares Comedies, Histories & Tragedies* (First Folio). London: Isaac Jaggard and Edward Blount, 1623.

Shakespeare, William. *The Riverside Shakespeare*. 2nd edition. Edited by G. Blakemore Evans et al. Boston: Houghton Mifflin Company, 1997.

Shirley, James. *The Dramatic Works and Poems of James Shirley*. 6 vols. Edited by Alexander Dyce and William Gifford. New York: Russell and Russell, 1966.

Sidney, Sir Philip. *Astrophel and Stella*. 1591. Menston: Scolar Press, 1970. Facsimile.

———. *The Poems of Sir Philip Sidney*. Edited by William A. Ringler. Oxford: Clarendon Press, 1962.

Smith, Bruce R. *Homosexual Desire in Shakespeare's England*. Chicago: University of Chicago Press, 1991.

Smith, William Henry. *Bacon and Shakespeare*. London: J. R. Smith, 1857.

Sobran, Joseph. *Alias Shakespeare*. New York: The Free Press, 1997.

Spenser, Edmund. *The Works of Edmund Spenser*. 11 vols. Edited by Charles Grosvenor Osgood and Henry Gibbons Lotspeich. Baltimore: The Johns Hopkins Press, 1947.

Spurgeon, Caroline F. E. *Shakespeare's Imagery and What It Tells Us*. 1935. Boston: Beacon Press, 1958.

Stephenson, Henry Thew. *The Elizabethan People*. New York: Henry Holt and Company, 1910.

Stern, Virginia F. *Gabriel Harvey: His Life, Marginalia, and Library*. Oxford: Clarendon Press, 1979.

Sweet, George Elliott. *Shake-speare: The Mystery*. Stanford: Stanford University Press, 1956.

Sykes, Claud W. *Alias William Shakespeare?* London: Francis Alton, 1947.

Sykes, H. Dugdale. *Sidelights on Elizabethan Drama*. 1924. New York: Barnes and Noble, 1966.

Thorndike, Ashley H. *The Influence of Beaumont and Fletcher on Shakspere*. 1901. New York: Russell and Russell, 1965.

Titherley, A. W. *Shakespeare's Identity: William Stanley, Sixth Earl of Derby*. Winchester: Warren and Son, 1952.

Twain, Mark. *Is Shakespeare Dead?: From My Autobiography*. New York: Harper and Row, 1909.

Vendler, Helen. *The Art of Shakespeare's Sonnets*. Cambridge, MA: Harvard University Press, 1997.

Vickers, Brian. *Shakespeare, Co-Author*. Oxford: Oxford University Press, 2002.

Viëtor, Wilhelm. *A Shakespeare Phonology*. 1906. New York: F. Ungar Publishing, 1963.

Wadsworth, Frank W. *The Poacher from Stratford*. Berkeley: University of California Press, 1958.

Ward, B. M. *The Seventeenth Earl of Oxford, 1550–1604, from Contemporary Documents*. London: John Murray, 1928.

Wells, Stanley W., and Gary Taylor, eds. *William Shakespeare: A Textual Companion*. Oxford: Clarendon Press, 1987.

Whalen, Richard F. *Shakespeare: Who Was He?* Westport, CT: Praeger, 1994.

Wilkes, George, and J. W. Tavener. *Shakespeare from an American Point of View: Including an Inquiry as to His Religious Faith and His Knowledge of Law with the Baconian Theory Considered*. London: Low, Marston, Seale and Rivington, 1877.

Willoby, Henry. *Willobie His Avisa*. 1594. New York: Barnes and Noble, 1966. Facsimile.

Wilson, Ian. *Shakespeare: The Evidence*. New York: St. Martin's Press, 1993.

Wilson, John Dover, ed. *Life in Shakespeare's England*. 1913. Cambridge: Cambridge University Press, 1978.

Wood, Michael. *Shakespeare*. New York: Basic Books, 2003.

Wraight, A. D. *The Story the Sonnets Tell*. London: Adam Hart, 1994.

Wraight, A. D., and Virginia F. Stern. *In Search of Christopher Marlowe*. New York: Vanguard Press, 1965.

Yates, Frances A. *John Florio: The Life of an Italian in Shakespeare's England*. Cambridge: Cambridge University Press, 1934.

Index

Acting companies: Admiral's Men, 169; Chandos's Men, 169; Derby's Men, 146–47, 168–69; Oxford's Boys, 160, 168; Oxford's Men, 160, 168, 169; Pembroke's Men, 169; Queen Anna's Men, 160; Sussex's Men, 169; Warwick's Men, 160; Worcester's Men, 160. *See also* Chamberlain's Men (later King's Men)

Actors: Marston on, 170; status of, 40, 99, 166. *See also individual names*

Ad Herennium, 64

Addenbrooke, John, 43

Admiral's Men, 169

Aeschylus, 10, 66

Aesop's Fables, 64, 194–95

Alleyn, Edward, 37, 39, 40, 170

All's Well That Ends Well, 44, 59, 70, 71, 73, 80, 164–65, 193, 235n81

American University, 221

Amurath III, 198

Amyot, Jacques, 66, 68, 156

Anna, Queen (of England, wife of James I), 119, 131

Anti-Stratfordianism: aristocratic sympathy and, 29, 94, 100; Beaumont and, 171, 226n8; biography of Shakespeare and, 14–15, 27, 32, 40, 41, 43, 46, 48, 218; characteristics of True Author and, 13–14, 53–55, 68, 80, 89, 100, 147, 153, 154; ciphers and, 132, 139, 182, 242n26; conspiracy and, xiii, 13, 16, 20–23, 26, 216, 217, 222; dating and, 194–97, 205–7; death of True Author before 1616 and, 180–87, 190–91; evidence of conspiracy, 169–75; false expectations and, xiii, 49; Fletcher and, 249n12; Gad's Hill incident and, 157–58, 244n14; *Groats-worth of Wit* and, 37; history of, 10–14; Italy and, 73–74, 76; Jonson and, 16–19, 21, 170–71; law and, 81; "Labeo" and, 137–38; logical fallacies of, 13, 26, 129–30, 146; Marston and, 138, 170; models for characters and, 130, 135, 146, 156, 161, 164–65; monument at Holy Trinity Church and, 22–23; omissions as evidence, 48, 95, 217, 218, 226n8; Oxford's Genevan Bible and, 177–79; parallelisms and, 139, 152–53, 242n25; posthumous evidence and, xii–xiii, 9; *Richard II* (play) and, 175–77; on Shakespeare of Stratford as inadequate, 13, 14,

About the Author

SCOTT McCREA is on the faculty of the Conservatory of Theatre Arts and Film at the State University of New York, Purchase College. He is also a playwright.